LEARNING
THEOLOGY
WITH THE
CHURCH
FATHERS

CHRISTOPHER
A. HALL

InterVarsity Press
Downers Grove, Illinois

InterVarsity Press
P.O. Box 1400, Downers Grove, IL 60515-1426
World Wide Web: www.ivpress.com
E-mail: mail@ivpress.com

InterVarsity Press* is the book-publishing division of InterVarsity Christian Fellowship/USA*, a student movement active on campus at hundreds of universities, colleges and schools of nursing in the United States of America, and a member movement of the International Fellowship of Evangelical Students. For information about local and regional activities, write Public Relations Dept., InterVarsity Christian Fellowship/USA, 6400 Schroeder Rd., P.O. Box 7895, Madison, WI 53707-7895, or visit the IVCF website at <www.ivcf.org>.

Scripture quotations, unless otherwise noted, are from the New Revised Standard Version of the Bible, copyright 1989 by the Division of Christian Education of the National Council of the Churches of Christ in the USA. Used by permission. All rights reserved.

Cover photograph: Vanni/Art Resource, NY

ISBN 0-8308-2686-6

Printed in the United States of America ∞

Library of Congress Cataloging-in-Publication Data

Hall, Christopher A. (Christopher Alan), 1950-
    Learning theology with the church fathers/Christopher A. Hall.
        p. cm.
Includes bibliographical references and indexes.
    ISBN-0-8308-2686-6 (pbk.: alk. paper)
    1. Theology, Doctrinal—History—Early church, ca. 30-600 2. Fathers
of the church. I. Title.
    BT25 .H33 2002
    230'.11—dc21
                                                                                    2002006755

| P | 19 | 18 | 17 | 16 | 15 | 14 | 13 | 12 | 11 | 10 | 9 | 8 | 7 | 6 | 5 | 4 | 3 | 2 |
| Y | 19 | 18 | 17 | 16 | 15 | 14 | 13 | 11 | 10 | 09 | 08 | 07 | 06 | 05 | 04 |

To two valued mentors in the faith:
W. Ward Gasque and
J. I. Packer

CONTENTS

Preface

Learning Theology with the Church Fathers is the second volume of a projected three-volume set: *Reading Scripture with the Church Fathers* (patristic biblical interpretation);[1] *Learning Theology with the Church Fathers* (patristic reflection on key theological topics and issues: Scripture, Christ, the Trinity, the Holy Spirit, sin and salvation, providence, the church and the resurrection); and a book provisionally titled *Praying with the Church Fathers* (patristic reflection and practice in the spectrum of Christian spirituality: prayer, worship, the Eucharist, baptism, Christian witness and service to the poor).

Reading Scripture with the Church Fathers, the first volume of the series, is a basic introduction to the manner and content of patristic biblical interpretation. In it I focus on the eight great doctors of the church—Athanasius, John Chrysostom, Basil the Great and Gregory of Nazianzus in the East; Ambrose, Augustine, Jerome and Gregory the Great in the West—using these masters of the faith as examples of how the fathers read and interpreted the Bible. I also provide basic biographical and bibliographical background for those who want to explore patristic hermeneutics further.

When I had finished writing *Reading Scripture with the Church Fathers* I knew there were still vast areas of patristic wisdom and insight that I had yet to touch. What, for example, of the thoughts of the fathers on key theological topics such as the authority of Scripture, tradition, the Trinity, the incarnation of the Son, the Holy Spirit, sin, grace, redemption, suffering and evil, providence, the church and the resurrection of the dead? These subjects in themselves called for a second book. Hence, the volume you now find in your hands, *Learning Theology with the Church Fathers*.

I acknowledge readily and immediately that the fathers never split theology off from spirituality, as though theology was an academic, mental exercise best practiced in one's study, while Christian spirituality was more appropriately focused on the heart and centered in a church sanctuary. Any split between mind and heart, theology and spirituality, study and sanctuary would have met with scant toleration from the fathers.

For the fathers, as for at least one of the three great ecclesiastical communions of the Christian world—Eastern Orthodoxy—theology and spirituality, the Christian mind and heart, worship and reflection are an inseparable whole. The fathers continually remind us that theology is at best broken speech about the transcendent, mysterious God who draws near to us in the incarnation of the Son and the presence of the Spirit. Within the context of worship, whether through the proclamation of the Word from the pages of Scripture or in the celebration of the sacraments, God draws near to us. Here we learn what we can and cannot know and speak within the inherent limitations of human language as we attempt to understand and express faithfully the wonder of who God is and what God is up to in human history. Our thoughts and words about God will always and inevitably fall short in their attempt to capture and explain God's nature and actions.

Anthony Ugolnik chides the West's tendency to "avoid" the "essentially mysterious nature of Christianity . . . rather than [to] adore it." He writes:

> We [Christians in the West] confess to doctrines profoundly mysterious by their nature—that a man should be God, that one God should be at the same time three persons, that we of corruptible flesh should also be temples of the living God. So we believe, but so we cannot comfortably *think*. For as "thoughts," these are in essence mystery. Mystery is what many contemporary minds are hungry for; it is what they seek far afield, in the non-Christian realms and such Eastern, Asiatic sources as the Bhagavad Gita and the Tibetan Book of the Dead. We Christians in the West have not shared what we possess. We have mystery in plenty, yet our discourse averts it, avoids it as if in embarrassment. For mystery is what we have been taught through our education to extinguish.[2]

Ugolnik is not arguing that all speech about God is necessarily impossible and unproductive. Thinking and speaking about God is surely a possible and praiseworthy endeavor, if our reflection and speech are formed and informed within the context of worship. For it is within worship, the fathers insist, that we encounter the mystery of God and God's acts on our behalf and learn to think, speak and reverently respond to divine realities—all the while acknowledging that our words fall far short of the wonder they are feebly attempting to encompass and describe.

Daniel Clendenin, an evangelical theologian, explains that Eastern Orthodox theology, a theology deeply rooted in the fathers, "is far removed from the theological abstractions common in the West. Adoration, contemplation, and vision, not rational intellection, characterize the Eastern tradition."[3] For instance, Clendenin directs us to the christological formulations of the Chalcedonian Creed as an example of how Eastern fathers went about their work.

The fathers describe "the union of the divine and human natures of Christ" by employing "a series of four negative words: the two natures of Christ exist 'without confusion, change, division, or separation.' " That is, as Clendenin explains, "the creed states the fact of the union of Christ's two natures in one person and does so in such a way that we avoid theological error, but it resists any temptation to provide a rational explanation of how this can be."[4] This reticence to speak beyond the boundaries revealed in Scripture, the church's reflection upon Scripture and the church's lived experience in worship illustrates well the patristic and Eastern refusal to separate "reason and experience, theology and spirituality, cognition and mystery."[5]

In this vein, John Climacus (A.D. 579-649) writes that the word spoken by the theologian remains hollow if not grounded in personal experience in worship:

> Do you imagine plain words can precisely or truly or appropriately describe the love of the Lord . . . and assurance of the heart? Do you imagine that *talk* of such matters will mean anything to someone who has never *experienced* them? If you think so, then you will be like a man who with words and examples tries to convey the sweetness of honey to people who have never tasted it. He talks uselessly. Indeed I would say he is simply prattling.[6]

And so to title a book *Learning Theology with the Church Fathers* entails the danger of perpetuating a tendency in Western theology to divide theology from spirituality, theological reflection from devotion. Having acknowledged this danger, however, I find that both the depth and the quantity of patristic thinking and writing on essential topics such as the Trinity and the incarnation demands that they be covered in a volume devoted to them alone. To try to combine them with the fathers' thoughts on matters such as prayer, the sacraments, worship, temptation, confession and other key areas of the spiritual life would lay too heavy a burden on both reader and author.

In the third volume of the series, we will focus on patristic spirituality.[7] There, for example, we will explore key sacraments such as the Eucharist and investigate its relationship to worship, prayer and the nature of the church itself. Readers expecting links such as these to be discussed thoroughly in the present volume will be disappointed. Best to be forewarned.

This volume, like its predecessor, is simply designed to be a primer for beginners. Perhaps you are a pastor longing to root yourself more deeply in the early church's understanding of the heart of the faith. Maybe you are a seminary student interested in hearing the fathers speak on various theological topics, but in an accessible, lively fashion. You have your doubts, though; earlier efforts to sample patristic offerings turned out to be fairly dusty and dry affairs, more like drinking sand than sampling fine wine. And then, of course, some of you are part of the vast Christian audience who have no plans or interest in becoming pastors (or theologians!) but desire to whet your appetite with the thoughts of the fathers. The fear lurks, though, that one might gag in the attempt or, to mix metaphors, find the terrain too rough to merit the journey.

These misgivings and fears are fair and, by observing the dust covering some patristic textbooks on library shelves, more than warranted. I am convinced, though, that the fathers themselves are rarely boring—strange perhaps, sometimes difficult to understand at a first reading, often opinionated and occasionally quirky—but almost always worthwhile companions for an evening's study, meditation and prayer. Thus, in *Learning Theology with the Church Fathers* I have tried to allow the fathers to speak for themselves, with as little extraneous comment from me as possible. Occasionally I develop a contemporary application. For instance, in chapter one I discuss the difficulty some modern readers have in addressing God as "Father" and how a church father such as Athanasius might coach those struggling in such a way. For the most part, though, I leave contemporary links and applications up to the reader. It goes without saying that you know your story better than I do and will be much more adept at recognizing particular connections to your life's narrative.

My advice for the pages to come? Read slowly, listen carefully and surround the entire process with prayer. If you find yourself drawn to meditation or worship as you read, accept this gift willingly and thankfully. Do not become discouraged, frustrated or disillusioned if the immediate relevance of a father's reflections, insights and arguments fails to appear. Patristic theology is occasionally complex, understandably so, because the God who reveals himself to us in the Scripture, worship, prayer and the sacraments is complex. Complexity, however, is different from confusion, and the reader who slowly chews on Athanasius's understanding of the incarnation or Augustine's thoughts on the Christian's hope for the future will discover flavors, textures and nourishment that may well last a lifetime. Welcome to the feast!

"This is true worship: when the mind of the worshipper presents itself
as an undefiled offering to God."
LACTANTIUS
The Divine Institutes

"We should consider what is said—
not with what eloquence it is said. Nor should we look at how it tickles the ears.
Instead, we should look at the benefits it confers upon its hearers."
ARNOBIUS
Against the Heathen

"Every place and every time in which we entertain the idea of God is in reality sacred."
CLEMENT OF ALEXANDRIA
The Stromata, or Miscellanies

"Sound doctrine does not enter into a hard and disobedient heart."
JUSTIN MARTYR
Fragments

ONE

PREPARING TO LEARN THEOLOGY WITH THE CHURCH FATHERS

Key Questions to Explore

The incarnation of the Word. The first five hundred years of the church's life were a period of intense biblical and theological ferment, reflection and development. Think of the momentous events of the first century A.D. itself. The early Christian community was birthed with the firm conviction that the God revealed to Abraham, Moses and David had acted finally and completely on humanity's behalf in Jesus Christ. In the incarnation of the divine Logos (Word), sent by the Father into the midst of this present evil age, the life of the age to come had been dramatically introduced and manifested.

"In the beginning was the Word," John writes, "and the Word was with God and the Word was God" (Jn 1:1). How could this be? What strange kind of theological arithmetic was this? How could God be God and the Word be distinct from God and yet, simultaneously, also God? Exactly what Word was this? How was the Word related to God? To further complicate matters, John writes that this Word "became flesh and lived among us, and we have seen his glory, the glory as of a father's only son, full of grace and truth" (Jn 1:14). In fact, this Son had become fully manifest in Jesus Christ, who as John puts it, "is close to the Father's heart" and has "made him known" (Jn 1:18).

Breathtaking, mysterious and complicated statements all. Of course, John's prologue to his Gospel is only the beginning of the story. The reader soon discovers that God has uniquely visited humanity in Christ. Here we have an incarnate God, one who comes to serve, suffer, die and rise again, conquering the awful reality of sin in the process. It is a wonderful story, at first glance seemingly simple, but increasingly complicated and troublesome the more one contemplates it. How was the early church to think through and resolve the many questions that would invariably rise, some almost immediately, others as the church reflected on the gospel narrative during the crucial formative years of its history?

The question of authority. We have, for example, the question of authority. Why were certain documents considered authoritative for the life and thought of the church? What was the source of this authority? What separates documents such as the four canonical Gospels from other texts that attempt to tell and interpret the meaning of Jesus' life? Not only is the question of the Scripture's own inherent authority highly significant, but so also is the issue of what one is to do when Christians read the text of Scripture and interpret it differently. How can one distinguish a correct interpretation of Scripture from an incorrect one? How did the early church handle this considerable problem?

The person and work of Christ. Or what of the person and work of Jesus himself? We have, for instance, the question of Jesus' divinity. If Jesus was God incarnate, as New Testament writers appeared to insist, in what way was he God? Were there actually three gods: the Father, the Son and the Holy Spirit? Or was Jesus perhaps a lesser god, not on the same plane as the Father, but in some mysterious and ineffable manner divine nonetheless? Maybe there was only one God, but that single God possessed the marvelous ability to manifest himself in various forms or roles, occasionally as the Father and at other times as the Son or the Spirit. How was one to make sense of the complex biblical testimony regarding Jesus' divinity?

And then we have the question of Jesus' humanity. The Gospel narratives surely seemed to portray Jesus as a human being. He had a human body—or at least appeared to have one—and thus ate food, drank wine, was tired after a long day's work, slept at night, spoke a human language those around him readily understood, possessed human emotions such as joy, sadness and fear, and finally experienced death, a reality only genuine biological life can undergo.

How could one make sense of Jesus' humanity in light of his divinity? Could genuine divinity and humanity be joined together? What kind of union was this? Was such a union even possible? Perhaps Jesus possessed a human body controlled by a divine mind. Or maybe his body was not real after all. Then again, perhaps Jesus possessed a real body and a genuinely human mind but a divine will. To what extent was Jesus human after all? Perhaps he was more like an angel, a third type of personal, created being—part human, part divine.

And what did Jesus come to accomplish? Apostles such as Paul, Peter and John were absolutely insistent that Jesus' life, death and resurrection had overcome sin and its destructive effects on humanity and God's creation at large. In what way had God conquered sin in the lives of those people who believed in Jesus? Apostolic teaching indicated that Christ's crucifixion and subsequent resurrection had broken the spine of sin. How? How did human faith and belief tap into the benefits of Christ's death and resurrection? In what way was the exercise of faith related to God's power? To human freedom? How were the glorious realities of Christ's work and person communicated to those who believed in him?

The Holy Spirit. Perhaps the greatest surprise of all was the ascension of Christ back to heaven, just when all seemed to have been accomplished and fulfilled. Jesus left his small band of brothers and sisters behind at the very moment when they appeared to need his guidance the most. Why would he do such a thing? Clearly Christ's departure surprised his early followers.

Luke records that, after the disciples had received extended postresurrection instruction from Jesus, they asked, "Lord, is this the time when you will restore the kingdom to Israel?" (Acts 1:6). Jesus' response no doubt caught them off guard: "It is not for you to know the times or periods that the Father has set by his own authority. But you will receive power when the Holy Spirit has come upon you; and you will be my witnesses in Jerusalem, in all Judea and Samaria, and to the ends of the earth" (Acts 1:7-8). Whereas the early postresurrection Christian community thought the story had reached its conclusion, it was only just beginning. There was work to be done, a witness to be proclaimed, and those left behind would inaugurate that work and witness. Moreover, the early Christian generations would play a key role in witnessing to, incarnating and interpreting the story of Jesus' life, death and resurrection. Though Christ was physically leaving, he promised the disciples that he would soon return to them through the Spirit, the Spirit who would empower them for ministry and form them into Christ's body on earth, the church.

Again, layers of questions present themselves. Who is this Holy Spirit who will infill and energize the church? How is the Holy Spirit related to Christ and to the Father? Are Father, Son and Spirit simply different manifestations of one divine being, or is the Father distinct from the Son, and the Son from the Spirit? If these distinctions exist, exactly who is the Holy Spirit? What is the Spirit's work and mission? And what of the witnessing community Jesus predicts the Spirit will form, infill, power and direct? How can the church, made up of sinful human beings, still be called by the apostle Paul Christ's "body, the fullness of him who fills all in all" (Eph 1:23)? In short, what is the church?

As the early church pondered these questions, its thinking coalesced around central theological *loci*:

- The question of authority: To what should the church look for its guiding authority? What is the relation between Scripture and the apostolic tradition, and how do these two relate to one another in the formation of doctrine?

- The question of the Trinity: Is Christ genuinely divine? If so, how is the divinity of Christ to be understood in relationship to the Father and the Spirit?

- The question of the incarnation: What is the relationship between Christ's deity and humanity? If Jesus was truly divine, was he also truly human? How can he simultaneously be both?

- The question of Christ's work: How has Jesus' ministry, death and resurrection overcome sin and introduced the life of the age to come into this present evil age?

- The question of humanity: What is a human being? What does the Scripture mean when it states that human beings have been created in the image of God? How and to what extent has sin affected and infected human nature?

- The question of the church: What is the church? How is the church related to Christ? What is the church's task on earth? How does one enter the church? What are the church's marks? How is the life of the church nourished and strengthened? What are the dangers the church can expect to encounter in its mission and ministry on earth?

- The question of the future: What will happen in the future? When will Christ return? What is the resurrection of the dead? What will occur at the last judgment?

How shall we work through these questions in this book? In the following pages I will attempt to act as a guide to the reflections of the church fathers—bishops, pastors and, occasionally, laypeople who ministered in the church from approximately A.D. 100 to 750. Readers familiar with my earlier book, *Reading Scripture with the Church Fathers*, will already be aware of why I think the church fathers are important and neglected to our own detriment and peril. Those unfamiliar with this earlier book will perhaps find a brief introduction to the fathers and a rationale for studying their exegesis and theological reflections to be helpful.[1]

A Brief Introduction to the Fathers

The idea of a "father in the faith" has a rich and fruitful background in the Bible and in the ancient world. Paul, for example, describes himself as a "father" to the members of the Corinthian congregation, distinguishing the role of a father from that of a mere guardian (1 Cor 4:15). The term *father* also occurred in rabbinic, Cynic and Pythagorean circles. Early Christian writers such as Clement of Rome, Irenaeus and Clement of Alexandria all employ the term. Irenaeus speaks, not only of the student as one "who has received the teaching from another's mouth" as a son, but also of one's instructor as a "father."[2] A father in the faith, then, is someone who is familiar with the teachings concerning the life and ministry of Jesus Christ and can be trusted to hand on faithfully and correctly the tradition that he himself has already received. Trustworthiness of character and rootedness in the gospel are nonnegotiables in the life of a father. There were also trusted mothers in the faith, but unfortunately we do not possess a large written corpus from their hands.[3]

The idea of preserving and faithfully passing on the apostolic teachings concerning the meaning of Jesus is clearly evident in the era of the trinitarian and christological controversies. Bishops who faithfully preserved and protected the conciliar decisions of key councils such as Nicaea (A.D. 325), Constantinople (381) and Chalcedon (451) received the title "father." The church considered these Christian leaders worthy of special honor and regard for preserving orthodox teaching during times marked by severe testing and occasional persecution.

Vincent of Lerins describes the fathers of the church as people who "each in his own time and place" remained "in the unity of communion and the faith" and were "accepted as approved masters." Vincent argues that "whatsoever these may be found to have held, with one mind and one consent . . . ought to be accounted the true and catholic doctrine of the Church, without any doubt or scruple."[4]

In addition, four key criteria are often employed to determine whether a particular Christian teacher qualifies as a father of the church.

Antiquity. A father lived and ministered from roughly the close of the first century (ca. A.D. 96) to the time of John of Damascus (750).

Holiness of life. By holiness we do not mean perfection, as though the fathers were angels in human form. Most, as I have elsewhere written, were intensely human and struggled with the same shortcomings and temptations common to humanity.

> The fathers exhibited a tremendous zeal for God and the Scriptures. And, often like us, their zeal manifested itself in both their strengths and weaknesses. They have much to teach us about reverence, awe, self-sacrifice, self-awareness and self-deception, worship, respect, prayer, study and meditation. Their theological contributions remain foundational for Christians in the Roman Catholic, Orthodox, Anglican and many Protestant communions. . . . Most often they wore their hearts and thoughts on their sleeves. At times they were impatient, short-tempered and narrow. Some had a very hard time listening to perspectives other than those they endorsed. Yet their hearts were set on fire by the gospel. They lived and breathed the Scriptures. And many willingly laid down their lives for the sake of Christ.[5]

Orthodox doctrine. Since the fathers were teachers of the church, two key points pertain here. First, a father must have left behind a body of teaching, however small it might be. Second, this teaching must line up with apostolic tradition. That is to say, whatever a father says in his teaching must be "orthodox" or in line with what the apostles themselves taught and modeled.[6] Many of the topics we will explore with the fathers in this book—the Trinity, the incarnation, the absolute authority and infallibility of Scripture, the fallen condition of humanity and Christ's redemptive death on the cross—were first affirmed and developed doctrinally by patristic exegetes. Indeed, as Boniface Ramsey notes, belief and trust in these essential, central doctrines is what precisely sets off Christian belief from other religious belief systems.[7]

Ecclesiastical approval. Finally, the church itself must identify and approve the teachings and lives of those who would receive the designation "church father." No one can autonomously claim the title for himself.[8] Some highly significant early Christian writers, such as Origen, failed to receive this designation from the church because their positions drifted beyond the bounds of orthodoxy.

So why should we spend the time and effort to learn theology with the church fathers? For one thing, the fathers can help us to understand what it means to be a Christian and how the early stages and models of Christian worship, practice and reflection have shaped Christian perspectives and practices throughout the church's history. The fathers were formative figures in the formulation and modeling of Christian faith and practice and can be a healthy antidote for the theological and ethical faddism and foolishness that marks too much of the modern Christian world. The fathers will insistently remind us that the content of Christian belief and its lived practice in worship, prayer and the many relationships of life must always remain one piece.

In fact, the fathers will insist that it is in the womb of worship and the experience of God's redemptive act in Christ that theology is born, nourished and developed. Athanasius's response to his Arian opponents, as we will shortly discover, was largely based on the Arians' inability to make sense of Christian worship. How, Athanasius asks, can the Arians deny the full divinity of Christ and yet still worship Christ? To do so is to worship a *creature*, however highly elevated in status, as God. Surely, Athanasius will argue, something is wrong here.

Not only were the fathers key figures in the formulation of Christian faith, but they were much nearer to the apostolic writers than we are, what I have called elsewhere *hermeneutical proximity*.[9] This proximity in time and space does not guarantee that the fathers heard and understood the biblical writers infallibly. It does mean, however, that they often hear melodies and harmonies in the biblical narrative that modern Christians fail to discern. The fathers hear tonal qualities in the text that might well remain muted for readers of another age. If we rely solely on modern commentaries and systematic theologies, we might well overlook wisdom, patterns, concerns and models that can supplement or correct the insights offered by modern theological reflection.

No Christian's ideas or practices have been shaped in a familial, cultural, ecclesiological or theological vacuum. Theological knowledge, awareness, practice and, occasionally, prejudice are formed within a number of contexts. Purposefully and systematically moving out of these familiar boundaries, that is, taking a theological voyage to other times, places and personalities, rebukes the tendency of us all to think that we are the only people who genuinely comprehend the truth and who practice it faithfully. Exposure to foreign theological terrain can surprisingly highlight the fissures in our own theological understanding and remind us of the continuing need to listen to other voices carefully and respectfully.

However, a broadening and deepening of theological perspective, insight and sympathy is not the only happy fruit of working outside of one's home theological turf. A thorough immersion in patristic theology will continually pull us toward the center of the gospel and help to guard against the danger of transforming peripheral issues into the heart of the matter.

A Personal Reflection

I, for instance, am a Protestant evangelical theologian who presently attends a local Episcopal church. My initial intense exposure to the gospel in the late 1960s was filtered through the lens of premillennial dispensationalism, a perspective for which I am grateful in many ways but which possesses its own blind spots. As a young Christian I possessed only vague recollections from childhood that Jesus had said he would come again. However, words, phrases and symbols such as "rapture," "the great tribulation," "pretribulation," "posttribulation," "millennium," "antichrist," "beast" and "666" were entirely new to me.

Hal Lindsey, one of my first Bible teachers, interpreted apocalyptic images from Daniel and Revelation in a manner that surprised and excited me.[10] As Hal explained matters, Jesus could come at any time for his church. Indeed, Hal argued, the signs indicating the imminent arrival of the last times had been fulfilled when Israel regained its status as a nation in 1948. The retaking of Jerusalem in the 1967 war between Israel and its Arab enemies only further confirmed God's timetable. And this had just occurred! Soon, according to Hal's timetable, the rapture would occur, the antichrist would be revealed, the great tribulation would break out, and finally Christ would return to establish his millennial kingdom for a thousand years.

The ideas I first heard from Hal soon made their way into print in *The Late Great Planet Earth*, and publishing history was made. Hal had unexpectedly

uncovered a deep vein of eschatological and apocalyptic longing in the fundamen-
talist-evangelical subculture and in the American culture at large. Perhaps more
important, he knew how to package the dispensational eschatology he had
learned at Dallas Theological Seminary in a fashion that Americans, many of
them young, countercultural types emerging from the turbulent 1960s, could
understand and embrace.

What I did not realize was that elements of Hal's premillennial perspective—
minus dispensational emphases such as the distinct separation of Israel from the
church in God's economy and a pretribulational rapture—represented a distinguished, though minority, view in the history of Christian exegesis. Justin Martyr, an early Christian apologist and martyr writing in the mid-second century,
was convinced that Christ would soon return in triumph. This "great and terrible
day" would include Christ's judgment of the entire world, his appearance in
Jerusalem and the destruction of "the man of sin." Why the delay in the return of
Christ? Justin argued that "the number of the just" to be included in the kingdom
was yet to be completed.[11]

Christ's return, as understood by Justin, would result in great blessing for the
saved, a beatitude to be enjoyed successively in two stages. First, believers in Jesus
would possess and inhabit the land of Canaan, reigning there for one thousand
years.[12] Second, upon the completion of the thousand years, "the general, and, to
put it briefly, eternal resurrection and judgment of all will . . . take place." Other
passages in Justin seem to indicate that after this second resurrection the saints
would eternally possess the Holy Land.[13]

Significantly, Justin was convinced that the reality of Christ's coming and its
attendant, severe judgments should be a spur to faithful, sober Christian living as
the church waited for its Lord. Brian Daley, author of *The Hope of the Early
Church*, explains that Justin's eschatology convinced him that Christians should
be "marked out from the rest of pleasure-loving human society . . . by their conviction that the wicked will be punished in eternal fire, and the Christ-like just
united with God, free from suffering . . . . This is the reason Christians are
truthful in affirming their faith . . . as well as the ground of their good citizenship
. . . and their ultimate fearlessness before the threat of persecution."[14]

Irenaeus of Lyons, another church father writing in the late second century
A.D., also represents a broadly premillennial perspective, describing a two-stage

resurrection in his great work, *Against Heresies*. Stages are necessary, Irenaeus argues, because "it is fitting for the righteous first to receive the promise of the inheritance which God promised the fathers, and to reign in it, when they rise again to behold God in this creation which is renewed, and that the judgment should take place afterward."[15] Daley points out that Irenaeus supports his interpretation on the basis of "many biblical passages that promise salvation to Israel in typical terms of peace, prosperity and material restoration, and he insists that these may not be allegorized away."[16] Hence, the necessity of a one-thousand-year millennium (following Rev 20), followed by a general resurrection. God will cast the resurrected unbelievers into Gehenna's eternal fire and create the habitation of the saints, "a new heaven and a new earth."[17]

As a young believer birthed during the Jesus Movement, I knew nothing of Justin or Irenaeus. The model of exegesis I had received and practiced as a young Christian was a highly individualistic affair. With the help of a gifted teacher—in this case, Lindsey—and supplementary interpretive tools, I felt prepared to unlock the eschatological mysteries of Daniel and Revelation. I was shockingly unaware of the Christians who had read, pondered and interpreted these texts before me. Indeed, a crippling aspect of the Jesus Movement as a whole was its drastically shortened exegetical perspective, a theological and historical amnesia that continues to trouble sectors of the evangelical world. The idea of biblical interpretation as a communal, ecclesial function and practice never entered my mind. I am ashamed to admit that many who excitedly discussed prophetic time-tables throughout the week, myself included, were asleep in bed on Sunday mornings. We simply saw little need for the church.

Most dispensationalists saw the church as a theological surprise, the unexpected result of Israel's rejection of the Messiah, a temporary characteristic of the interim "church age." The church, it was believed, would be raptured before the tribulation. Then God's salvific dealings with Israel would recommence during the tribulation. I ended up assuming, almost by osmosis, that God's primary concern was with me and my personal salvation. The idea that my salvation was part of a larger, grander story, the formation of Christ's body, the church—Christ's hands and feet in history and in the future—went largely unrecognized and unexpressed.

Church fathers, whether premillennialists such as Justin or Irenaeus or amillennialists such as Augustine, at best would have been puzzled by this state of affairs, more likely horrified. Augustine, in fact, contended in his *City of God* that the premillennialism advocated by other Christian teachers too easily fed the desire for material rather than spiritual delights. He clearly felt uncomfortable, perhaps because of his immersion in Platonic philosophy, with eschatological expectations that fed a desire for pleasures rooted in the material world. In referring to "chiliasts," the ancient forerunners of the modern premillennialists, Augustine writes:

> Those people assert that those who have risen again will spend their rest in the most unrestrained material feasts, in which there will be so much to eat and drink that not only will those supplies keep within no bounds of moderation but will also exceed the limits even of incredibility. But this can only be believed by materialists; and those with spiritual interests give the name "Chiliasts" to the believers in this picture, a term which we can translate by a word derived from the equivalent Latin, "Millenarians."[18]

Augustine, then, distanced himself from the premillennialism of a Justin or Irenaeus, arguing that John's one thousand years "can be interpreted in two ways." The first possibility was that the thousand years represented the sixth day or sixth millennium, based upon the Roman conception of history as a "cosmic week" of six ages. The second possible interpretation, one that Augustine himself seems to have more strongly supported, was that John "may have intended the thousand years to stand for the whole period of this world's history, signifying the entirety of time by a perfect number."[19] As Brian Daley summarizes Augustine's thought, the thousand years come to represent "all the years of the Christian era." Most significantly, Augustine comes to identify the kingdom of God with the church in the world. During this thousand years the church struggles "against the forces of evil both outside and inside her own ranks." Augustine's ecclesiological interpretation of Revelation 20 became the majority interpretive position, leading, as Daley puts it, to the "widespread tendency of later Latin theology to identify the Kingdom of God, at least in its first stage of existence, with the institutional Catholic church."[20] Hence, while in dispensational premillennialism the church appears somewhat peripheral to God's overarching purposes, in the development of Augustinian amillennialism the church and God's kingdom become virtually identified.

Among all the church fathers, though, whether they were the premillennialist minority or the amillennialist majority, unity reigned in the call to holiness in the light of Christ's imminent coming. John Chrysostom, for example, archbishop of Constantinople in the late fourth century, firmly believed that Jesus' return to earth was soon to take place. He identified the preaching of the gospel throughout the world as a sign of Jesus' imminent return. Chrysostom warned, however, of the dangers of an eschatological curiosity divorced from a life centered in the gospel. He reminded his listeners that their lives would end with the consummation of this age. Were they prepared to greet their Lord? Had their words and lives faithfully reflected the life of the one they so eagerly awaited? A life of Christian integrity far outweighed the value of a detailed prophecy chart. Thus he writes, "Is not the consummation of the world, for each of us, the end of his own life? Why are you concerned and worried about the common end? . . . The time of consummation took its beginning with Adam, and the end of each of our lives is an image of the consummation. One would not be wrong, then, in calling it the end of the world."[21]

My exposure to patristic teaching has helped me understand that the premillennial eschatological position possessed its own respected lineage in the history of the church. While certain aspects of premillennialism are more recent developments, particularly dispensational emphases, its overall perspective goes back to the second century to Justin and Irenaeus.

Patristic theology and history, however, also taught me that other distinguished fathers such as Augustine clearly believed premillennialism reflected a poor reading of Scripture. These fathers force me to listen continually to other voices that I might too quickly overlook or ignore, voices that have proven themselves over hundreds of years to be reliable guides. The benefit of listening to them will be at least threefold for modern readers.

First, interaction with these voices might actually strengthen our present perspectives and convictions. Those who advocate a premillennial eschatology can find allies in fathers such as Justin and Irenaeus. If no fathers defended a premillennial position, however, modern premillennialists would clearly be swimming upstream theologically and would have to ask themselves, what are the odds that we are the only people in the history of the church who have discovered the truth concerning Christ's second coming?

Second, learning theology with the church fathers continually rebukes the fallen human inclination toward theological and spiritual pride, an exaggerated and overblown appreciation and advocacy of what we perceive the truth to be. For instance, as we read the fathers we will quickly realize that we do not need to reinvent the wheel. We are not the first Christians to read Scripture—a surprise to no one but me on my worst days—and those who have come before us have much to offer, if only we will open ourselves to their advice and insight. In fact, I am increasingly convinced that the task of theology is the constant, nuanced, prayerful reappropriation of the heart of the Christian faith and its careful and sensitive communication to the modern world in which we live. The soundest theology will protect, preserve and effectively communicate the church's theological legacy, rather than succumbing to the temptation to create compulsively new theological models out of whole cloth. Vincent of Lerins, for instance, argues that the soundest and safest Christian reflection consists in

> what you have received, not what you have thought up; a matter not of ingenuity, but of doctrine; not of private acquisition, but of public Tradition; a matter brought to you, not put forth by you, in which you must be not the author but the guardian, not the founder but the sharer, not the leader, but the follower.[22]

I am not arguing that there will never be progress in comprehending or communicating Christian truth, but as Thomas C. Oden puts it, "true progress is not change. True progress is an advance in understanding of that which has been fully given in the deposit of faith."[23]

Third, the fathers will consistently prod us to focus on the heart of the matter. They themselves were forced to pray and think through communally the meaning of the gospel, frequently in response to other teachers who were exaggerating, ignoring, distorting or undercutting important aspects of Christian truth. The doctrines of the incarnation and Trinity, for instance, were largely forged against the anvil of the teaching of Arius, a presbyter in the fourth century who believed Jesus to be a highly exalted creature. Arius's teaching forced early Christian leaders such as Athanasius to focus on the heart of the matter, and Christ's deity was affirmed at Nicaea (A.D. 325) and reaffirmed at Constantinople (381). Surprisingly, heretical teaching helps the church to clarify its own understanding of the gospel, a dynamic worthy of further exploration.

The Surprising Role of Heresy

We have previously commented that error can often spur one to seek the truth. Heresy has often performed this troubling function for the church. Surely faulty teaching prodded the church to understand Christ more clearly, both in his deity and humanity.

Exactly what is heresy? Tertullian, writing in the early third century A.D., argued that heresy could be identified by its divergence from apostolic teaching and doctrine. He describes a distinct paradigm of revelation and authority. First, Jesus in his earthly ministry "declared what he was, what he had been, what was the Father's will which he was carrying out, what was the conduct he laid down for humankind: all this he declared either openly to the people or privately to the disciples."[24]

Second, Tertullian explains that Jesus "chose twelve leading ones to be his close companions, appointed as leaders of the nations." These men proceeded to plant churches throughout the Mediterranean basin and in doing so "published the same doctrine of the same faith." These churches, founded by apostles who had in turn been selected by Jesus as his authoritative representatives and interpreters, were all part of one connected plant or vine. Indeed, Tertullian contends, newer churches "borrowed the shoot of faith and the seeds of doctrine" from those previously planted. It is this shared seed, a dissemination of common apostolic life and doctrine, that identifies a church as "apostolic, as being the offspring of apostolic churches. Every kind of thing must needs be classed with its origin. And so the churches, many and great as they are, are identical with that one primitive Church issuing from the Apostles, for thence they are all derived. So all are primitive and all apostolic, while all are one."[25]

Third, Tertullian believes that only preaching and doctrine that matches apostolic teaching should be received in the church.

> Now the substance of their preaching, that is, Christ's revelation to them, must be approved, on my ruling, only through the testimony of those churches which the Apostles founded by preaching to them both *viva voce* and afterwards by their letters. If this is so, it is likewise clear that all doctrine which accords with these apostolic churches, the sources and origins of the faith, must be reckoned as truth, since it maintains without doubt what the churches received from the Apostles, the Apostles from Christ, and Christ from God. . . . We are in communion with the

apostolic churches because there is no difference of doctrine. This is our guarantee of truth.[26]

What, then, is heresy? For Tertullian at least, heresy is teaching that can be identified by its diversity and contrariety. That is, as Tertullian puts it, "it originates neither from an apostle nor from an apostolic man; for the Apostles would not have diverged from one another in doctrine; no more would the apostolic man have put out teaching at variance with that of the Apostles."[27]

Irenaeus, a gifted father writing in the second century, also emphasized the importance of apostolic teaching and tradition in the propagation of the gospel and particularly stressed the important role bishops played in preserving and protecting apostolic truth. "By 'knowledge of the truth,'" Irenaeus writes, "we mean the teaching of the Apostles; the order of the Church as established from the earliest times throughout the world." Irenaeus contends that the "distinctive stamp of the Body of Christ" is "preserved through the episcopal succession: for to the bishops the Apostles committed the care of the church which is in each place, which has come down to our own time."[28] Heresy can be identified, Irenaeus believes, by the willingness of the heretic to proclaim a message "that he himself has discovered by himself—or rather invented." When the heretic is presented with the tradition derived "from the Apostles, and which is preserved in the churches by the successions of presbyters, then they oppose tradition, claiming to be wiser not only than the presbyters but even than the Apostles, and to have discovered the truth undefiled."[29] Irenaeus explains that in distinction from the heretic—a theological maverick of sorts—the genuinely "talented theologian . . . will not say anything different from these beliefs (for 'no one is above his teacher'): nor will the feeble diminish the tradition."[30]

Athanasius, bishop of Alexandria in the fourth century, says much the same thing in his critique of his Arian adversaries. "How," Athanasius asks, "can they deny that this heresy is foreign, and not from our fathers? But what is not from our fathers, but has come to light in this day, how can it be but that of which the blessed Paul has foretold, that 'in the latter times some shall depart from the sound faith, giving heed to seducing spirits and doctrines of devils'?"[31]

Heresy, then, is the willful propagation of a position or perspective that runs against the grain of apostolic teaching and tradition. It is frequently linked to specific personalities, precisely because at the core of heresy is often an individual's intentional choice to advocate and promote a teaching that the church has not communally received and cannot discover in or reconcile with the teaching of the apostles. Athanasius himself comments that heresy is often marked by the name of its teacher, specifically because it is that teacher's unique doctrine that sets a group apart from the church at large. Orthodox Christians, on the other hand, are marked by their refusal to link themselves with any other name than that of Christ.

> For never at any time did Christian people take their title from the bishops among them, but from the Lord, on whom we rest our faith. Thus, though the blessed Apostles have become our teachers, and have ministered the Savior's gospel, yet not from them have we our title, but from Christ we are and are named Christians. But for those who derive the faith that they profess from others, it is with good reason that they should bear [their teacher's name], for they have become his property.[32]

Athanasius lists various splinter groups that have adopted their leader's name: the Marcionites, Valentinians, Basilidians, Manichees, Simonians and Novatians. Such identification with a particular leader, Athanasius insists, is a flashing warning signal:

> When Alexander of blessed memory [Athanasius's predecessor as bishop of Alexandria] had cast out Arius, those who remained with Alexander remained Christians; but those who went out with Arius left the Savior's name to us who were with Alexander, and as for them they were henceforward called Arians. Note that after Alexander's death those in fellowship with his successor Athanasius are instances of the same rule. None of them bears his name, nor is he named from them, but all in a similar manner and as is custom are called Christians. For though we have a succession of teachers and become their disciples, yet, because we are taught by them the things of Christ, we both are, and are called Christians all the same.[33]

As we will investigate in some detail in chapter two, the teaching of individuals such as Arius, ultimately deemed heretical by the church, ends up performing the positive function of forcing the church to reflect more deeply on the wonder of the incarnation. The fruit? The production of a theological model—in this case, the Trinity—that more effectively preserves and communicates the wonder of the gospel itself.

Is Theology Really Necessary?

"But why," some will ask, "is there a need for theology at all? Why can't we simply preserve and proclaim the simplicity of the gospel?" On more than one occasion I have encountered students frustrated with the complexities of the Trinity or the hypostatic union who asked me, "Why do we need to bother with this? Isn't the gospel really more simple? After all, even a child can understand Jesus' message. All theology does is unnecessarily complicate matters and create an intellectual elite. It's a recipe for spiritual pride and deception. Can we skip it altogether and get back to the message of Christ?"

These are fair questions all, and it is a comfort to me to know that the fathers themselves occasionally felt these same tensions and frustrations. Hilary of Poitiers, for instance, demonstrates a similar longing for the simplicity of the gospel in his treatise on the Trinity. He almost wistfully recalls the simplicity of the baptismal formula in Jesus' commandment to the disciples in Matthew 28:19: "Go therefore and make disciples of all nations, baptizing them in the name of the Father and of the Son and of the Holy Spirit." Hilary comments: "What element in the mystery of man's salvation is not included in those words? What is forgotten, what left in darkness?"[34] Why, Hilary asks, must we tread the more difficult and complex path of theological reflection?

Such a difficult endeavor would not be necessary, Hilary responds, were it not for those teachers who distort the message of the gospel, undercutting the very truths that make the simple proclamation possible. Hence, there will always be the need to explain, clarify and protect the basic message of the gospel. As Hilary explains,

> We must strain the poor resources of our language to express thoughts too great for words. The error of others compels us to err in daring to embody in human terms truths which ought to be hidden in the silent veneration of the heart.
>
> For there have risen many who have given to the plain words of holy Writ some arbitrary interpretation of their own, instead of its true and only sense. . . . Heresy lies in the sense assigned, not in the word written; the guilt is that of the expositor, not of the text. . . . Since, therefore, they cannot make any change in the facts

recorded, they bring novel principles and theories of man's device to bear upon them. . . .We must set a limit to their license of interpretation. Since their malice, inspired by [the Adversary's] cunning, empties the doctrine of its meaning, while it retains the Names which convey the truth, we must emphasize the truth which those Names convey. [35]

Hilary urges us, then, not to abandon the need for theological clarity in a misguided longing for simplicity. It is best to acknowledge from the beginning the tendency of us all to err in our understanding of the gospel and of the need to study carefully the questions, struggles and responses of the church as it worshiped, read Scripture and clarified its understanding of the gospel in light of the errors it encountered through the years.

How can we best learn theology with the church fathers in a book such as this? Various possibilities and strategies present themselves for consideration. We might divide the book topically, discussing chapter by chapter subjects such as the Trinity, the incarnation and the atonement and drawing on the broad patristic corpus in our discussion. Such an approach would no doubt cover a broad terrain, but it runs the risk of sacrificing depth for breadth. That is, we might discover what a wide range of fathers thought about a given theological topic but never get to know individual fathers or works well. In addition, books already exist that excellently introduce patristic figures and theology in such a topical, survey form.[36]

A second approach would be to focus on many of the same doctrinal topics, but by looking in depth at the thoughts of two or three key fathers. That is, rather than covering the incarnation or the Trinity by casting a net across seven hundred years of patristic reflection, one can offer a *theological sampler* of sorts. In short, spending an evening in deep conversation with Athanasius or Cyril of Alexandria on the incarnation might well supplement the riches we can gain by a wider overview. By doing so, the reader will become acquainted with a father in some depth, with the additional benefit of accompanying that same father as he explores and explains a key subject. While in *Reading Scripture with the Church Fathers* I focused on the eight great doctors of the church, in this volume I will cast a wider net. Ante-Nicene fathers such as Justin and Irenaeus will appear alongside post-Nicene luminaries such as Augustine and Chrysostom.

Finally, readers should realize from the very beginning that I have no interest in presenting my own thoughts to you in the present volume. Rather, my goal is to act as a guide, hopefully presenting the reflections of key church fathers on central Christian doctrines in such a way that you will desire to get to know the fathers' reflections and lives even more intimately. As for the topics covered, we will attempt to center on the doctrinal heart of the Christian faith. Peripheral issues will remain just that, peripheral.

How will I identify the heart of the matter doctrinally? The best route is simply to follow the outline offered by the great creeds of the church. The roadmap presented, for example, by the Nicene Creed will keep us from wandering off the main highway on to less important side streets. And how does the creed begin?

> We believe in one God, the Father, the Almighty, maker of heaven and earth, of all that is, seen and unseen. We believe in one Lord, Jesus Christ, the only Son of God, eternally begotten of the Father, God from God, Light from Light, true God from true God, begotten, not made, of one Being with the Father.[37]

Immediately the creed focuses our attention on God the Father, God the Son and the eternal relationship between the two. Why? Why the insistence on "one God" and "one Lord"? And what of the emphasis that the Son is "begotten, not made"? How can the Son be "God from God, Light from Light, true God from true God," and Christians still claim to worship only one God? Is Christ indeed God incarnate? How could this be? Clearly the question of Christ and his relationship with the Father is of utmost significance for the Christian, whether one is young in the faith or long in the tooth. The question of Christ will not go away. How might the fathers help us to answer it?

*"Brothers, it is fitting that you should think of Jesus Christ as of God—
as the Judge of the living and the dead."*
CLEMENT OF ROME
2 Clement

"I pray for your happiness forever in our God, Jesus Christ."
IGNATIUS
Epistle of Ignatius to Polycarp

"For Christ is King, Priest, God, Lord, Angel, and Man."
JUSTIN MARTYR
Dialogue with Trypho

*"Christ Himself, therefore, together with the Father,
is the God of the living, who spoke to Moses,
and who was also manifested to the fathers."*
IRENAEUS
Against Heresies

"Our Instructor is the holy God Jesus, the Word."
CLEMENT OF ALEXANDRIA
The Instructor

Two

Christ the Son, Begotten and Not Made

The Arian Controversy

While for years the church had reflected fruitfully on the person and work of Christ, it took a specific individual to prod the church to formalize or crystallize its teaching regarding the divinity of Jesus. How so? At Alexandria in the early fourth century a presbyter by the name of Arius began to question seriously the possibility that Jesus could be divine, at least in the same sense that God or the Father was divine.

We can best understand Arius's position by sneaking a peek at his own mail. In a letter written to his friend Eusebius of Nicomedia, Arius complains of the trouble that has engulfed him in Alexandria. Arius relates that "the bishop greatly injures and persecutes us and does all he can against us, trying to drive us out of the city as godless men."[1] Why was Arius encountering such opposition? Arius writes that

> we do not agree with him [Alexander, the bishop of Alexandria] when he says publicly, "Always Father, always Son," "Father and Son together," "The Son exists unbegottenly with God," "The eternal begotten," "Unbegotten-only-one," "Neither in thought nor by a single instant is God before the Son," "Always God, always Son," "The Son is of God himself."[2]

Arius is displeased with Bishop Alexander's description of the Son, largely because Alexander is leaning over backwards in his insistence that the Son has always been with the Father. There is "no instant," as Alexander phrases it, when the Father was without the Son. Indeed, to be Father is to have a Son: "always God, always Son." If so, the Son must be divine in essence, just as the Father is. Or so it would seem.

Arius refuses to accept Alexander's formulations. Alexander's position raises a number of problems that appear insurmountable to Arius. If the Son possesses the same divine nature as the Father—is "consubstantial" with him—then "the Father is compound and divisible and alterable and a body, and according to them presumably, the bodiless God [is thought of as] suffering what belongs to a body."[3]

The Father, Arius insists, cannot share his divine nature with another. He is by definition simple (not made up of parts) and indivisible (incapable of division into parts). Hence, whoever and whatever the Son is, he cannot be eternally God, uncreated and consubstantial with the Father. Some other definition regarding the Son will have to be formulated, and Arius appoints himself for the task.

"What is it that we say, and think, and have taught, and teach?" Arius asks Eusebius.

> That the Son is not unbegotten, nor a part of the unbegotten in any way, nor [formed out] of any substratum, but that he was constituted by [God's] will and counsel, before times and before ages, full (of grace and truth), divine, unique, unchangeable. *And before he was begotten or created or ordained or founded, he was not.* For he was not unbegotten. We are persecuted because we say, "The Son has a beginning, but God is without beginning." For this we are persecuted, and because we say, "he is [made] out of things that were not." But this is what we say, since he is neither a part of God nor [formed] out of any substratum. For this we are persecuted, and you know the rest.[4]

Frankly, Arius seems to want his cake and to eat it, too. On the one hand, he wants to affirm that the Son is in some way divine. On the other hand, if Arius is to preserve God's simplicity and indivisibility, he must affirm that the Son has a beginning, even if he posits this as a beginning outside of time as we know it. Arius asserts, then, that the Son was "begotten timelessly by the Father and cre-

ated before ages and established." Arius admits that the Son is utterly unique—
"He alone was constituted by the Father"—yet the Son is "neither eternal nor co-
eternal nor co-unbegotten with the Father, nor does he have his being together
with the Father."[5]

As much as Arius struggles to maintain the unique status of the Son, he is
still left with a creature, however exalted such a one may be. Can such a creature be worshiped? Can such a creature save humanity from the awful reality of
sin? If not, if the Son indeed shares the same divine nature with the Father and
the Spirit, how can the church best think and speak of such a mysterious reality?

The Response of Athanasius

Athanasius's response to the Arian position is a deft mixture of biblical exegesis and
theological insight.[6] Athanasius insists that Arius's explanation of the Son's relationship to the Father is fundamentally flawed. Athanasius argues, particularly in
his great work *Orationes contra Arianos*, that Arius has failed to think through the
implications of his assertion that "the Son is from nothing" and "did not exist before
he was begotten."[7] If Arius is correct, how could the Son rightly receive such names
as "Son," "God" and "Wisdom"? If these names do not pertain to the Son by nature,
that is, because of what he essentially is, they must be attributed to him because he
participates in something beyond himself. Exactly what?

Perhaps, Arius suggests, such names can be attributed because of the Son's
"participation" in the Holy Spirit. That is, the Holy Spirit has communicated to
the Son attributes the Son himself does not possess by nature. But does not this
participation and communication reverse the order of giving and receiving that
Jesus teaches in the Gospel of John? Jesus states that the Spirit "will glorify me,
because he will take what is mine and declare it to you" (Jn 16:14). Yes, Athanasius insists, the Son does receive by participation, but this is an eternal, essential
participation, one that characterizes the relationship *between Father and Son alone*.
"This is the only possibility."[8]

Arius seems to be picturing the Father and Son as bottles or decanters that are
filled by each other's contents; in a similar fashion a prophet of God experienced
this type of participation when filled with the Spirit. In this way Arius hopes to
preserve the uniqueness of God while simultaneously elevating the "Son" to

divine status, by participation rather than nature. For instance, when Jesus gently rebukes Philip for not recognizing "that I am in the Father and the Father is in me" (Jn 14:10), Arius understands this participation or indwelling to be similar to that which other human beings have at times experienced, though Jesus experiences it to a much greater extent or degree.

Athanasius will have none of this. Participation simply does not do justice to the biblical testimony concerning Christ, nor does it provide humanity with the savior it needs to be redeemed from sin.

> "I in the Father and the Father in me" does not mean (as the Arians suppose) that they are decanted into each other, being each filled from the other, as in the case of empty vessels, so that the Son fills the Father's emptiness, and the Father the Son's, each of them separately not being full and perfect . . . for the Father is full and perfect, and the Son is "the fulness of the godhead" [Col 2:9]. Again, God is not in the Son in the same way as he comes into the saints and thus strengthens them.[9]

Of what, then, does the Son partake in his relationship with the Father? Since this partaking or sharing takes place only between the Father and the Son, it must be a sharing of "the substance of the Father," as difficult as this may be to conceive or understand. Any other kind of sharing or partaking would be external and by definition outside of the filial relationship of the Son to the Father. The Son, Athanasius argues, needs no other intermediary to communicate the Father to him. The unique status he possesses as Son in itself entails an immediate, timeless, eternal sharing, partaking and communion of identical substance.

Indeed, Athanasius believes, the eternal reality of God as Father demands that his Son also be eternally in relationship with him, a relationship predicated on the common substance and relationship shared. If this were not eternal and substantial, the reality of God as *Father* would be an imperfect one, one requiring a further addition, that of the Son in time. As Athanasius puts it, "To beget in time is characteristic of man: for man's nature is incomplete; God's offspring is eternal, for his nature is always perfect."[10]

An *eternal* Father, in short, demands an *eternal* Son. Was, Athanasius asks, God ever without his Word? How could he be? "Was he, who is light, without radiance? . . . God is, eternally; then since the Father always is, his brightness exists eternally." The relationship between the sun and its own light illustrates the point well.

> If a man looked at the sun and asked about its radiance, "Did that which 'is' make something which did not exist before, or something which already existed" [a frequent Arian question regarding the Father and Son] he would not be regarded as reasoning sensibly; he would in fact be crazy in supposing that what comes from the light is something external to it.[11]

Athanasius's point is that just as the sun is inseparable from its rays—to be the sun is to shed light—so for the Father to be Father is to possess a Son. How could things be otherwise? And, as he later writes in *Orations Against the Arians*, whatever kind of "begetting" is involved in the relationship between Father and Son, this begetting cannot be external to their natural, inherent paternal and filial relationship.

> We see that the radiance from the sun is integral to it, and that the substance of the sun is not divided or diminished; but its substance is entire, and its radiance perfect and entire, and the radiance does not diminish the substance of the light, but is as it were a genuine offspring from it. Thus we see that the Son is begotten not from without, but "from the Father," and that Father remains entire, while the "stamp of his substance" [Heb 1:3] exists always and preserves the likeness and image without alteration.[12]

Of course, Athanasius's argument and illustration run directly against the Arian insistence that the generation of the Son is external to the Father, that is, a generation that takes place at some "time," even if that time is before the creation of the heavens and the earth. As long as Arius insists that there was a time when the Son did not exist, such must be the case. Hence, Athanasius's use of the illustration of the sun and its rays. The two are, Athanasius insists, inseparable, as are the Father and Son.

Athanasius believes that at least part of the Arian error can be linked to the kinds of questions Arian theologians tend to ask. Think of the following two questions:

1. How can the Son exist eternally with the Father? Do not human fathers beget sons "in the course of time"? No human son existed before his father begat him in time. "The father is, say, thirty years old, and the son is begotten then and starts his

existence. In fact, every human son 'did not exist before he was begotten.'"

2. How can the Son be the Word, or the Word be the image of God?[13] Human "speech is a combination of syllables," signifying a speaker's meaning as one speaks that meaning into the air. The words did not exist before the speaker chose to speak them, and they cease to exist once they have been uttered. How, then, Arian thinkers ask, can God's Word always exist and continue to exist once it has been spoken? No human analogies exist to demonstrate that this can be possible.

That, Athanasius responds, is precisely the point. The Arians fundamentally err in limiting their thinking and speaking about God to what seems possible from a human perspective. Athanasius concedes that if the Scripture were describing a human man or relationship, the Arians would be correct. "Now if they are discussing a *man*, then they may argue about his word and his son on the human level. But if they are talking of God, man's creator, they must not think of him on the human level."[14]

This, Athanasius contends, is the Arians' fundamental mistake. Human procreation does take place in time and space. Human fathers are both older and separate from their children. Begetting does involve division and separation. Not so, however, with God. The Arians have forgotten who the subject of the discussion actually is: "The character of the parent determines the character of the offspring. Man is begotten in time and begets in time; he comes into being from non-existence." The same is true of human speech: "his word ceases and does not remain. . . . A human word is a combination of syllables, and has no independent life or activity; it merely signifies the speaker's meaning, and just issues and passes away and disappears, *since it had no existence at all before it was uttered*; therefore a man's word has no independent life and activity; in short it is not a man."[15]

The Arians are guilty of a serious category error. They have applied human categories to God in an inappropriate and illogical fashion. "God," Athanasius insists, "is not like man." Rather, "he is 'he who exists' [Ex 3:14] and exists forever." Furthermore, "his Word is 'that which exists,' and exists eternally with the Father, *as radiance from a light*. . . . But God's word is not merely 'emitted,' as one might say, nor is it just an articulate noise; nor is 'the Son of God' just a synonym for 'the command of God,' but he is the perfect offspring of the perfect."[16]

God's divine Word is, indeed, utterly unique. A human word is spoken, communicates and disappears into the air. In itself it has no capability "to affect anything." Not so with God and his Word. God, as Athanasius puts it, does not speak his Word so that a subordinate might hear God's command and then carry it out. No, "this is what happens in human affairs. But the Word of God is creator and maker, and he *is* the Father's will."[17]

The errors of Arius and his followers, Athanasius firmly believes, can be laid at the doorstep of theological and spiritual presumption. They are either asking the wrong questions or asking questions that should not be asked at all, questions such as: Why is the Word of God not like our word? How is the Word of God from God? How is he God's radiance? How does God beget? and What is the manner of his begetting? Asking such questions is much like asking: Where is God? How does God exist? and What is the nature of the Father? "It is enough merely to write down the kind of things they say," Athanasius scolds, "to show their reckless impiety. They ask such nonsensical questions as, 'Has he free will, or not?' 'Is he good from choice, of free will, and can he change, if he so will, being by nature capable of change?'. . . It is blasphemy even to utter such things."[18]

Such questions cannot be adequately asked or answered because the human mind and its accompanying speech is inadequate for explaining the deep mystery of God. As Athanasius explains, these questions "demand to have explained in words something ineffable and proper to God's nature, known only to him and to the Son."[19]

Some readers might remember Wittgenstein's example of the limitations of human language to express and explain fully even the most simple phenomena. He would ask his students to describe in words the smell of coffee. I have also repeated this language experiment with class after class of beginning theology students. The responses I have received are remarkable. What does coffee smell like? "Dirt." "Warmth." "A spring morning." "Something sweet." "Something bitter." "Wet mud." Even some of the most common human experiences, it seems, are incapable of description apart from metaphor and simile. How much more so, Athanasius argues, with the reality of God.

The Arians have forgotten with whom they are dealing, a theological and spiritual shortness of memory that reflects a serious spiritual malady Athanasius diagnoses as "a lack of reverence and ignorance of God."[20] When we measure

God by ourselves, we will inevitably fall into error. Here the link between theology and worship becomes immediate.

In fact, Athanasius argues that Christian worship makes little sense, is indeed blasphemous, if Christ is a creature, however elevated he may be. Yet Christ must be worshiped if the church is to remain true to the Scripture. "The whole earth," Athanasius reminds his reader, "sings the praises of the Creator and the truth, and blesses him and trembles before him."[21] Rightly so. But who is this Creator? Does not both Old and New Testament point to the Word, the Word now incarnate in Christ?

John's prologue to his Gospel comes to mind: "In the beginning was the Word, and the Word was with God, and the Word was God. . . . All things came into being through him, and without him not one thing came into being" (Jn 1:1, 3). Jesus himself had taught, Athanasius reminds his reader, that "my Father is still working, and I also am working" (Jn 5:17). And had not the Old Testament wisdom literature averred that "when he [God] marked out the foundations of the earth, then I [God's Wisdom] was beside him, like a master worker; and I was daily his delight, rejoicing before him always, rejoicing in his inhabited world and delighting in the human race" (Prov 8:29-31)?

The logic of worship, then, seems to be plain. If God's Wisdom and Word creates, as Creator he is worthy of praise and adoration. And if God's Wisdom and Word is worthy of the church's worship, he must be God, though in an ineffable, mysterious fashion.

The Arians felt that Athanasius was moving much too quickly. Did Proverbs 8 really teach what Athanasius was saying? What of Proverbs 8:22? "The LORD created me at the beginning of his work, the first of his acts of long ago." Surely if the text spoke of God's Wisdom as created, it must have a beginning, even if that beginning was somehow before time itself. Here, at least from Athanasius's perspective, we approach the heart of the Arians' error. Had not the apostle Paul described the Son as "before all things" (Col 1:17)? Athanasius reasons that if the Son is "before all things," the creation of Wisdom mentioned in Proverbs must be pointing to a specific purpose in the "economy" of God, that is, God's plan for human salvation.

> If he is before all things, yet says, "he created me"—not "that I might make the works" but—"for the works," then either "he created" refers to something later

than himself, or he will clearly be later than the works, finding them already in existence when he is created, and created "for" them. If so, how can he be before all things? And how were all things "made through him" and "are established in him"?[22]

Clearly Athanasius believes that if we compare Scripture with Scripture, Paul with the text of Proverbs, we are driven to discover a different interpretation for Proverbs 8:22 than that of the Arians. Athanasius finds his answer in the rhyme and reason of the incarnation and Christ's redemption of humanity.

Proverbs 8:22 does speak of God's Wisdom as created. When did this creation take place? At the time of the incarnation, Athanasius contends, when the Word "put on created flesh." The Wisdom of God was "created for his works," in the sense that in the incarnation the Son becomes what we are to save us from what we have become. "If he says that he was 'created for the works' it is clear that he means to signify not his substance but the dispensation [incarnation] which happened 'for his works.' "[23]

To sum up, Athanasius's defense of the Son's essential deity contains the following key points.

1. The Son's entire being belongs to and shares in the substance of the Father, "as radiance from light, and stream from source. . . . For the Father is in the Son as the sun is in its radiance, the thought in the word, the source in the stream."[24] The Son, then, is both *in* the Father substantially and derives his being *from* the Father. Both John 10:10, "the Father and I are one," and John 14:10, "I am in the Father and the Father is in me," point to "the identity of the godhead and the unity of the substance."

2. If the relationship between the Father and Son is not carefully articulated and nuanced, any number of errors can occur. For example, we can think that God possesses parts, the Father being one part and the Son another. No, Athanasius teaches, they are "one thing."[25] God does not have parts, as though God were a composite being constructed out of building blocks.

The moment we insist on the essential unity of the Father and Son, however, we risk thinking that no true or essential distinctions exist between Father and Son. "Father" and "Son" simply become "two names" with no essential distinctions behind them, "one thing with two names . . . the Son is at one time Father, at another time his own Son." The names "Father" and "Son" become merely masks

God wears as God plays out certain roles. Here, Athanasius reminds us, we encounter the heresy of Sabellius. No, "they are two, in that the Father is father and not also son; the Son is son and not also father, but the nature is one."[26] The true doctrine holds to essential unity and essential distinctions.

If we conceptualize the distinction between Father and Son at the expense of their substantial unity, we quickly end up with—counting the Holy Spirit—three separate gods, the heresy of tritheism. "The Son is not another God, for he was not devised from outside [the Father]; for then there might surely be many gods, if we assume a godhead besides the Father."[27]

The deity of the Son, that is, finds its source or fount in the deity of the Father. As the "offspring" of the Father, Athanasius writes, the Son is indeed distinct. But we must not allow this fundamental distinction to blur "the identity of the one godhead":

> For the radiance also is light, not a second light besides the sun, nor a different light, nor a light by participation in the sun, but a whole proper offspring of it. No one would say that there are two lights, but that the sun and its radiance are two, while the light from the sun, which illuminates things everywhere, is one. In the same way the godhead of the Son is the Father's.[28]

3. The essential oneness of the Father and Son indicates, Athanasius argues, that whatever is predicated of the Father must be predicated of the Son, "except the title of 'Father.' " That is, if the Father is sovereign as an attribute of deity, the Son possesses that same attribute. If the Father is Lord, the Son is Lord. If the Father is Light, the Son is Light. "Thus, since they are one, and the godhead itself is one, the same things are predicated of the Son as of the Father, except the title of 'Father.' "[29]

Further Questions to Explore

What might the implications of Athanasius's thought be for key issues facing the church today? For one thing, the theology of Athanasius demonstrates how careful we must be in pondering thoroughly the language we employ in our theological reflection, speech and worship of God. Think, for example, of the debates that have raged in recent years concerning the use of inclusive language in the translation of Scripture and the church's liturgy. Can or should we continue to use language such as "Father" in describing God, particularly in light of the rampant sexual abuse many women have experienced in the modern world? Would not a change to "Creator" rather than "Father" be more than appropriate?

Those of us who have never experienced abuse related to gender issues are liable to roll our eyes at this point. Before we do so, however, allow me to share from my own experience as a college professor. Over the past ten years I have regularly taught an undergraduate course titled "Foundations of Christian Spirituality." I teach this course at a Christian liberal arts university that is firmly rooted in the values and ethos of the evangelical tradition. Most of our students come from an evangelical background. Many have been raised in families and church environments where their parents and pastors have consistently affirmed the inspiration and authority of the Bible, faithfully preached the necessity of repentance from sin and faith in Christ as Savior and Lord, and fervently urged the necessity of sharing the good news of Christ with friends and strangers. Some of my students sense a distinct call to ministry. Not a few are planning to pursue this call in seminary, youth ministry or service in parachurch agencies within the evangelical spectrum. This remains extremely encouraging to me.

However, I am increasingly aware that all is not well in the evangelical heart. A disturbing, shadow side of the evangelical world has opened up to me as I have read the journals kept by students as a central course requirement in Foundations. I ask students to record and reflect upon key individuals, groups, perceptions, questions, struggles, barriers and life experiences that have shaped their understanding of God and themselves. For example, I might ask a class to note in their journals the good and bad habits that nourish or strangle their spiritual lives. Another entry might explore how their surrounding culture has "squeezed them into its mold" (Rom 12:2 Phillips). Further entries could investigate how relationships with parents, siblings, pastors and other significant mentors continue to shape my students' understanding of God or their relationship with Christ. As the semester progresses, this process of spiritual exploration and discovery continues.

The first time I read my students' journals I was overcome with surprise and dismay. I quickly learned that the level of pain, tragedy and sin that my students had experienced, not infrequently at home or in a church setting, was elevated far beyond my unsuspecting expectations. The journals I read spoke of incest, child molestation, rape, abortion, greed, materialism and widespread, deep-seated spiritual confusion and disillusionment. Not all journals presented this picture of spiritual infection. Some students were clearly growing spiritually and demonstrated a healthy and expanded self-understanding. Many, though, freely admitted a radical disjunction between what they confessed with their minds and mouths, and what they actually believed in their private, hidden world and experienced in their daily patterns of living. As shocking as this first experience in journal reading was for me, I comforted myself with the thought that perhaps this initial grouping of students were particularly troubled folk and did not represent a fair sample of the evangelical student population.

As time passed, however, the same pattern consistently duplicated itself. In fact, I have come to the point where I fully expect that, within a group of forty to sixty evangelical students, one-fourth to one-third will be sexually active, struggling with substance abuse, alienated from parents, addicted to pornography, wounded by divorce, or the victims of rape or incest. Some students, particularly women, recurrently relate their distrust of pastors because of the emotional and occasional sexual abuse they have suffered from their church leaders.

Consider, for example, the story of Susan, who grew up in an ostensibly Christian home, the daughter of an evangelical pastor. From an early age Susan heard the gospel preached by her father. She learned well the story of Jesus and the language, narratives and key concepts of the Bible. Behind the appearance of healthy spirituality and life, however, festered a darker reality. For years Susan's father sexually and physically abused her. One sad result is that Susan experiences a continuing struggle to perceive the gospel apart from the intense feelings of anger, hatred, guilt, confusion and disjunction that she feels toward her father.

Susan has experienced the love of Christ and by God's grace is slowly breaking free from the horror of her past. Nevertheless, the damage inflicted by her father, the glaring incongruity of the preacher's words and the father's lust, lingers. It was from her father that Susan first learned of Christ, one who loves her infinitely and calls for trust and commitment in response, yet it was her abuser who issued Christ's call to faith and discipleship. Susan offers a chilling analysis of her predicament: "It seems that I have two choices. Either I choose to die or I choose to deny God. If I choose to affirm God I encounter the face of my father, the terrorist of my existence. It seems my only escape is to die myself. If I choose to deny God I free myself from my father, but also lose the safe haven and love I long for. My own death seems the only alternative."

Cornelius Plantinga Jr. describes the terrible dynamic operative in the lives of women such as Susan who have suffered sexual abuse in a "Christian" context:

> A faithful father . . . accepts his small daughter's trust and love, strengthens them, and tries to extend them toward God and out toward the world. A sexually abusive father also accepts his daughter's trust and love, but he uses them to bind his daughter to his lust. Sooner or later, he converts trust to fear and love to resentment. He strengthens *these* emotions with each episode of abuse, and, whether he wants to or not, may extend them toward God and out toward the world.[30]

A spiral of disjunction seems to be operative here. First, a pastor or "Christian" father speaks of Christ while simultaneously sexually exploiting his "audience." Second, the spiral of disjunction deepens as the victim of this abuse in turn experiences deep disjunction in her relationship with God and her father. God, the source of all light, life and love, comes to represent the exact opposite. As Susan explains, she finds herself boxed in with no escape route. The only apparent alternatives are God (i.e., her father) or death itself. What might Athanasius have to say to a woman such as Susan, a woman for whom the word *father* represents the abuser who robbed her of her innocence?

First, Athanasius would have to address the issue of Susan's abuse and acknowledge her difficulty in addressing God as Father. On a pastoral level, he might well suggest other scriptural titles and metaphors for God as apt alternatives for Susan. I also think Athanasius would emphasize that words such as *Father* and *Son* are models that the Scripture uses to describe relationships that are in reality indescribable or ineffable. That is to say, out of the various alternatives human language offers us to describe relationships within the Godhead, God through apostolic testimony and interpretation has indicated that certain words describe intratrinitarian relationships more effectively than others.

Some of Athanasius's Greek opponents, for example, contended that using "Unoriginate" instead of "Father" would help to erase many of the theological conundrums Father and Son language seemed to pose. Athanasius rejected such a substitution on both biblical and theological grounds. To substitute *Unoriginate* for *Father* is to use "unscriptural" language, whereas the use of *Father* is "simple and scriptural and more accurate."[31]

If we begin to substitute words such as *Unoriginate* or *Maker* in place of *Father*, we inevitably will end up substituting one model or picture of God for another. *Unoriginate*, a term that would make sense to many Greeks, nevertheless cannot picture or describe adequately the wonder of intratrinitarian relationships. Perhaps the following chart will help to map out the difference between calling God "Unoriginate" or "Maker" and calling God "Father," together with the implications of each model or term for relations within the Trinity.

Athanasius would also readily admit that certain aspects of the word *Father* when used in a human context certainly do not apply when the term is used of God. In fact, Athanasius insists that the Arians consistently misunderstand how human language and conceptual models apply to divine realities. We misunderstand what we mean when we speak of God as Father if we apply or transfer human patterns to the divine reality. God as Father, for instance, does not procreate a Son as human fathers produce children.

Unoriginate/Maker and Work	Father and Son
A "work is external" to the nature of the one who has created or made it. [32]	"A son is the proper offspring" of his father's "essence."
There is no need for a work to be in any sense "eternal" or outside time. "A work need not have been always, for the workman frames it when he will."	"An offspring is not subject to will, but is proper to the essence."
A person can receive the name "Maker," though the works are not as yet," that is, yet to be created.	A person cannot "be called" nor "be" a father "unless a son exist."
God, then, can be called "Maker" or "Creator" before any created reality has come into existence. No created thing must be viewed as eternal simply because God has the name "Maker" or "Creator," "although God always had the power to make, yet the things originated had not the power of being eternal. For they are out of nothing, and therefore were not before their origination; but things which were not before their origination, how could these coexist with the everlasting God?"	The Son is not a work, a created reality that has come into existence in time and thus by nature separated from the Father. No, the Son "not being a work, but proper to the Father's offspring, always is." Why? The Father himself always is and cannot exist as Father apart from his Son. To describe the Father apart from the Son is both an ontological and relational impossibility. "For the offspring not to be ever with the Father, is a disparagement of the perfection of His essence."

In other words, the Son is "the eternal offspring of the Father." As such, whatever the generation of the Son by the Father means, it cannot mean that the

Father generated the Son as a human father procreates children, "as man to man," or from one human to another. "For whereas it is proper to men to beget in time, from the imperfection of their nature, God's offspring is eternal, for His nature is ever perfect."[33] How, Athanasius asks, could God ever be without his Word, the sun without its rays? To exist in such a state would mean that God was not Father, the sun a dead star.

To fail to see the limitations of human language or to reduce divine intratrinitarian relationships to human linguistic or conceptual boundaries is to think and theologize in a "material" manner.

> And is it not a grievous error, to have material thoughts about what is immaterial, and because of the weakness of their proper nature to deny what is natural and proper to the Father? It does but remain, that they should deny Him also, because they understand not how God is, and what the Father is, now that, foolish men, *they measure by themselves* the Offspring of the Father.[34]

Some readers might well be thinking, "Take a reality pill! Speak in plain English to Susan. Help her to understand Athanasius. What he has to say is important, but only if it reaches Susan's ears in a manner she can understand. If you worked hard to build a bridge between Susan and Athanasius, what would it look like?"

First, I think I would emphasize to Susan that Athanasius—and the church through the ages—would want her to know that *Father* in reference to God does not mean the same thing as "father" when referred to human beings. Consider the following contrasts. A human father, in distinction from God as Father, is created, finite, human, male, and begets offspring through human procreation. In addition, all human fathers are infected with sin and apart from the grace of God apt to manifest that sinfulness in awful ways. A catalogue of abuse characterizes fallen human fatherhood. In modern North American culture this abuse frequently appears in the form of domestic violence and sexual abuse of women and children.

However, when Athanasius—or Scripture for that matter—uses the word *Father* in referring to God, some aspects of human fatherhood would still apply. The idea of a good father as a protector or provider comes to mind. Other aspects of human fatherhood, however, will have to be left behind. God is not an exploitive male, for instance. God is not finite, human, male or infected with sin. God does not beget sons or daughters through sexual procreation.

It is easier to explain what we do not mean when we speak of God as Father than to explain well what we do mean. Such is often the case when we try to wrap human language around divine realities. They consistently, inevitably elude our attempt to capture them. Perhaps words such as *Father* and *Son* are best seen as a kind of theological shorthand, words that always point beyond themselves to a mysterious, ineffable reality that defies description.

By *Father* and *Son*—words borrowed from the household language of everyday human life—we mean that God is much more wonderfully complex than we would have ever imagined. For one thing, these words teach us that God is personal. God, before creation ever occurred, was giving and receiving love within the divine essence itself. God has always existed as a community of love, a love expressed not only between Father and Son but, as we will shortly see, between Father, Son and Holy Spirit.

Not only does God exist in a communion of love, but the words *Father* and *Son* teach us that God has eternally existed in such a way. God has always been and will always be Father. He has not become Father at a certain point in time. There was never a time when he was not Father. If so, God as Father must always have had a Son, a Son who finds his origin in the Father, a Son "begotten" by the Father, but in a generation that is eternal and ineffable.

All analogies and metaphors begin to break down at this point, precisely because we have no realities within creation that can describe such a mysterious communion. It is, indeed, indescribable. If Susan is still following Athanasius's argument, she might well ask at this juncture, "Then why bother trying to speak of such a mysterious reality at all?"

I can hear Athanasius respond, "I would rather have remained silent and simply adored the mystery and wonder of God in worship. Unfortunately, certain teachers began to speak of this mystery in such a way that the gospel itself was desperately threatened. How could I remain silent when Arius began to teach that the Son was an exalted creature? Can a creature save us from sin? Susan, could a creature save you—or, by the grace of God—your father? Never. Yes, reverent silence and adoring worship is much more the proper response to the wonder and mystery of God. But there comes a time to speak, if only to build a boundary around the mystery itself. And that is what I have attempted to do. But do know, Susan, that the Father I present to you includes all that you had hoped for in a human father and much, much more. He has chosen to manifest his love by sending his Son into the world of your pain and suffering to redeem that world. But God could only do so if he is genuinely Father, Son and Holy Spirit."

Ah, yes, the Holy Spirit. How are we to speak well of the Spirit? Not only does the Spirit pose a challenge if we are to worship and think well of God, but how can we faithfully affirm that we worship only one God if God is as complex as both Scripture and Athanasius contend? Here we face the wonder, mystery and challenge of the Trinity.

"Let us now enter upon theological questions,
setting at the head thereof the Father, the Son, and the Holy Ghost,
of whom we are to treat; that the Father may be well pleased,
and the Son may help us, and the Holy Spirit may inspire us;
or rather that one illumination may come upon us from the one God,
one in diversity, diverse in unity, wherein is a marvel."

GREGORY OF NAZIANZUS
The Second Theological Oration—On God

"For it is known with complete certainty from the scriptures
and is thus to be devoutly believed . . .
that the Father is and the Son is and the Holy Spirit is,
and that the Son is not the same as the Father is,
nor is the Holy Spirit the same as the Father or the Son.
So human inadequacy searched for a word to express three what,
and it said substances or persons.
By these names it did not wish to give any idea of diversity,
but it wished to avoid any idea of singleness;
so that as well as understanding unity in God,
whereby there is said to be one being, we might also understand trinity,
whereby there are also said to be three substances or persons."

AUGUSTINE
The Trinity

THREE

THE MYSTERY
AND WONDER OF
THE TRINITY

The Puzzle of Trinitarian Arithmetic

Times have changed. In the theologically charged atmosphere of the fourth century, Gregory of Nyssa grumbled that it was impossible to accomplish even simple tasks without being challenged to doctrinal debate by the local banker or baker. "If you ask for the price of bread, you're told the Father is greater and the Son inferior. If you ask is the bath ready, someone answers the Son was created from nothing."

By way of contrast to Gregory's complaint, compare the frustration and skepticism of Enlightenment figures such as Immanuel Kant and Thomas Jefferson over the logic and practical value of the doctrine of the Trinity. Kant, for example, argued that the doctrine had no practical significance: "The doctrine of the Trinity provides nothing, absolutely nothing, of practical value, even if one claims to understand it; still less when one is convinced that it far surpasses our understanding. It costs the student nothing to accept that we adore three or ten persons in the divinity. . . . Furthermore, this distinction offers absolutely no guidance for his conduct."

Jefferson seems particularly irritated by the complexities of trinitarian arithmetic, a theological mathematics that only served to blur our vision of who Jesus truly was: "When we shall have done away with the incomprehensible jargon of the Trinitarian arithmetic, that three are one, and one is three; when we shall have knocked down the artificial scaffolding, reared to mask from view the very simple structure of Jesus; when, in short, we shall have unlearned everything which has been taught since his day, and got back to the pure and simple doctrines he inculcated, we shall then be truly and worthily his disciples."[1]

So who is correct? Gregory of Nyssa or Kant and Jefferson? Most conservative Christians would say Gregory, but perhaps in the back of our minds doubts linger. What difference, we ask ourselves, does such an apparently esoteric doctrine really make after all? Is the Trinity not, in the final analysis, more a theological mind game than a creedal statement by which orthodox belief stands or falls? In *Knowing the Name of God: A Trinitarian Tapestry of Grace, Faith and Community*, Roderick T. Leupp captures well our hidden reservations about the Trinity:

> For most people and, sadly, for most Christians also, the Trinity is the great unknown. The Trinity, to use a familiar equation, is viewed as a riddle wrapped up inside a puzzle and buried in an enigma. A riddle, for how can any entity be at the same time multiple (three) yet singular (one)? A puzzle, for the Trinity is so clearly contrary to any rational thought as not to warrant a second thought from sensible people. An enigma, for even if the Trinity could be understood, of what practical value, even what religious value, would it have for ordinary people?[2]

Not much, many of us might be tempted to say. As Karl Rahner notes, "Despite their orthodox confession of the Trinity, Christians are, in their practical life, almost mere monotheists."[3]

I sympathize with the frustrations many Christians experience when it comes to the doctrine of the Trinity. "What difference does it really make whether one believes in the Trinity or not?" many ask. "I've never found the word 'Trinity' in the Bible," others complain. "If this doctrine were so crucial for our understanding of God and a healthy spiritual life, wouldn't writers such as Paul or John have been more explicit in their teaching?"

These are all good questions, and we would be mistaken to think that we are the first Christians to have asked them. From the moment believers in Christ began to read and ponder apostolic teaching and its implications, questions about the nature of God quickly rose to the surface. Fourth-century bishops such as Athanasius were not the first to realize that the apostles' understanding of God seemed to lead to mysterious and complex conclusions. How could the teaching of the Bible be expressed in a theological model that preserved both the monotheistic roots of Christianity and the Christ worshiped by the church? Richard P. C. Hanson comments:

> The subjects under discussion between 318 and 381 were not, as has sometimes been alleged, those raised by Greek theology or philosophy and such as could only have been raised by people thinking in Greek terms. . . . In the fourth century there came to a head a crisis . . . which was not created by either Arius or Athanasius. It was the problem of how to reconcile two factors which were part of the very fabric of Christianity: monotheism, and the worship of Christ as divine. . . . The theologians of the Christian Church were slowly driven to a realization that the deepest questions which face Christianity *cannot be answered in purely biblical language, because the questions are about the meaning of biblical language itself.* In the course of this search the Church was impelled reluctantly to form dogma. It was the first great and authentic example of the development of doctrine.[4]

Hanson's point must be remembered. The fathers of the church formulated the doctrine of the Trinity because they believed a faithful and careful reading of the Bible drove them to do so. Patristic theology, then, is first and foremost based on careful exegesis. In short, patristic writers develop and affirm the complex trinitarian model because they are convinced such a paradigm faithfully reflects and illustrates the teaching of Jesus and the apostles concerning the nature of God. The God they have encountered in Christ through the Spirit has proven by divine actions and the inspired interpretation of those actions to be mysterious, complex and intensely relational. For years church fathers and early Christian writers interpreted, described, analyzed and debated the biblical data itself. The final conclusion, framed toward the end of the fourth century, was that God must exist and act as both a unity and a Trinity—a shocking and surprising conclusion for defenders of the Nicene Creed and its opponents.

Defenders of the Nicene Creed such as Athanasius argued that Scripture and the necessities of salvation itself demonstrated the validity and appropriateness of a trinitarian model, one founded on biblical exegesis but free to employ new terms not found in the Bible—among them *homoousios*—to explain and elucidate the implications of the biblical data concerning the Father, Son and Holy Spirit. That is to say, Athanasius contended that, if the Bible is reliable and the church was reading it well, a trinitarian model was unavoidable, indeed absolutely necessary.

The conclusions reached at the Council of Nicaea were debated and frequently rejected by many for a period of more than fifty years. Some theologians rejected Nicaea because they felt its newly coined terms—again, *homoousios* comes to mind—went too far beyond the boundaries of the biblical testimony itself. These writers, sympathetic to Nicaea and theologically conservative, longed to see the church more firmly tied to the Bible.

Other theologians and early Christian leaders such as the Alexandrian presbyter Arius believed the biblical testimony surely spoke of Christ in an exalted fashion but, as we have seen, pictured him as an exalted creature. Perhaps the best way to explore these issues is to investigate the work of two key fathers on trinitarian concerns: Gregory of Nazianzus and Augustine.[5]

Gregory of Nazianzus—The Theological Orations

Foundational considerations. From the very outset of his theological orations, Gregory warns his audience that they and he are attempting a high and holy task. Theology, while employing the mind, also involves the heart. A pure heart, one grounded in the worship of the church and a life of prayer, will produce clear and fruitful theological reflection. A murky heart and a dark mind, on the other hand, will produce a sick, thorny theology; it will offer no nourishment, only harm.

Because of the intimate connection between mind and heart, Gregory counsels that those who choose to write on the Father, Son and Holy Spirit "ought to be, as far as may be, pure, in order that light may be apprehended by light." Theologians who would unfold Scripture can do so safely and sanely only if they themselves have been "molded" and shaped by it.[6] Only then can they "enter upon theological questions, setting at the head thereof the Father, the Son, and the Holy Ghost . . . one in diversity, diverse in unity, wherein is a marvel."[7]

Not only is a pure heart a prerequisite necessary for thinking well about God, but Gregory warns us that we must remember that there are definite limits to theological perception and understanding. Alluding to Moses' experience on Mount Sinai, Gregory describes himself as drawing "aside the curtain of the cloud," only to withdraw. "And then when I looked up, I scarce saw the back parts of God; although I was sheltered by the rock, the Word that was made flesh for us." In the shelter of the Word Gregory looks "a little closer" but does not see "the first and unmingled nature, known to itself, to the Trinity, I mean."[8] No, he views "only that nature, which at last reaches even to us." This is the "glory which is manifested among the creatures. . . . These are the back parts of God, which he leaves behind him, as tokens of himself, like the shadows and reflection of the sun in the water, which show the sun to our weak eyes, because we cannot look at the sun himself, for by his unmixed light he is too strong for our power of perception."[9] Thus, whatever we choose to write about the Father, Son and Holy Spirit is necessarily bounded by the fence God erects for our own protection. We can approach God, but only through the safeguards the Word provides.

Gregory insists that these theological boundaries include the inherent limitations of human thought and speech about God. Any discussion of the Trinity must begin with the ready and humble acknowledgment of human reason's inability to conceive and describe God's nature adequately: "It is difficult to conceive God, but to define him in words is an impossibility. . . . In my opinion it is impossible to express him, and yet more impossible to conceive him."[10]

> For that which may be conceived may perhaps be made clear by language, if not fairly well, at any rate imperfectly, to anyone who is not quite deprived of his hearing, or lazy in understanding. But to comprehend the whole of so great a subject as this is quite impossible and impracticable, not merely to the utterly careless and ignorant, but even to those who are highly exalted, and who love God.[11]

These limitations apply to "every created nature; seeing that the darkness of this world and the thick covering of the flesh is an obstacle to the full understanding." Gregory is not denying the existence of God, but he insists that the knowledge of God's essence, the nature of God, is sharply limited because God's nature is by definition "incomprehensible and illimitable."[12]

If so, what can be said? Are we left entirely in a wordless vacuum? No, Gregory insists. Both "our very eyes and the law of nature" clearly communicate to us the reality of God's existence and "that he is the efficient and maintaining cause of all things." As we gaze upon "visible objects," we see their "beautiful stability and progress, immovably moving and revolving if I may so say." Natural law in turn manifests itself because through these visible things and their order it reasons back to their author. For how could this universe have come into being or been put together unless God had called it into existence, and held it together? For everyone who sees a beautifully made lute, and considers the skill with which it has been fitted together and arranged, or who hears its melody, would think of none but the lutemaker, or the luteplayer, and would recur to him in mind, though he might not know him by sight. *And thus to us also is manifested that which made and moves and preserves all created things, even though he is not comprehended by the mind.*[13]

The difficulty that knowledge of God poses, Gregory continues, is that the "approximations" of reason will always fall short of the glory of the subject it is trying to encompass, understand and explain. Yet there are certain things we can know about God, even if our knowledge is largely a series of negations. For example, Gregory comments, we can know that God does not have a body. If God did, how could God possibly be "infinite and limitless, and formless, and intangible, and invisible"? None of these characteristics could possibly apply to one who existed within a body's confinement. How, Gregory asks, could we worship God "if he is circumscribed"? Divine embodiment would mean that God must "be made up of elements, . . . subject to be resolved into them again," or perhaps even "dissolved." Indeed, the elements themselves that formed the parts of such a strange divine composition would be more basic and fundamental than God. "Thus also there must be no body, that there may be no composition, and so the argument is established by going back from last to first."[14] That is to say, the implications of a faulty theological model—God as possessing a body—will ultimately demonstrate foundational cracks.

If God does not possess a body, then God must be "incorporeal," a conclusion Gregory readily admits. But the fact that God is incorporeal still does not tell us what God's essence is. The term *incorporeal* "does not yet set before us—or contain within itself—his essence." Neither do other terms such as unbegotten, unoriginate, unchanging, incorruptible or "any other predicate which is used concerning God or in reference to him. For what effect is produced upon his being or substance by his having no beginning, and being incapable of change or limitation?"[15] Other predicates we sometimes employ, such as "corporeal, begotten, [or] mortal," fall short unless one "clearly and adequately" describes the subject to which they apply. All, for example, could equally apply to "a man, or a cow, or a horse."

Hence, Gregory believes, those who would speak well of God must reverently and humbly move beyond a merely negative or apophatic theology. To describe God only in negative terms would be much like a mathematician "who, when asked how many twice five make, should answer, 'Not two, nor three, nor four, nor five, nor twenty, nor thirty, nor in short any number below ten, nor any multiple of ten,' " but refused to answer, "ten." A better path to follow, both in mathematics and in theology, is to broaden our knowledge "both by the elimination of negatives and the assertion of positives to arrive at a comprehension of the truth."[16] The best theologians, then, will know both when to speak and when to remain silent.

Further warnings. On the basis of this methodology, Gregory begins to add to and arrange his fundamental building blocks concerning God. Having concluded that God is incorporeal, Gregory explores the relationship of God to space. Is God "nowhere or somewhere"? If God is nowhere, is it reasonable or coherent to speak of God as existing at all? Gregory thinks not. "For if the nonexistent is nowhere, then that which is nowhere is also perhaps nonexistent." On the other hand, if God is somewhere, where is he? The only two options seem to be a spatial location within the universe or existence "above the universe."

How, Gregory wonders, can God be *in* the universe? God must either be "in some part" of the universe or "in the whole." If he inhabits only a part of the universe, however, God will end up "circumscribed by that part which is less than himself," hardly a satisfactory state of affairs. Problems also accompany placing God within the universe as a whole. For instance, "Where was he before the universe was created"?[17] If we describe God as being above the universe, what do we mean by "above"? To describe God as above something seems to demand that we still think spatially concerning where God is, a position Gregory has already found untenable.

By this time, Gregory, you and I are tempted to scream. Our linguistic and spatial categories are proving incapable of adequately describing God, which turns out to be exactly Gregory's point: "For my purpose in doing so was . . . to make clear the point at which my argument has aimed from the first. And what was this? That the divine nature cannot be apprehended by human reason, and that we cannot even represent to ourselves all its greatness."[18] Human beings in their present state are simply unable to gaze directly upon God. As embodied creatures we naturally gravitate to picturing God through the analogies in the visible world around us. Gregory, however, is insistent that the vision of God is an "object of pure thought apart altogether from bodily objects." "Thus," Gregory states, "our mind faints to transcend corporeal things, and to consort with the incorporeal, stripped of all clothing of corporeal ideas, as long as it has to look with its inherent weakness at things above its strength."[19]

Still, God has planted reason within us, "reason that proceeds from God, that is implanted in all from the beginning and is the first law in us, and is bound up in all," the reason that "leads us up to God through visible things."[20] Yet, our knowledge of God for the present will remain fragmentary at best. Why?

In this life we simply are too weak to view God's nature and essence directly. Gregory holds the hope that such will not always be the case. He refers, for instance, to Paul's words in 1 Corinthians that in the future "I will know fully, even as I have been fully known" (1 Cor 13:12). What does Paul mean?

> What God is in nature and essence . . . will be discovered when that within us which is godlike and divine, I mean our mind and reason, shall have mingled with its like, and the image shall have ascended to the archetype, of which it has now the desire. And this I think is the solution of that vexed problem as to "We shall know even as we are known." But in our present life all that comes to us is but a little effluence, and as it were a small effulgence from a great light.[21]

Hence, because of the inherent limitations of human nature, at least in its present state, there is nothing more difficult than coming to know and speak of God well. As Gregory puts it, "the truth, then—and the whole word—is full of difficulty and obscurity; and as it were, with a small instrument we are undertaking a great work, when with merely human wisdom we pursue the knowledge of the self-existent."[22]

Having warned both his audience and himself as to the pitfalls surrounding the practice of theological reflection, a thinking and speaking focused on the mystery and wonder of God, Gregory moves to an analysis of the Godhead in his third theological oration.

The Third Theological Oration—On the Son. Gregory begins by describing God in trinitarian terms. God is a "monarchy" and a "unity," a unity grounded in an "equality of nature, and a union of mind, and an identity of motion, and a convergence of its elements to unity."

Fine, we respond to Gregory, but to speak frankly, we have no idea what you are talking about. "Fair enough," Gregory might respond. Trinitarian language is inherently difficult, precisely because we have no genuine correspondences in creation to the reality of God's nature. Motion in the created order, for example, means something different from motion within the Godhead. Why, then, does Gregory use the word *motion*? It manages to convey, at least partially, the eternal movement of love between Father, Son and Holy Spirit. In Gregory's expression, "The Father is the begetter and the emitter; without passion, of course, and without reference to time, and not in a corporeal manner. The Son is the begotten, and the Holy Ghost the emission; for I know not how this could be expressed in terms altogether excluding visible things."[23]

The Father begets the Son, but not in a human manner and not in time. The Son is begotten, but has always been begotten. And the Spirit is emitted and always has been emitted. Thus, we have an eternal movement of love grounded in the essence of God himself. Nothing in our world or the wider created order matches up to such a wonder.

"When," Gregory asks, "did these come into being?" He responds, "They are above all 'when.'" There was never a time when there was not a Father, a Son and a Holy Spirit. The Father has always been unbegotten, the Son always begotten and the Spirit always proceeding from the Father and Son. This relationship of love, whose movement Gregory describes using the technical theological vocabulary of "unbegotten," "begotten," and "proceeding," is "beyond the sphere of time, and above the grasp of reason."[24]

If this relationship is above time, how are Father, Son and Spirit "not alike unoriginates"? That is, the very language of begetting and proceeding seems to demand some kind of beginning for the Son and the Holy Spirit. Here Gregory turns to the well-known patristic illustration of the sun and its rays.

Yes, the Son and Spirit find their origin in the Father, who is "unoriginate." Yet the "origin" of the Son and Spirit is eternal and timeless, without beginning and without end. Neither comes into existence after the Father. The analogy of the sun and its rays illustrates this point. Can one imagine the sun as existing apart from the light rays it constantly emits? The rays find their source, their origin, in the sun. Still, the rays and the sun came into existence at the same time.

The rays are not "after" the sun. They are part and parcel of what it means to be the sun. Granted, the analogy does break down when referring to trinitarian relationships, for the Trinity has always existed outside of time. Still, the analogy serves well in illustrating what the church means when it teaches that the Son and Spirit find their origin in the Father. The Father *must* beget the Son and spirate the Spirit, just as the sun *must* shed light.

Other questions come to mind. For instance, the only kind of generation or begetting familiar to humans entails physical bodies of some sort. God, as we have seen, has no body. How, then, can the Father generate the Son? In Gregory's expression, "How can this generation be passionless?" Gregory answers that only "corporeal generation involves passion." God's generation of the Son is "incorporeal" and outside of time.

Again, we sense that trinitarian language is stretching the capabilities of human reason and language. Precisely so. God's generation or begetting of the Son is indescribable or "ineffable." Just as the Son's "generation according to the flesh differs from all others (for where among men do you know of a virgin mother?), so does he differ also in his spiritual generation; or rather he, whose existence is not the same as ours, differs from us also in his generation."[25]

"Who, then, is that Father who had no beginning?" Gregory asks. Well, for one thing, he is a father unlike any other. For while other fathers must first be born, grow into maturity and then father children, this Father has always been a Father. It is his nature to be Father, to generate the Son and to emit, spirate or breath the Spirit.[26] In addition, the Father is Father as distinct from the Son. He is neither the Son nor the Spirit, just as the Son and Spirit are not the Father. While a human being may occasionally function as a father or a son, within the wonder of trinitarian relationships, the Father is Father in an absolute sense, as is the Son as Son, and the Spirit as Spirit. Thus, the fatherhood of God, while occasionally analogous to human fatherhood, is utterly unique.

Gregory rebukes the tendency in all of us to reject that which we cannot comprehend. Gregory's theological opponents insist, for instance, that the Son could not be "begotten," because such a generation fits no reasonable categories. Part of the problem, Gregory responds, is that the model these theologians use to picture the divine generation is itself faulty.

"First," Gregory advises, "cast away your notions of flow and divisions and sections, and your conceptions of immaterial as if it were material birth, and then you may perhaps worthily conceive of the divine generation."[27] And what is a worthy conception of such a mysterious generation? Who can say? "The begetting of God must be honored by silence. It is a great thing for you to learn that he was begotten. But the manner of his generation we will not admit that even angels can conceive, much less you." Only the Father, Son and Spirit could possibly comprehend it. "It was in a manner known to the Father who begot, and to the Son who was begotten. Anything more than this is hidden by a cloud, and escapes your dim sight."[28]

A key question. A further question presents itself. If the Father as unbegotten and the Son as begotten are indeed distinct from one another, they are obviously not the same. How can they both be the same God? Gregory poses the question as follows: "For if to be unbegotten is the essence of God, to be begotten is not that essence; if the opposite is the case, the unbegotten is excluded. What argument can contradict this?"[29]

All depends, Gregory argues, on what we mean when we say that the unbegotten and the begotten are not the same. Certainly, he agrees, "the unoriginate and the created are not of the same nature." Is such the case with the Father and the Son? "But if you say that he that begot and that which is begotten are not the same, the statement is inaccurate. For it is in fact a necessary truth that they are the same. For the relation of father to child is this: that the offspring is of the same nature with the parent."[30] Think, Gregory coaches, of Adam. "Was he not alone the direct creature of God," created in a unique manner by God? Does this mean that Adam was the only human being? Hardly. Other humans "begotten" by normal procreative means are clearly also human. What is Gregory's point? "Just so neither is he who is unbegotten alone God, though he alone is Father."

If so, how are terms such as *unbegotten* and *begotten* to be understood in terms of the unity of God? What are the possibilities? Well, "if the Son is the same as the Father in respect of essence," perhaps the Son is unbegotten. Such might be true, but only "if the essence of God consists in being unbegotten." Then the Son becomes a "strange mixture, begottenly unbegotten." Scratch one possibility off the list of possible models.

What, however, if the difference between the Father and the Son, between the unbegotten and the begotten, "is outside the essence"? On a human level, for instance, I can be a father within certain relationships, but my fatherhood is not part of the essence of what it means to be a human being. If it were, as Gregory observes, I would end up being my father's father, since I would be "the same with him in essence."[31]

Gregory comments that to investigate the "nature of the essence of God" might leave issues concerning personality or individuality "absolutely unaffected." We perhaps are on the right track here, particularly because if we describe God's nature itself as unbegotten and begotten, we end up with "contradictory essences, which is impossible."

What, however, if the names "Father" and "Son" *describe a relation*, a relation existing eternally in the nature of God?

> Father is not a name either of an essence or of an action. . . . But it is the name of the relation in which the Father stands to the Son, and the Son to the Father. For as with us these names make known a genuine and intimate relation, so in the case before us too they denote an identity of nature between him that is begotten and him that begets.[32]

Both Father and Son share a common essence. They are *homoousios*. Simultaneously they are eternally distinct in the relationship of Father and Son, unbegotten and begotten. As Gregory puts it, "there never was a time when he was without the Word, or when he was not the Father, or when he was not true, or not wise, or not powerful, or devoid of life, or of splendor, or of goodness."[33]

Further difficulties. How are we to make sense of those biblical texts that seem to picture the Son as inferior to the Father? If the Son is inferior, how can he share the same essence with the Father? The Son sleeps, hungers, struggles in Gethsemane and dies on the cross. At times Jesus' knowledge seems limited. For instance, in speaking of the last day and hour, Jesus comments that, "But about that day or hour no one knows, neither the angels in heaven, nor the Son, but only the Father" (Mk 13:32). If the Son's knowledge is less than the Father's, how can he share a common nature with him? Is the possibility of a trinitarian model undercut by texts such as these?

These are significant questions regarding the incarnate Son that must not be sidestepped, yet Gregory dares to answer them "in one sentence. What is lofty you are to apply to the Godhead, and to that nature in him which is superior to sufferings and incorporeal; but all that is lowly to the composite condition of him who for your sakes made himself of no reputation and was incarnate—yes, for it is no worse thing to say—was made man, and afterwards was also exalted."[34] The key to these difficult biblical texts is learning "to know which passages refer to his [divine] nature, and which to his assumption of human nature."

Of course, the Son was not always incarnate. "He who is now man was once the uncompounded. What he was he continued to be; what he was not he took to himself."[35] In his saving descent into our world, human nature is "united to God, and became one [person]." In a series of vibrant, shining contrasts Gregory highlights the dual nature of Christ's person and actions.

> He was baptized as man—but he remitted sins as God. . . . He was tempted as man, but he conquered as God. . . . He hungered—but he fed thousands. . . . He was wearied, but he is the rest of them that are weary and heavy-laden. . . . He prays, but he hears prayer. He weeps, but he causes tears to cease. He asks where Lazarus was laid, for he was man; but he raises Lazarus, for he was God. He is sold, and very cheap, for it is only for thirty pieces of silver; but he redeems the world, and that at a great price, for the price was his own blood. . . . As a sheep he is led to the slaughter, but he is the shepherd of Israel, and now of the whole world also. As a lamb he is silent, yet he is the Word, and is proclaimed by the voice of one crying in the wilderness. He is bruised and wounded, but he heals every disease and every infirmity. . . . He dies, but gives life, and by his death destroys death.[36]

Biblical passages, then, that contain "the higher and diviner expressions" must be attributed to Christ's deity, while we attribute "the lower and more human to Him who for us men was the second Adam, and was God made capable of suffering [to strive] against sin."[37]

A crucial hermeneutical principle. Gregory lays down a crucial hermeneutical principle in his analysis of Proverbs 8:22, "The Lord created me at the beginning of his ways with a view to his works."[38] Many early Christian exegetes saw this text as pointing to the divine Logos (Word), "the true Wisdom." If so, the text appears to teach that the Son was created, a problem for all who would affirm his timeless, eternal nature. Gregory solves the difficulty by teaching that when biblical texts such as Proverbs 8:22 speak of the Son as caused or created, they are referring to the economy or dispensation of salvation. The Son, God's Wisdom, is sent by the Father "with a view to his works," that is, "our salvation." Thus, those texts in which we find the Son described as caused or created "we are to refer to the humanity [assumed by the Son], but all that is absolute and unoriginate we are to reckon to the account of his Godhead."[39]

What of those texts in which the Son is described as a servant? Can one who is truly God rightfully be described in such a fashion? Yes, Gregory replies, if the Son's service is linked to his incarnation, "to birth and to the conditions of our life with a view to our liberation, and to that of all those whom he has saved, who were in bondage under sin."[40]

One by one Gregory leads his audience through the problematic biblical texts that appear at first glance to threaten Christ's deity, an analysis that goes beyond the space we can fairly allot it. The basic underlying principle remains the same. Some texts highlight "that nature which is unchangeable and above all capacity of suffering," and others center on Christ's "passible humanity. . . . This, then, is the argument concerning these objections, so far as to be a sort of foundation and memorandum for the use of those who are better able to conduct the inquiry to a more complete working out."[41]

Gregory closes his fourth oration by analyzing the actual titles of the Son. While the being of God "cannot be expressed in words," Gregory does believe it is possible to "sketch him by his attributes, and so obtain a certain faint and feeble and partial idea concerning him."[42] Gregory's catalogue of divine names and attributes includes the following:

1. *He Who Is* and *God*. Both are "the special names of his essence."[43]

2. *Father, Son and Holy Spirit*. Within the Godhead itself, "the proper name of the unoriginate is 'Father,' and that of the unoriginately begotten is 'Son,' and that of the unbegottenly proceeding or going forth is 'the Holy Ghost.' " More particularly, the Son is called "Son because he is identical with the Father in essence; and not only for this reason, but also because he is of him."

3. *Only Begotten*. When the Son is called Only Begotten, both his uniqueness as "the only Son" and "the manner of his Sonship" are in view. This, as we have seen, is an incorporeal, eternal and timeless generation, one "not shared by bodies."[44]

4. *Word*. The Son is called Word in relationship "to the Father as word to mind; not only on account of his passionless generation, but also because of the union, and of his declaratory function." In a manner of speaking, the Son is the

definition or "demonstration . . . of the Father's nature, [as] everything that is begotten is a silent word of him that begot it."[45]

5. *Wisdom.* The Son is "the knowledge of things divine and human. For how is it possible that he who made all things should be ignorant of the reasons of what he has made?"

6. *Power.* The Son sustains "all created things, and [provides] to them . . . power to keep themselves together."

7. *Truth.* The Son is truth "as being in nature one and not many (for truth is one and falsehood is manifold) and as the pure seal of the Father and his most unerring impress."

8. *Image.* Because the Son is of one substance with the Father, he exactly reproduces the "archetype." While normally an image "is a motionless representation," the Son as image of the Father "is the living reproduction of the living one, and is more exactly like than was Seth to Adam, or any son to his father."[46]

9. *Light.* The Son is "the brightness of souls cleansed by word and life. For if ignorance and sin be darkness, knowledge and a godly life will be light."

10. *Life.* As Life, the Son "is the constituting and creating power of every reasonable soul." The Son provides not only the breath by which we live, but "as many of us as were capable of it, and in so far as we open the mouth of our mind, with the Holy Ghost."[47]

11. *Righteousness.* The Son is a righteous judge "both for those who are under the law and for those who are under grace, for soul and body, so that the former should rule, and the latter obey, and the higher have supremacy over the lower."

12. *Sanctification.* The Son is "purity, that the pure may be contained by purity."

13. *Redemption.* The Son has set us free, for we "were held captive under sin." He gave "himself a ransom for us, the sacrifice to make expiation for the world."

14. *Resurrection.* The Son is resurrection in a twofold sense: he has himself risen from the dead, and he "brings to life again us who were slain by sin."[48]

15. *Man.* The Son's body enables he who was "incomprehensible" in his divine nature to "be apprehended by embodied creatures." In addition, through the incarnation the Son sanctifies humanity, "as it were a leaven to the whole lump." Gregory explains:

By uniting to himself that which was condemned [the Son] may release it from all condemnation, becoming for all people all things that we are, except sin— body, soul, mind, and all through which death reaches—and thus he became

man, who is the combination of all these; God in visible form, because he
retained that which is perceived by mind alone. He is son of man, both on
account of Adam, and of the Virgin from whom he came: from the one as a fore-
father, from the other as his mother, both in accordance with the law of generation, and apart from it.[49]

Finally, at the end of the fourth oration, Gregory groups together a series of
titles and names, most from the Gospel of John and Hebrews: the way ("because he
leads us through himself"), the door ("as letting us in"), the shepherd ("as making us
dwell in a place of green pastures, and bringing us up by waters of rest"), the sheep
("as the victim"), the lamb ("as being perfect"), the high priest ("as the offerer") and
Melchizedek ("as without mother in that nature which is above us, and without
father in ours; and without genealogy above . . . and, moreover, as king of Salem,
which means peace, and king of righteousness, and as receiving tithes from patriarchs, when they prevail over powers of evil").[50]

The Son, then, as demonstrated by Gregory's detailed listing of titles and
characteristics, is both divine and human, the eternal begotten Son, and—in the
economy of the incarnation and salvation—the incarnate Word who has come
to save fallen humanity. Gregory has said little, however, to this point concerning
the Holy Spirit, the third person of the Trinity.

What of the Holy Spirit? Gregory seems a bit wearied by his detailed discussion
of the Son. Yet his detailed analysis was necessary, precisely because of those in
the church who were muddled in their understanding of the Son. Even more
people, Gregory writes, are confused in their understanding of the Spirit. "But,
they go on, what have you to say about the Holy Ghost? From whence are you
bringing in upon us this strange God, of whom Scripture is silent?"[51]

Thus, even though Gregory is "worn out by the multitude of their questions,"
he sets out determinedly to examine closely Scripture's teaching on the Holy
Spirit. Gregory begins by defending the Spirit's deity. He will "begin our teaching
concerning his Godhead by fitting to him the names which belong to the Trinity,
even though some persons may think us too bold."

Gregory turns to the Gospel of John and identifies three separate lights: the
Father, the "true Light," who lights every person who comes into the world; the
Son, "the true Light"; and the Spirit, "the true Light, which gives light to every
one coming into the world" (see Jn 1:9; 14:16). "Was and was and was, but one

thing," Gregory comments. "Light thrice repeated; but one light and one God."[52]
Here in a nutshell is the doctrine of the Trinity, "simply the doctrine of God the
Trinity, comprehending out of light [the Father], light [the Son], in light [the
Spirit]."[53]

The implications of this undivided light ripple into Gregory's analysis. For
instance, this is a light outside of time that has invaded time. Father, Son and
Spirit have always existed.

> If ever there was a time when the Father was not, then there was a time when the Son
> was not. If ever there was a time when the Son was not, then there was a time when
> the Spirit was not. If the one was from the beginning, then the three were so too. If
> you throw down the one, I am bold to assert that you do not set up the other two.[54]

The only alternative to this trinitarian model, Gregory argues, would be to
place the Holy Spirit among created beings, but what good would that do? "If he
is not from the beginning, he is in the same rank with myself, even though a little
before me; for we are both parted from Godhead by time."[55]

Gregory reminds his audience of the beliefs of the Sadducees, who "denied the
existence of the Holy Spirit, just as they did that of angels and the resurrection."
The Greeks, at least those who "are more inclined to speak of God," have "some
conception of him, . . . though they differed as to his name, and have addressed
him as the mind of the world, or the external mind, and the like." Even "the wise
men among ourselves," Gregory admits, disagree regarding the Spirit. Some
"have conceived of him as an activity, some as a creature, some as God; and some
have been uncertain which to call him, out of reverence for Scripture, they say, as
though it did not make the matter clear either way."[56]

This confusion leads to the unhappy state of neither worshiping the Spirit nor
dishonoring him, the "miserable" state of neutrality. Some are so confused as to
separate Father, Son and Spirit "so completely as to make one of them infinite
both in essence and power, and the second in power but not in essence, and the
third circumscribed in both; thus imitating in another way those who call them
the creator, the co-operator, and the minister."[57]

Is the Spirit a self-existent substance, a created substance, or an accident or
divine activity? If the Spirit is merely "an accident, he would be an activity of
God" and not substantially related to the Godhead. This model does not really

work. As an activity or accident of God, the Spirit would cease to exist the moment the divine activity was finished and could not be said to experience the emotions attributed to him such as grief or anger. If not an activity, what kind of substance is the Spirit, created or uncreated? If created, "how do we believe in him, how are we made perfect in him? For it is not the same thing to believe in a thing or to believe about it. The one belongs to deity, the other to—any thing." Hence, the Spirit must be a self-existent substance and thus divine. And "if he is God, then he is neither a creature, nor a thing made, nor a fellow servant, nor any of these lowly appellations."[58]

Having established the deity of the Spirit, at least to his own satisfaction, Gregory proceeds to analyze the relationship between Father, Son and Spirit. For example, would it be appropriate to describe the Spirit as begotten, just as the church speaks of the Son as begotten by the Father? No, Gregory responds, for to do so would result in "two Sons." In turn, if we say the Spirit is begotten by the Son, we end up with a "grandson God, than which nothing could be more absurd."[59] How best can we describe the Spirit?

Gregory proposes the term *proceeds* as an apt description for the relationship of the Spirit to the Father and draws our attention to John 15:26. Jesus describes the Counselor as one he "will send to you from the Father, the Spirit of truth *who goes out* from the Father" (NIV, emphasis added). This "going out" or procession of the Spirit distinguishes the Spirit from the Son. Whereas the Son is begotten by the Father, the Spirit proceeds from the Father. The Spirit, "who, inasmuch as he proceeds from that source, is no creature; and inasmuch as he is between the unbegotten and the begotten is God." To try to say more than this is impossible, for just as the generation of the Son is ineffable, so is the procession of the Spirit. "What, then, is procession? Do you tell me what is the unbegottenness of the Father, and I will explain to you the physiology of the generation of the Son and the procession of the Spirit, and we shall both of us be frenzy-stricken for prying into the mystery of God."[60]

Gregory then expresses a common question of those who dispute the Spirit's divinity. If the Spirit is not the Son, must this not mean that the Spirit lacks what the Son possesses, pointing to a deficiency in the Spirit? If the Spirit is deficient in such a manner, how can he be considered equal to the Father and Son? Good question, but one that indicates a failure to distinguish between a deficiency and a difference in manifestation. That is to say, the names Father, Son and Spirit within the Trinity designate how the three persons relate to each other. In Gregory's words, "the difference in manifestation, if I may so express myself, or *rather of their mutual relations* one to another, has caused the difference of their names."[61]

For indeed it is not some deficiency in the Son which prevents his being Father (for Sonship is not a deficiency), and yet he is not Father. . . . For the Father is not Son, and yet this is not due to either deficiency or subjection of essence; but the very fact of being unbegotten or begotten, or proceeding, has given the name of Father to the first, of the Son to the second, and to the third, him of whom we are speaking, of the Holy Ghost, that the distinction of the three persons may be preserved in the one nature and dignity of the Godhead.[62]

Is, then, the Spirit God? "Most certainly," Gregory responds. Is he then consubstantial—that is, having the same nature or essence—with the Father and Son? "Yes, if he is God."[63] The central problem, of course, is how to maintain the unity within the Trinity without falling into Sabellianism, or how to maintain the proper distinctions between Father, Son and Spirit without falling into tritheism.

Gregory now comes to what he calls the "principal point" of his argument. His opponents, those who would deny the deity of the Holy Spirit, do so out of a misplaced desire to maintain the unity of God. "If, say they, there is God and God and God, how is it that there are not three Gods, or how is it that what is glorified is not a plurality of principles?"[64] Gregory responds, "There is one God, for the Godhead is one, and all that proceeds from him is referred to one, though we believe in three Persons."

Among the three persons of the Trinity, there is "not [one] more and another less God." That is, the Spirit is God as fully as the Son and the Father. Whatever pertains to deity, apart from the distinction between the persons, is genuinely true of all three. In terms of existence, all exist eternally. The persons are one in will as well as power. As far as essence or Godhead goes, it is "undivided in separate Persons; and there is one mingling of lights, as it were of three suns joined to each other." If we speak, then, of the Godhead, the First Cause or the *monarchia*, we conceive of God as one. However, "when we look at the Persons in whom the Godhead dwells, and at those who timelessly and with equal glory have their being from the first cause, there are three whom we worship."[65]

God's unity of essence and plurality of persons would seem to provide a reliable model for understanding what the church means by the Trinity, but Gregory realizes that the comparative silence of the Scripture regarding the deity of the Spirit will remain a problem for some. If the Holy Spirit is God, why do not biblical writers emphasize this truth more thoroughly? It is a fair question, and Gregory answers it by focusing on how "things and names" are treated in the Scripture.

For instance, sometimes the Bible speaks of *things that have no real existence as actually existing*. Think, for example, of the figures of speech used in Scripture to describe God. "According to Scripture, God sleeps and is awake, is angry, walks, [and] has the cherubim for his throne." If God actually existed in such a manner, Gregory argues, God would possess human passions and a body of some kind. If God does not possess a body, then the biblical expressions describing him as having one must be figures of speech. "For we have given names according to our own comprehension from our own attributes to those of God." For instance, God "remaining silent apart from us, and as it were not caring for us, for reasons known to himself, is what we call his sleeping; for our own sleep is such a state of inactivity."[66]

Conversely, other theological terms used to describe God are never mentioned in the Bible but are implied by scriptural teaching. For example, one will never find the term *unbegotten* or *unoriginate* in the Bible, yet they appear to be implied by biblical passages such as "I am the first and I am the last," or "Before me no God was formed, nor shall there be any after me" (Is 44:6; 43:10). "When you accept this, that nothing is before him, and that he has not an older cause, you have implicitly given him the titles 'unbegotten' and 'unoriginate.' "[67] Hence, it is perfectly valid to use words not found in the Bible to construct theological models of God, if those words faithfully communicate what Scripture implies.

Why has it taken so long for the church to formulate a doctrine of the Trinity or to clearly understand the relationship of the Holy Spirit to the Father and the Son? Theology has its own pace, Gregory contends. That is, in theology "perfection is reached by additions." During the time of the Old Testament dispensation or economy, writers "proclaimed the Father openly, and the Son more obscurely." As we move into the period of the New Testament, the Son is manifested more clearly and the deity of the Spirit suggested. Now that the Son has ascended into heaven and sent the Spirit to the church on the Day of Pentecost, we have an even clearer demonstration of the Spirit:

> For it was not safe, when the Godhead of the Father was not yet acknowledged, plainly to proclaim the Son; nor when that of the Son was not yet received, to burden us further (if I may use so bold an expression) with the Holy Ghost; lest perhaps people might, like men loaded with food beyond their strength, and presenting eyes as yet too weak to bear it to the sun's light, risk the loss even of that which was within the reach of their powers; but that by gradual additions . . . the light of the Trinity might shine upon the more illuminated.[68]

Gregory wisely writes that there is an "order of theology," one in which we "see lights" slowly, gradually "breaking upon us." Thus, when we speak of God, there is a rhyme and rhythm to our speech. We must not speak too quickly, speaking before God has chosen to reveal, nor must we be hesitant to speak where God has not remained silent. To speak too quickly would be "unscientific." To refuse to speak would be "atheistical." If God has chosen to reveal himself as marvelously, mysteriously complex in the wonder of the Trinity, so be it. If the Holy Spirit has been revealed as divine with the Father and Son, to fail to affirm his divinity is at best a misplaced modesty on the theologian's part.

Gregory himself unreservedly affirms his belief in the Trinity. The church is called "to worship God the Father, God the Son, and God the Holy Ghost, three persons, one Godhead, undivided in honor and glory and substance and kingdom."[69] If the church worships these three persons, all must be God in "a truly golden and saving chain. And indeed from the Spirit comes our new birth, and from the new birth our new creation, and from the new creation our deeper knowledge of the dignity of Him from whom it is derived."[70]

Yes, Gregory admits, every illustration of Trinity ultimately breaks down: "I have been unable to discover anything on earth with which to compare the nature of the Godhead." However we model God, whatever analogies we apply to the Trinity, all will ultimately fall short. Gregory again is drawn to his illustration of "the sun and a ray and light." To a degree the illustration suffices, but people will err if it leads them to think of God as composed of different elements, "such as there is in the sun and the things that are in the sun." The second danger is that we would make the Father the sun, with the Son and Spirit as only "powers of God, existing in him and not personal. For neither the ray nor the light is another sun, but they are only effulgences from the sun, and qualities of his essence."[71]

Finally, all human and earthly analogies must break down, for they cannot encompass or illustrate completely the wonder and mystery of God. Perhaps in the long run, it is wisest "to let the images and the shadows go, as being deceitful and very far short of the truth; and clinging myself to the more reverent conception, and resting upon few words, using the guidance of the Holy Ghost, keeping to the end as my genuine comrade and companion."[72]

Augustine on the Trinity

Augustine's reflections on the Trinity are both illuminating and intimidating. More than one reader has turned to Augustine's *The Trinity*, only to walk away discouraged and daunted.[73] A better place for students who are unfamiliar with Augustine's thought to begin might be one of Augustine's sermons. We choose to focus on a sermon in which Augustine discusses the Trinity, one of a series of sermons Augustine preached on significant New Testament texts.[74] Augustine quite evidently felt his parishioners needed a sound, basic understanding of the Trinity, and he saw in Jesus' baptism by John in the Jordan an apt opportunity for deepening his congregation's understanding. Indeed, in Jesus' baptism "we behold and see as it were in a divine spectacle exhibited to us the notice of our God in Trinity, conveyed to us at the river Jordan."[75] Jesus is baptized, the Spirit descends upon him as a dove, and the Father affirms his love for his only Son. "Here then we have the Trinity in a certain sort distinguished. The Father in the Voice,—the Son in the Man,—the Holy Spirit in the Dove. . . . The notice of the Trinity is here conveyed to us plainly and without leaving room for doubt or hesitation."[76]

At first glance, it appears that the Father, Son and Spirit are "in a manner separable," for Jesus comes "from one place to another; and the Dove descended from heaven to earth, from one place to another; and the very voice of the Father sounded . . . from heaven."[77] Yet as Augustine ruminates over the possibility of separation within the Trinity, his mind is drawn to the "right Catholic faith," one "gathered not by the opinion of private judgment, but by the witness of the Scriptures . . . grounded on Apostolic truth: this we know, this we believe." And what does that faith proclaim? "That the Father, Son, and Holy Spirit are a Trinity inseparable; One God, not three Gods. But yet so One God, as that the Son is not the Father, and the Father is not the Son, and the Holy Spirit is neither the Father nor the Son, but the Spirit of the Father and of the Son."[78] Such, indeed, is "this ineffable Divinity, abiding ever in itself, making all things new, creating, creating anew, sending, recalling, judging, delivering, this Trinity, I say, we know to be at once ineffable and inseparable."[79]

Quickly, it seems, Augustine leaves behind Jesus' baptism as he begins to address common questions and misperceptions Christians have concerning the Trinity. For instance, Is there anything the Father does that the Son does not do? Augustine answers "No." How could such be the case if it is through the Son that "all things were made" (see Jn 1:3)? It is by means of the Word that the Father creates. In fact, the Father through the Word not only creates, but governs his creation: "The Father does nothing without the Son, nor the Son without the Father."[80]

If the work of the Father and Son is inseparable, however, does this not lead to greater difficulties? As Augustine states, "If the Father does nothing without the Son, nor the Son without the Father, will it not follow, that we must say that the Father also was born of the Virgin Mary, the Father suffered under Pontius Pilate, the Father rose again and ascended into heaven?"[81] Such cannot be the case, Augustine argues, for to so mix the work and persons of the Father and Son would be to simply change them into "names" for an indistinguishable reality. The persons of the Trinity must be distinguished. If so, they are separate. But in what way?

On the one hand, the Father does nothing apart from the Son. On the other hand, the Father did not become incarnate, did not die on the cross, was not resurrected from the dead and did not ascend to himself! Yet the Father was intimately involved in the work of the Son. The Son's birth from the Virgin Mary, for example, "was the work both of the Father and the Son." The Father did not suffer and die with the Son on the cross, "yet the suffering of the Son was the work of the Father and the Son." The Father was not raised from the dead, "yet the resurrection of the Son was the work of the Father and the Son."[82] Only one person of the Trinity—the Son—is actually crucified and resurrected. The Father and Son (and, of course, the Spirit) are involved and mutually engaged in this great redemptive event.

In what way is the birth of Christ, for instance, the work of both the Father and Son? As for the Father, it is the Father who sent the Son on his redemptive mission. Augustine points his audience to Paul's teaching in Galatians: "When the fullness of time had come, *God sent his Son*, born of a woman, born under the law, in order to redeem those who were under the law" (Gal 4:4-5, emphasis added). Yet the incarnation is clearly also the Son's work. For it is the Son himself who assumes "the form of a servant in the Virgin's womb. Is the birth of the Son anything else, but the taking of the form of a servant in the womb of the Virgin?"[83]

What of the crucifixion? Christ's death on the cross was surely the work of his Father, for he "did not withhold his own Son, but gave him up for all of us" (Rom 8:32). Still, it is the Son "who loved me and gave himself for me" (Gal 2:20). "The Father delivered up the Son," Augustine observes, "and the Son delivered up Himself. This Passion was wrought out for one, but by both."[84]

And the resurrection? It is the Father who in the resurrection "exalted him and gave him the name that is above every name" (Phil 2:9). "The Father therefore raised the Son to life again, in exalting, and awakening Him from the dead." Yet, Augustine asks, "Did the Son also raise Himself?" Augustine answers, "Assuredly He did. For He said of the temple, as the figure of His own body, 'Destroy this temple, and in three days I will raise it again' [Jn 2:19]."[85]

Augustine summarizes his trinitarian argument thus far as follows:

> The Father was not born of the Virgin; yet this birth of the Son from the Virgin was the work both of the Father and the Son. The Father suffered not on the Cross; yet the Passion of the Son was the work both of the Father and the Son. The Father rose not again from the dead; yet the resurrection of the Son was the work both of the Father and the Son. You see then a distinction of Persons, and an inseparableness of operation. Let us not say therefore that the Father does any thing without the Son, or the Son any thing without the Father.[86]

Augustine senses that his teaching, although possessing its own trinitarian coherence, still falls far short of the divine reality. How, though, can a human being hope to grasp the God who lives and acts in a manner that infinitely surpasses human categories and conceptions? We think and act, Augustine writes, in a manner "suited to the nature of bodies." Such is far from the case with God.

For God is "beyond all such places." God, for instance, cannot be found in space. Rather, God is "everywhere invisible and inseparably present; not in one part greater, and another smaller; but whole everywhere, and nowhere divided."

How can we possibly wrap our minds around such a wonder? How can we possibly think it through? In the end, the wisest course is to "restrain ourselves: let us remember who we are, and of Whom we speak." Our thoughts and speech must be formed by faith and a "holy respect. . . . Let words be hushed: let the tongue be silent, let the heart be aroused, let the heart be lifted up above. For it is not of such a nature that it can ascend into the human heart, but the human heart must ascend to it."[87]

Augustine suggests that we can attempt to understand divine realities by way of analogy, studying God's creation for clues that lead beyond themselves. By sifting through creation we may find "some resemblance, whereby we may prove that there are some three things which be exhibited" as being both separate and yet inseparable in their work or operation.[88] If we discover trinitarian hints embedded in the created order, we may be able to extrapolate modestly from them as we attempt to understand God's complex being.

As we plumb the depths of trinitarian relationships, however, we should remember that God "is far above, and I am far below." If ever we feel we have captured God, fully understood God, finally stretched our minds fully around God's being and work, we delude ourselves terribly. "For if you have been able to fully comprehend what you would say, it is not God. If you have been able to comprehend it, you have comprehended something else instead of God. If you have been able to comprehend him as you think, by so thinking you have deceived yourself."[89]

With this warning against theological self-deception, Augustine turns to creation for hints of realities much greater than itself. Where in creation might one find the clearest markers to aid us in understanding the Trinity? Augustine is convinced that creation's clearest road map lies close at hand, in human nature itself. "How long," Augustine asks, "will you roam over the creation? Return to yourself, see, consider, examine your own self." In human nature, Augustine believes, we will find the trinitarian resemblance we have been searching for. How so?

Humanity alone has been created in the image of God. "You were speaking of the Trinity of Majesty ineffable, and because you did fail in contemplating the divine nature, and with becoming humility did confess your infirmity, you did come down to human nature. . . . For God made humankind after his own image and likeness."[90] Perhaps the "image of the Trinity" might well reflect "some vestige of the Trinity."

If so, it is best to take a closer look at the image of God, humanity itself. What do we find there? On the one hand, "it is an image very different from its model." For instance, it is not the image of God "in the same way as the Son is the Image, being the Same which the Father is." A mirror will reflect an image in one way, the son of a father in another. "There is a great difference between them. Your image in your son is your own self, for the son is by nature what you are. In substance the same as you, in person other than you." The image of God in humanity, then, will be different from the image of God as seen in the Son. Still, if we look closely at human nature, can we find "three things that are exhibited separately, whose operation is yet inseparable"? If Augustine can find a solution to this question, perhaps the relationship between the Father, Son and Spirit can be clarified, at least within the limitations inherent in human nature and the exercise of human reason.

First of all, all humans have a body. In and through our bodies we occupy space, move about, listen to others and view the world around us. Augustine urges us to look even deeper, though. When we listen, for instance, who is doing the listening? When we look at another, who is doing the seeing? Augustine observes that the eye does not see by itself. Rather, "is it not another that sees by means of the eye?"[91] Hence, Augustine urges us to look into our inner selves, "for there it is rather that the resemblance must be sought for of some three things which are exhibited separately, whose operation is yet inseparable." What is this inner world we must explore? The human mind.

Take a look at your own soul, Augustine advises. What do you find there? If humanity is the image of the entire Trinity—Father, Son and Holy Spirit—a Trinity who acts in unity and yet separately, how does human nature reflect this? In what way does it bear a "distant resemblance"?[92] Augustine is convinced that "in the very creatures of the lowest order, and subject to change, we do find three things which may be separately exhibited, whose operation is yet inseparable."

These three include our own memory, our understanding and the human will. "These are the three things which I promised I would bring home to your ears and minds. These three things are in you, which you can number, but cannot separate. These three then, memory, understanding, and will—these three, I say, consider how they are separately exhibited, yet is their operation inseparable."[93]

Can we doubt that we have a memory? Even the doubts we formulate are constructed from words stored in our memories. Could we analyze Augustine's thoughts on the Trinity if we had no memory? Obviously not, "for if you had no memory, you could not retain what I said." The same is true of the understanding. "Had you not understanding, you could not understand what you had stored in your memory."[94] Memory and understanding are inextricably linked, yet separate in their function and operation. "You recall your understanding to that which you have retained within, and so see it [in your memory]." Knowledge, the fruit of understanding and memory, is the happy result. How does the will tie in? It is through the will, Augustine argues, that we retain information in our memory and choose to exercise our understanding upon it. "Have you not with your will retained and understood?"[95]

Augustine appears to have established his point. He had "promised to show . . . three things which are separately exhibited whose operation is yet inseparable."[96] We have three aspects of human nature that can be numbered: memory, understanding and will. Each presents itself to us separately. Each has its own proper name. They are each a distinct aspect of human nature. However, when it comes to their function and operation, they are inseparable. If one is at work, so are the others. Indeed, Augustine contends, we cannot think of any of these three— memory, understanding and will—apart from also recalling to our minds the other two.

"Memory" is the name of one only of those three, yet all the three concurred in producing the name of this single one of the three. The single word *memory* could not be expressed, but by the operation of the will, and the understanding, and the memory. The single word *understanding* could not be expressed, but by the operation of the memory, the will, and the understanding; and the single word *will* could not be expressed, but by the operation of the memory and the understanding and the will.[97]

Memory itself is produced by the relationship between all three aspects, but "has reference to none but the memory alone." In the same way the word *understanding* is produced by will, memory and itself, "but it has reference to none but the understanding only." Finally, "the three together have produced the word 'will,' but it has reference to none but the will only." That is, the will is not the memory or the understanding. It is clearly separate from them but also inextricably linked to their operations.

By way of analogy from the created order to trinitarian relationships, the distinct persons of the Trinity can be numbered and are clearly separate as Father, Son and Spirit, each with his own characteristics. Each, for instance, has its own proper name. Each has a distinct role in the economy of salvation. Simultaneously, though, their "operations" in saving humanity from sin are inseparable. "So the Trinity concurred in the formation of the body of Christ," Augustine writes, but that body "belongs to none but Christ alone." Similarly, the "Trinity concurred in the formation of the Dove from heaven, but [the dove] belongs to none but the Holy Spirit only." When a divine voice identifies Jesus as the "one in whom I am well pleased," that voice is formed by the Trinity, "but this Voice belongs to none but the Father only."[98]

Augustine's final conclusion? If within the created order, indeed, within humanity itself, we have instances of realities both separate and inseparable, we should "believe that the Father, Son, and Holy Spirit may be exhibited separately, by certain visible symbols, by certain forms borrowed from the creatures, and still be in their operations be inseparable."[99]

Augustine makes no attempt to force the analogy to the breaking point. He does not try, for instance, to identify the Father with the memory, the Son with the understanding or the will with the Holy Spirit. "I do not say that these things are in any sort to be equaled with the Holy Trinity, to be squared after an analogy; that is, a kind of exact rule of comparison."[100] Rather, through his comparison Augustine simply wants us to believe in the Trinity, allowing the analogy to pass away in the worship of the incomprehensible God. We can know certain things about human nature, Augustine admits, but how can we know "what is in him" who created us? Even if in the future we possess such knowledge, we are not able yet to comprehend fully such wonders. Even when we possess perfect knowledge, we will not know God as "God knows himself."[101]

Indeed, illustrations and analogies drawn from human nature will always break down when applied to divine realities. Yet as the church reflected on the biblical portrayal of Christ and its theological implications, it realized that in Jesus humanity and divinity had been joined in a wondrous way. How could the church best speak of such a mysterious, indeed, incomprehensible union? To this question, one destined for prolonged and heated debate, we now turn.

"Indeed, the mystery of Christ runs the risk of being disbelieved
precisely because it is so incredibly wonderful.
For God was in humanity. He who was above all creation was in our human condition;
the invisible one was made visible in the flesh;
he who is from the heavens and from on high was in the likeness of earthly things;
the immaterial one could be touched;
he who is free in his own nature came in the form of a slave;
he who blesses all creation became accursed; he who is all righteousness
was numbered among transgressors; life itself came in the appearance of death.
All this followed because the body which tasted death belonged
to no other but to him who is the Son by nature."
CYRIL OF ALEXANDRIA
On the Unity of Christ

FOUR

CHRIST DIVINE
AND HUMAN

Continuing Christological Struggles

We have already explored the mystery of Christ's divinity in our discussion of
Athanasius's fervent, consistent and deliberate defense that in Jesus of Nazareth
we actually encounter God incarnate. Athanasius often describes this truth as
ineffable, that is, incapable of description. Yet, on the basis of what he considered
to be incontrovertible biblical testimony, Athanasius defended Christ's deity
throughout the many years he served as bishop of Alexandria. The church confirmed its belief in Jesus' deity at the Council of Constantinople (A.D. 381), and
many hoped that the dust of theological battle might finally settle. This hope was
not to be realized, and for good reason. Why?

The moment that one asserts that Jesus of Nazareth is God incarnate, a new
collection of questions immediately present themselves. For example, if Jesus is
God, how can we simultaneously assert that he is human? Is he genuinely
human? Did Jesus possess a human mind, will, soul and body? For well into the
fifth century these questions would be debated vigorously.

The humanity of Christ was not the only issue destined to be a topic of heated
theological discussion. If Jesus was human, how was his humanity to be reconciled
or related to his divinity? What kind of model or paradigm could best describe or
explain a reality that at its heart and core was ineffable? How could deity and
humanity fully and genuinely exist in the same individual? What was the nature of

such a union? How might it best be described? What possible errors might erupt in the effort to describe what appeared to be indescribable?

A number of possibilities presented themselves. To illustrate and explore both the difficulty of the issues involved and the theology that finally emerged is our task in this chapter. Rather than viewing and analyzing developments broadly through the eyes of many church fathers, we will center instead on the ideas of a father who played a central role in this key debate and discussion, Cyril of Alexandria.

Cyril, bishop of Alexandria from 412 to 444, engendered a wide variety of responses to his life and teaching, both in his own lifetime and down through the ages. As Frances Young comments, many thought that Cyril was simply "an unscrupulous political operator, a true successor to his uncle Theophilus who contrived the downfall of John Chrysostom, a nasty piece of work out to achieve maximum power for the Alexandrian see by whatever means possible."[1]

Cyril described himself quite differently. "I love peace," Cyril writes. "There is nothing that I detest more than quarrels and disputes. I love everybody, and if I could heal one of the brethren by losing all my possessions and goods, I am willing to do so joyfully; because it is concord that I value most."[2] One can sense Cyril's opponents rolling their eyes.

Yet Cyril insists that he involves himself in controversy only when the faith of the church is threatened by inadequate or clearly false teaching. And Cyril believes that Nestorius, the chief theological antagonist of Cyril, represents just such a threat. Even though he will battle Nestorius for years, Cyril affirms his love for his nemesis. Still, as Cyril describes matters, false teaching must be opposed. To do any less would be to desert his post as a shepherd of the church.

> But there is a question of the faith and of a scandal which concerns all the churches of the Roman Empire. . . . The sacred doctrine is entrusted to us. . . . How can we remedy these evils? . . . I am ready to endure with tranquillity all blame, all humiliations, all injuries provided that the faith is not endangered. I am filled with love for Nestorius; nobody loves him more than I do. . . . If, in accordance with Christ's commandment, we must love our very enemies themselves, is it not natural that we should be united in special affection to those who are our friends and brethren in the priesthood? But when the faith is attacked, we must not hesitate to sacrifice

our life itself. And if we fear to preach the truth because that causes us some incon-venience, how, in our gatherings, can we chant the combats and triumphs of our holy martyrs?[3]

What was Nestorius teaching that had Cyril so upset? Perhaps we might be wiser to glance at wider issues before addressing the question of Nestorius's teaching itself. Theology is not formed in a vacuum. How had Nestorius been formed and shaped theologically? Moreover, what kind of a person was Nesto-rius? How might his personality and, indeed, that of Cyril, have fed the theologi-cal controversy that erupted between the two? Both had their rough edges. Both were convinced that their positions regarding Christ faithfully preserved the truth. Consider the following words of Nestorius:

> It is my earnest desire that even by anathematizing me they may escape from blaspheming God [and that those who so escape may confess God, holy, almighty and immortal, and not change the image of the incorruptible God for the image of corruptible man, and mingle heathenism with Christianity . . . but that Christ may be confessed to be in truth and in nature God and Man, being by nature immortal and impassible as God, and mortal and passible by nature as Man—not God in both natures, nor again Man in both natures. The goal of my earnest wish is that God may be blessed on earth as in heaven]; but as for Nesto-rius, let him be anathema; only let men speak of God as I pray for them that they may speak. For I am with those who are for God, and not with those who are against God, who with an outward show of religion reproach God and cause him to cease from being God.[4]

Whatever we might end up concluding concerning Nestorius's theology, the man we meet in these words is, as Frances Young observes, "a great Christian."[5] Quite often, though, spiritual greatness manifests itself in human weakness and brokenness. Nestorius's own personality seems to have been abrasive and insen-sitive. Here was a man too quick to jump to conclusions, too apt to overestimate his own abilities and perspective.

Young points us to the estimate of Socrates, an early church historian who attributes Nestorius's difficulties as bishop and theologian to "his own conten-tious spirit." Socrates recalls an overconfident Nestorius ready to hound out her-esy soon after his consecration as bishop of Constantinople. "Give me, my prince, the earth purged of heretics, and I will give you heaven as a recompense. Assist me in destroying heretics, and I will assist you in vanquishing the Persians."[6] Nestorius soon earned the nickname "Firebrand" for his ardent pursuit of heretics. Socrates, less than enthusiastic in his estimation of Nestorius, links Nestorius's troubles not so much to bad theology as to a lack of knowledge.

> Having myself perused the writings of Nestorius, I have found him an unlearned man and shall candidly express the conviction of my mind concerning him. . . . I cannot concede that he was either a follower of Paul of Samosata or of Photinus, or that he denied the divinity of Christ; but he seemed scared at the term *Theotokos* as though it were some terrible "bugbear." The fact is, the causeless alarm he manifested on this subject just exposed his extreme ignorance; for being a man of natural fluency as a speaker, he was considered well-educated, but in reality he was disgracefully illiterate.[7]

Even a sympathetic observer such as Frances Young describes Nestorius as "over-sure of his own position," "high-handed," possessing a "total lack of tact" and a tendency to "act in haste," unable to "accept advice or meddling from his fellow-patriarchs," and "determined and impetuous in dispute and liable to make strong statements open to misunderstanding."[8]

One senses that even if Nestorius and Cyril had agreed theologically, they would have struggled to get along. Both had strong personalities, both too closely identified themselves with whatever position they chose to defend as orthodoxy, and both had a hard time listening attentively to others. But what of the theological debate that raged for years between the two? What were they arguing about? Were the issues worth the strife and bitterness that resulted? Were they actually saying the same thing but in a different way? What were they trying to make sense of? Were they both speaking well of Christ, or were Nestorius's ideas genuinely dangerous?

Nestorius, the *Theotokos*, and the Unity of Christ

Exactly what occurred in the incarnation of the Son of God? By the time of the Nestorian conflict, the Council of Nicaea had already chosen to use the Greek word *homoousios* to declare that the Father and Son shared the same divine essence. Jesus of Nazareth was indeed Immanuel, God with us. But how was the church theologically to describe and understand the person of Christ? When the church described the Son as *homoousios* with the Father, what was the church affirming and denying? What language and models best represented a reality that was genuinely indescribable? And how was the clear declaration of Christ's divinity related to Christ's humanity? What was the nature of this wondrous union of the divine and human in Christ?

Harold O. J. Brown refers to three fundamental test questions that surrounded the question of Jesus' deity and humanity: (1) "Was God born of Mary, or only a man?" (2) "Did God die on the cross, or only a man?" and (3) "Should the human nature of Christ be worshiped?"[9] All three questions are directly related to the dispute between Cyril and Nestorius, for all are related to the question of Jesus' deity and humanity. That is, in what way or manner does Jesus' deity indwell his humanity? Is "indwell" even a good choice of words, since it seems to imply a blending or mixing of the divine with the human, producing a strange third sort of creation. How can one faithfully, safely and biblically speak of such a mysterious union?

Not only is the question of the relationship of Christ's deity and humanity at issue, but there is the question of Jesus' humanity itself. Theologians centered in Antioch were particularly concerned that the reality of Jesus' humanity be preserved in any theological paradigm modeling the relationship between his deity and humanity. They, like the fathers in Cyril's camp, realized that Jesus must be human if salvation was to be communicated through his person to fallen humanity. For example, the fathers realized that Jesus must possess a human soul along with a human body if a human being was to be saved. Why? Not only was a soul a constituent element of a human person, but the soul as well as the body had become intertwined and enveloped in sin and was therefore genuinely culpable before God. Brown writes:

> The deep concern of these early Fathers with the fact that the soul and the intellect are culpable clearly shows that they did not think that sin was simply a matter of the body and its appetites. . . . Only as Christ became what we human beings are did he reunite us with God. . . . This is in a sense the counterpart to the earlier argument that Christ had to possess deity in order to have the power to transform us; now the orthodox are concerned to show that he had to be fully human in order that his transforming power actually be transmitted to mankind.[10]

Once we assert that Jesus must be both God and human, the problem of how these two natures can be joined immediately presents itself. Nestorius and Antiochene theologians such as Theodore of Mopsuestia were greatly concerned that Jesus' genuine humanity be maintained in the theological language and paradigms employed by the church. Nestorius, for instance, hesitated to use the word *theotokos* to describe Mary, the mother of Jesus. Why? *Theotokos* ("God-bearing one") seemed to Nestorius to threaten the reality of Christ's humanity. "Nestorius was willing to say that the Christ born of Mary is God, but did not want to say, 'God is born,' because to do so implied in his mind that the One born was not a true man."[11]

Instead, Nestorius preferred to describe Mary as *christotokos* because "Christ-bearer" appeared to him faithfully to preserve the reality of both Christ's deity and humanity. If *christotokos* proved unsatisfactory, Nestorius proposed, what about complementing *theotokos* with *anthropotokos* ("man-bearing one")? Mary, after all, had given birth to more than God.

Such a proposal was unsatisfactory to Cyril and other fathers centered in Alexandria. As John McGuckin writes in his introduction to Cyril's work *On the Unity of Christ*, to call Mary both "God-bearer" and "man-bearer" was deficient because "she was not the mother merely of God, or merely of a man, but the Mother of Christ, and Christ was not merely God, and not merely man, but was God conjoined to man, or if one liked, man conjoined to God."[12]

But was Cyril's thinking at this juncture significantly different from that of Nestorius? Did not Nestorius favor the designation *christotokos* to describe the mother of Jesus? We need to take a closer look at Cyril's response to Nestorius to answer this question adequately, and by doing so we will hopefully gain a greater understanding and appreciation of how the fathers thought and worked theologically.

Cyril's Response to Nestorius

As we will soon see in some detail, Cyril was upset by Nestorius's use of the word *christotokos*. He will argue that *christotokos* is deficient on a number of fronts as a description of the mother of Jesus. Before tackling Nestorius's theological language, however, Cyril finds fault with his methodology. How so?

As far as Cyril is concerned, Nestorius is fundamentally a theological innovator. That is, Cyril is convinced that Nestorius has ignored the previous theological reflections of the church in the construction of his theological proposal regarding the relationship of Christ's deity and humanity. Nestorius does not, Cyril writes, "welcome the tradition of all the initiates throughout the world," that is, the tradition passed on to new Christians at the time of their baptism. Rather, Cyril argues, "he innovates as seems fit to him."[13] He "denies that the holy virgin is the Mother of God, and calls her Christ-Mother instead, or Mother-of-the-Man."[14] Cyril has problems with the theology these titles seem to present. In addition, Cyril is deeply offended that a Christian bishop would take it upon himself to invent new theological language that seems to ignore or bypass the language the church has traditionally used to describe the great mystery of the Son's incarnation.

Having charged Nestorius with theological innovation, Cyril proceeds to evaluate critically the theological implications of Nestorius's theology. Nestorius errs by undercutting "the mystery of the fleshly economy of the Only begotten."[15] In other words, the titles Nestorius suggests as helpfully describing the incarnate Son actually twist or distort what is taking place in the incarnation. Whereas the Arians dragged "down the Word born of God the Father from the heights of divinity even before the incarnation," Nestorius and his followers "wage war against the Word even in his incarnation."[16] The term *christotokos*, Cyril insists, simply cannot preserve the wonder and mystery of the incarnate Son.

After all, Cyril writes, does not the title "Immanuel" clearly communicate that in the incarnation *God* is with us? And in the incarnational economy or dispensation, God is present in a human being in an utterly unique way. God's Spirit had filled and guided great prophets such as Moses, but not in the intimate manner and union manifested in Christ. Neither Moses nor Joshua were called "God with us" or "Immanuel."[17]

How, then, should we speak of God as born of a woman? This is a particularly difficult question to ask, Cyril comments, in light of God's immutable nature. Because God cannot cease being God or blend the divine nature with anything else, whatever the incarnation is, whatever John meant by "the Word [becoming] flesh" *cannot mean that the Word has changed into a human being* ("flesh"). Neither is the incarnation a "mixture or blending" of divine and human natures into a third sort of being. Within these incarnational boundaries, how can we best describe this indescribable union?

The Union of the Divine and Human in the Incarnation

Cyril responds by writing that the Word (Logos) "did not disdain the poverty of human nature" precisely because "he wished to make that flesh which was held in the grip of sin and death evidently superior to sin and death."[18] Cyril adds, "He thought it good to be made man and in his own person to reveal our nature honored in the dignities of the divinity." It was God the Word who entered the world, joined God's divine nature to human nature and through such an appropriation communicated salvation to that nature. Cyril illustrates his point by referring to Paul's words in Philippians 2. The Word, in an astonishing emptying, has assumed the "form of a slave" (the incarnation). "He as God in an appearance like ours. . . . This is what we mean when we say that he became flesh, and for the same reasons we affirm that the holy virgin is the Mother of God."[19]

Cyril, rightly or wrongly, interprets Nestorius's reluctance to describe Mary as *theotokos* as a threat to the reality of the union of God with human nature, a reluctance that in turn threatens the benefits obtained through such a union. For it is through the appropriation of human nature that the benefits of salvation are communicated to that nature by *God and no other*. In Cyril's words: "since it was his own [the Word's] and personal flesh, that of the incorruptible God, he set it beyond death and corruption." Hence, all human nature, or, as Cyril puts it, "human bodies," can be revitalized through "participation in his holy flesh and blood."[20]

Cyril is angry with Nestorius because he believes him to be unnecessarily fighting against such a union and appropriation, what Cyril describes as the "birth of the Word." Nestorius, perhaps in an overly rationalistic turn of phrase, had described the union of the Word with the man Jesus as an *association*. Such language deeply disturbs Cyril, since he feels it falls far short of what is meant by the self-emptying of the Word described by Paul. If we have only an association of sorts, Cyril asks, "are they not implying that the Only Begotten's wonderful economy in the flesh served no purpose for the inhabitants of the earth?"[21] In other words, only an appropriation of human nature—not a mere association—can communicate the Son's benefits to us in our terribly troubled condition.

Cyril on the Purpose of the Incarnation

To drive this point home, Cyril turns his attention to a more detailed discussion of the incarnation. *For what end* did the Word become incarnate? "For this end, that by the likeness that the Word born from God had with us, the law of sin in the members of our flesh could be condemned, and so that in the likeness of the death of the one who knew not death, death might be destroyed."[22]

> It follows, therefore, that He Who Is, the One Who Exists, is necessarily born of the flesh, taking all that is ours into himself, so that all that is born of the flesh, that is us corruptible and perishing beings, might rest in him. In short, he took what was ours to be his very own so that we might have all that was his.[23]

Therefore, to assert, as Nestorius seemed to do, that "the Word of God did not become flesh, or rather did not undergo birth from a woman according to the flesh," could only serve to "bankrupt the economy of salvation."[24] That is, the Word must become what we are if we are to obtain the deliverance and riches he can and desires to give us. Apart from such an intimate union, we would remain tied to Adam, "deprived of any return to a better condition."[25]

Thus, Cyril writes, the economy demonstrated in the incarnation must be affirmed. Nestorius's language, the language of mere association, fails to do this. Or at least such is the case as Cyril reads him. One will be tempted to accuse Cyril of theological nitpicking if we overlook the fundamental rationale of his argument: we cannot be saved if the Word did not become what we are. For example, Cyril asks, how can Christ's blood save us "if it was in reality only that of an ordinary man subject to sin?"[26]

Cyril insists that it is through the ineffable union of human nature with the "personal riches of the Word [that sin] is condemned and conquered." It is in this union with the Word incarnate, a union "full of divine energy," that sin is overcome.[27] Thus, when Cyril hears of Nestorius's reluctance to speak of Mary as the mother of God (*theotokos*), he interprets this reluctance as demonstrating a failure to understand the nature of salvation itself.

We see, accept and adore the mystery of the incarnation by faith, the mystery that the Word remains what he has always been while simultaneously joining himself to us by becoming what we are. Indeed, Cyril writes, "this is why the mystery of Christ is truly wonderful."[28] Paradoxically, Cyril argues, it is the mystery and wonder of the economy that is apt to cause us to disbelieve in its reality.

Indeed the mystery of Christ runs the risk of being disbelieved precisely because it is so incredibly wonderful. For God was in humanity. He who was above all creation was in our human condition; the invisible one was made visible in the flesh; he who is from the heavens and from on high was in the likeness of earthly things; the immaterial one could be touched; he who is free in his own nature came in the form of a slave; he who blesses all creation became accursed; he who is all righteousness was numbered among transgressors; life itself came in the appearance of death.[29]

How is this possible? "All this followed because the body which tasted death belonged to no other but to him who is the Son by nature."[30]

The Son's birth from the Virgin Mary, his supernatural conception through the Holy Spirit, ties in closely with the *purpose* of his entrance into human history. The purpose of that coming is that sin might be conquered and human nature joined to his divine nature. As Cyril puts it, the Son became a human being "in order to reconstitute our condition within himself; first of all in his holy, wonderful, and truly amazing birth and life. This is why he himself became the first one to be born from the Holy Spirit (I mean of course after the flesh) so that he could trace a path for grace to come to us."[31]

Through the union of the Son with genuine human nature, "he transmits the grace of sonship even to us so that we too can become children of the Spirit, insofar as human nature had first achieved this possibility in him."[32] Christ has become a new "rootstock" for the human race, "a new beginning."

Although Cyril often talks of God joining himself to a human body, he is insistent that this body possessed a human soul. He is well aware that, if humanity is to be saved, God must join himself to all that a human being is and not simply to a human body. Thus Cyril writes, "the body which he united to himself was endowed with a rational soul, for the Word, who is God, would hardly neglect our finer part, the soul, and have regard only for the earthly body."[33] Again, "he made the limits of the manhood his own, and all the things that pertain to it."[34]

Only a genuine union between the Word and human nature can accomplish the wonder of the economy. The centrality of the *union* of divine and human in Christ explains Cyril's frustration with Nestorius's unwillingness to employ the term *union* in describing the incarnation. Rather than accepting this union, Nestorius maintains that "God the Word assumed a perfect man,"[35] that "God the Word conjoined this man to himself in an entirely new way."[36] This man, Nestorius believes, "received the worship of all the creation insofar as he had an inseparable conjunction with the divine nature."[37] He adds, "this man is connected with him and participates in him and thereby shares in the very title and honor of the Son."[38] Finally, Nestorius argues that "it is obvious that he who is Lord and Son by nature has, for the sake of salvation, assumed a man into an inseparable conjunction with himself which thereby elevates him to the title and honor of both Son and Lord."[39]

Cyril is adamant in his insistence that Nestorius's language simply does not do justice to what is occurring in the incarnation of the Son. Words and phrases such as "assumed," "conjoined," "inseparable conjunction" and "connected" fail to capture the reality of what has taken place. In the incarnation we do not have simply a conjunction or an assumption of the man Jesus by the Word. Rather, Cyril contends, it is the "same one" who is "equally God and man," and to this same person "alone apply all the divine and human characteristics."

> For he who is and exists from all eternity, as he is God, underwent birth from a woman according to the flesh. This means that it pertains to one and the same both to exist and subsist eternally, and also to have been born after the flesh in these last times. . . . He who as God is Life and Life-Giver is said to have been brought to life by the Father in terms of his manifestation as man. . . . He did not disdain the economy.[40]

Is Cyril simply quarreling unnecessarily about words? What, after all, is the difference between union and conjunction? Cyril would likely respond by asking: "So you wish to use the word *conjunction* to describe the incarnation? *What* exactly is being conjoined? The Son and the man Jesus? If so, do we not have two persons? Are we not in danger of idolatry? For if the man Jesus is not God, but merely joined to God in a conjunction or association, how can we genuinely speak of him as divine?" To use Cyril's own words, is the mere conjunction of David's descendant with the Word sufficient "to allow him to grasp the proper glory of God and rise above the bounds of the created order? . . . Does this not make him an object of worship even though he is not God?"[41]

> It seems to us that there are two sons in this argument, who are unequal in nature, and that a slave is crowned with the glory that is proper to God, and that some bastard son is decked out with the selfsame dignities as the one who is really God's natural Son. . . . How can someone who has only been honored with a mere conjunction fail to be "other" to the true and natural Son?[42]

Cyril, then, understands Nestorius to argue that in the economy of the incarnation the Son assumes or conjoins his person to a man (Jesus of Nazareth) and subsequently raises that man to the glory of the Godhead. Such a construction, Cyril believes, turns the incarnation on its head. Rather than the elevation of a man through assumption or conjunction, the incarnation is actually the union of the Son with human nature itself.

Furthermore, what of the biblical testimony concerning the incarnation? Cyril asks rhetorically: "Surely our exposition follows the mind of the scriptures?"[43] He points his reader to the apostle Paul. Think, for example, of 2 Corinthians 5:21: "For our sake he made him to be sin who knew no sin, so that in him we might become the righteousness of God." Cyril takes it as self-evident that Paul is referring to the incarnate Son. Does not Paul write in Romans 8:32 that God "did not withhold his own Son, but gave him up for all of us [so that] with him [he might] also give us everything else"? It is the Son, in union with human nature, who suffered and died. Again Cyril refers the reader to John 1:14: "the Word became flesh." It is "God the Word, born of God, and God by nature [who] abased himself to a self-emptying and humbled himself to assume the form of a slave."[44]

Cyril wonders why his opponents cannot clearly perceive the implications of their position, for if in the incarnation the Son has only *assumed* a man or *conjoined* himself to a man, is not the Son actually despising the economy by refusing to enter fully into the human condition? In addition, "if it was true that he assumed a man, brought him to the trial of death, raised him to the heavens and made him sit alongside the Father, then where would the Only Begotten position his own throne after this?"[45] Cyril believes Nestorius's theology must inevitably lead to the conclusion that we have two Sons, the Only Begotten and the man the Only Begotten has assumed.

Does Cyril's Position Blend or Mix the Human with the Divine?

Cyril realizes that at least one reason Nestorius is reluctant to speak of a genuine union of the Son with human nature is that one could easily understand such a union to imply a mixing, blending or confusing of the divine and human natures. Cyril readily agrees that one must preserve the ontological distinction between these two natures.

But who would be so misguided and stupid as to think that the divine nature of the Word had changed into something which formerly it was not? Or that the flesh was changed by some kind of transformation into the nature of the Word himself? This is impossible. We say that there is one Son, and that he has one nature even when he is considered as having assumed flesh endowed with a rational soul. As I have already said, he has made the human element his own. And this is the way, not otherwise, that we must consider that the same one is at once God and man.[46]

Cyril advocates genuine union, but no confusion. "The term union in no way causes the confusion of the things it refers to, but rather signifies the concurrence in one reality of those things which are understood to be united."[47]

This concurrence in the mystery of the incarnation is genuinely inexplicable. That is to say, "Godhead is one thing, and manhood is another thing, considered in the perspective of their respective and intrinsic beings." One would never have imagined that divinity and humanity could have been joined in a union that simultaneously preserved their distinction, yet in the incarnation this is exactly what has occurred. Cyril explains, "in the case of Christ they came together in a mysterious and incomprehensible union without confusion or change. The manner of this union is entirely beyond conception."[48] In light of the revelation Scripture provides, though, Cyril is willing to accept the conceptual enigmas inherent in the incarnation.

In a sense, Cyril is asking us to hold truths concurrently, to think thoughts side by side that logic alone would demand that we separate. Deity is one thing, humanity another. Still, in a manner Cyril describes as beyond all conception, "Godhood and manhood have come together with each other in an indivisible union."[49] He adds, "After the union (I mean with the flesh) even if anyone calls him Only Begotten, or God from God, this does not mean he is thought of as being separated from the flesh or indeed the manhood. Similarly if one calls him a man, this is not to take away the fact that he is God and Lord."[50]

How a genuine union can occur without a blending or mixing of the divine and human natures of Christ is inexplicable. Nor can we understand how the human nature can remain intact in light of such an intimate union with the Son's deity. But, Cyril insists, such a mystery is the teaching of the Scripture and must be upheld and preserved. "It was not impossible to God, in his loving-kindness, to make himself capable of bearing the limitations of the manhood."[51]

Earlier biblical narratives point to the surprising ability of God to accommo-
date himself to the limitations of the created order. In fact, Cyril believes that a
number of "enigmas" surrounding the life of Moses serve aptly as depictions of
"the manner of the incarnation in types." Think of Moses' encounter with God in
the epiphany of the burning bush.

> For he came down in the form of fire onto the bush in the desert, and the fire
> played upon the shrub but did not consume it. When he saw this Moses was
> amazed. Why was there no incompatibility here between the wood and the fire?
> How did this inflammable substance endure the assaults of the flame? Well, as I
> have already said, this event was a type of a mystery, of how the divine nature of
> the Word supported the limitations of the manhood; because he chose to. Abso-
> lutely nothing is impossible to him [Mk 10:27].[52]

If God can manifest the divine presence in a bush without consuming it, how
much more can God draw close to humanity in the mystery of the incarnation
without overwhelming human nature. Cyril admits, however, that such a "true
unity . . . transcends speech and understanding."[53]

The reality of the incarnation simply refuses to fit within an entirely coherent
logical framework. But should this surprise us? Cyril has already encouraged us
to think concurrently, holding seemingly contradictory thoughts side by side and
allowing the tension between them to remain rather than attempting to resolve
the tension through a premature rationalistic maneuver.

In the twentieth century Robert Oppenheimer advocated much the same methodology, but for use in a different discipline, contemporary physics. Why is there a
need for occasionally logical inconsistency? Huston Smith notes the presence of
"many findings in contemporary physics that refuse to be correlated in a single logical framework." Hence, Oppenheimer's proposal that physicists employ a "Law of
Complementarity as the basic working concept in the field, meaning by this (in
part) that opposing facts must be held in tension even where logically they are at
odds if they can help account for phenomena observed. In more than one field, it
seems, reality can be more subtle than man's logic at any given moment."[54]

Another example Cyril provides of two opposing truths or facts that must be
held in tension concerns Jesus' experience of pain and suffering. Cyril has consistently argued that God the Word has been joined to human nature in Jesus of
Nazareth. If so, sooner or later Cyril must address the thorny question of Jesus'

suffering. When Jesus suffered, did God suffer? When Jesus experienced pain, did God the Word experience that same pain? On the one hand, Cyril reaffirms the patristic consensus that God cannot suffer.

> We say, then, that the Word who shines forth from God's essence is his proper Son, but that he is not given on behalf of us nakedly, as it were, or as yet without flesh, but rather when he became flesh. To say that he suffered does no disgrace to him, for he did not suffer in the nature of the godhead, but in his own flesh.[55]

Yet at least some of Cyril's opponents wondered how the same one could both suffer and not suffer, that is, suffer in his flesh without suffering in his divinity. To assert both truths was to assert a "fairy tale, and indeed verges on the incredible. For either, as God, he has not suffered at all, or alternatively, if he is said to have suffered, then how can he be God?"[56] Cyril pictures at least some of his opponents as deducing, on the basis of this rationalistic syllogism, that the one born of Mary must be of David's line of descent, but no more.

This position, Cyril asserts, demonstrates no more than "feebleness of mind." Why? One can only deduce that the child born of Mary is "any common man taken up in the rank of mediator and artificially holding the glory of sonship," a rank and title Cyril pictures as the result of the "conjunction" of the human Jesus and the divine Son. It is doubtful whether this represents Nestorius's own position fairly. Cyril clearly believed, however, that Nestorius's hesitancy in calling Mary *theotokos* could only lead to these conclusions.

On the contrary, Cyril argues, the one born of Mary is the Word of God, the eternal Logos, who "did not disdain the economy, and became flesh."[57] Further, "the manner of the economy allows him blamelessly to choose both to suffer in the flesh, and not to suffer in the Godhead." Cyril then quickly adds that how such could be the case was "altogether ineffable. . . . There is no mind that can attain to such subtle and transcendent ideas."[58] Yet on the basis of biblical testimony and the tradition he has inherited, Cyril deduces that the Son must be both impassible in his deity and passible in his humanity. Thus, *in his humanity* the Word genuinely suffers. If such were not the case, "the birth in the flesh was not his but someone else's."

Mary as *Theotokos* and Other Key Doctrines

Cyril believes that the theological affirmation of Mary as *theotokos* (bearer of God), inexplicable as this reality might be, preserves and clarifies other key doctrines. Think, for example, of the resurrection. The resurrection illustrates the glory of the incarnation, for it proves that the incarnate Son "is greater than death and corruption. As God he is life and life-giver, and so raised up his own temple."[59]

> We say that the destruction of death and the banishing of corruption from the bodies of men was certainly something that the Son wanted to do. . . . But there was no other way to shake off the gloomy dominion of death, only by the incarnation of the Only Begotten. This was why he appeared as we are and made his own a body subject to corruption according to the inherent system of its nature. In so far as he himself is life, for he was born from the life of the Father, he intended to implant his own benefit within it, that is life itself.[60]

How two diametrically opposed truths—the Son's divine, impassible nature and the suffering of the Son in his passible humanity—could both be true remains rationally inexplicable to Cyril. He admits that the "force of any comparison falters here and falls short of the truth." All Cyril can offer is a "feeble image [that might] lead us from something tangible, as it were, to the very heights and to what is beyond all speech."[61] For example, the relationship between the Son's impassible nature, impervious to suffering, and his human nature, in which genuine suffering occurs, must be something like the relationship between iron and fire.

> It receives the fire into itself, and when it is in the very heart of the fire, if someone should beat it, then the material itself takes the battering but the nature of the fire is in no way injured by the one who strikes. This is how you should understand the way in which the Son is said both to suffer in the flesh and not to suffer in the Godhead.[62]

Cyril readily concedes that "the force of my comparison is feeble," though intelligible "if we have not deliberately chosen to disbelieve the holy scriptures."[63] This last phrase is telling. As far as Cyril is concerned, the entire controversy revolves around the interpretation of Scripture as the church has traditionally understood its meaning. Nestorius, in his quest for rational consistency, has been unnecessarily innovative in his theology.

Cyril, perhaps unfairly or through an unwillingness to listen carefully to Nestorius, argues that Nestorius is unwilling to live with the mystery of the incarnation. Rather than worshiping the mystery the incarnation represents,

Nestorius is actually diluting that mystery through his unwillingness to use *theotokos* to refer to Mary, the mother of Jesus.

It is doubtful whether this is actually the case. Nestorius has never denied the divinity of Jesus, nor has he denied his humanity. If he is guilty of anything, we might call it rationalistic scrupulousness. Is Mary bearing God? Yes. Is she bearing a human being? Yes. Is she bearing the anointed one of Israel? Yes. And so the title *christotokos* is surely theologically correct. Mary *is* the mother of the Christ, the anointed one of Israel.

But, we must ask, was this the place for Nestorius to draw a line in the sand? Could he not have called Mary *theotokos*? Surely so, for not only does *theotokos* preserve the wonder of God's coming to us in union with human nature, but it also preserves the mystery involved in such an incarnation. That is to say, the appellation *theotokos* forces us to think theologically and devotionally in a manner that *christotokos* does not. It declares loudly, indeed blatantly, that in this birth God has entered his creation to redeem and renew. It refuses any attempt to rationalize theologically or to backpedal. Perhaps most importantly, it preserves the heart of the gospel more effectively than does *christotokos*, for in Jesus of Nazareth we encounter "God with us." He is both human and the Word of God incarnate. He must be so if the benefits of his deity are to be communicated to his humanity and in this communication to the human race itself. In Cyril's words:

> He made our poverty his own, and we see in Christ the strange and rare paradox of Lordship in servant's form and divine glory in human abasement. That which was under the yoke in terms of the limitations of manhood was crowned with royal dignities, and that which was humble was raised to the most supreme excellence. The Only Begotten did not become man only to remain in the limits of the emptying. The point was that he who was God by nature should, in the act of self-emptying, assume everything that went along with it. This was how he would be revealed as ennobling the nature of man in himself by making it participate in his own sacred and divine honors.[64]

Readers well may have noticed that in our discussion of trinitarian relationships one person of the blessed Trinity has been largely overlooked, at least to this juncture. It is surely time to focus our attention on the Holy Spirit, the very person who delights in illuminating our understanding of the Father and the Son.

"One cannot see the Father without the Spirit!
It would be like living in a house at night when the lamps are extinguished;
one's eyes would be darkened and could not exercise their function.
Unable to distinguish the value of objects, one might very well treat gold as if it were iron.
It is the same with the spiritual world; it is impossible to maintain a life of holiness
without the Spirit. It would be easier for an army to continue its maneuvers
without a general, or for a choir to sing on key without its director."
BASIL THE GREAT
On the Holy Spirit

FIVE

ON THE
HOLY SPIRIT

Four Key Groups

As we have already seen in our discussion of the early church's struggle to understand the person and work of Jesus Christ, the incarnate Son, for years the
church debated the central question of Jesus' deity: Was Jesus God? If so, how
was the church best to describe his relationship to the Father and, most importantly for the present chapter, to the Spirit? David Anderson observes four distinct groups within the church who responded to these key questions. [1]

The *"old" Nicenes.* These Christians insisted that the formula *homoousios*,
declared at Nicaea and confirming "that the Son is of one essence *(homoousios)*
with the Father," was the best and final word on the subject. That is, "acceptance
of the word *homoousios* was the only sure proof of orthodoxy."

The *"new" Nicenes.* Members of this group felt that *homoousios* could be too easily misconstrued or misinterpreted. While they affirmed the deity of the Son,
they argued that *homoousios* or "same essence" could be interpreted to mean that
the Son and Father were actually the same person. Better, they believed, to use
the word *homoiousios* to describe the relationship between the Father and the Son,
"meaning that the Son is of a *like* or *similar* essence with the Father."

The *semi-Arians.* Anderson notes that *homoiousios* was not without its own difficulties, it also being somewhat ambiguous and leading to the question: "to what
extent was He [the Son] like the Father?" The semi-Arians "accepted the use of

homoiousios, but nevertheless stressed the differences between Father and Son so much that if the divinity of the Son was not denied, it certainly was not affirmed very strongly."

The radical Arians. This group, grounded in the thought of the presbyter Arius, "placed the Son in the created order, denying that He was similar or equal to the Father in any way."

What of the Holy Spirit?

Despite the affirmation of the Son's divinity at the Council of Nicaea (A.D. 325), the controversy between these different groupings raged for years. It was not too long before people realized that the question of the nature of the Son and his relationship to the Father was not the only issue at hand. What of the Holy Spirit?

Of course, earlier Christian thinkers had reflected deeply on the Holy Spirit. For example, Clement of Rome, writing toward the end of the first century, comments: "Have we not one God and one Christ and one Spirit of Grace shed upon us?"[2] Irenaeus states that the Spirit is "our means of communion with Christ . . . the pledge of immortality, the strengthening of our faith, the ladder by which we ascend to God."[3] Indeed, Irenaeus affirms in a well-known phrase that humanity "was fashioned in the likeness of God and was formed by the hands of God, that is, by the Son and the Spirit, to whom he said, 'Let us make man.' "[4]

Origen's reading of John's Gospel and Paul's epistles convinced him of the personal nature of the Holy Spirit.

> "The Spirit blows where it wills" [Jn 3:8]. This signifies that the Spirit is a substantial being. It is not, as some imagine, an activity of God without individual existence. And the Apostle, after enumerating the gifts of the Spirit, proceeds thus: "And all these things come from the activity of the one same Spirit, distributing to each individually as he wills" [1 Cor 12:11]; if he "wills" and "is active" and "distributes," he is therefore an active substance, not a mere activity.[5]

Yet, despite significant instances of profound early Christian reflection upon the Holy Spirit, it was during the controversies of the fourth century, particularly between the years 325 and 381, that the church's understanding of the person and work of the Spirit developed and matured. The Council of Nicaea almost seems to treat the Spirit as an addendum. After the Nicene Creed's significant reflection on Christ, we encounter the phrase "We believe in the Holy Spirit" and nothing more. It was only in subsequent years that the church realized "such vagueness would not do, that the Church of Christ was disintegrating into a jumble of warring factions, and that . . . words adequate for God, were necessary to define the catholic faith."[6] Basil the Great, bishop of Caesarea, was to prove to be a key figure in helping the church to find the linguistic and conceptual models necessary for understanding and speaking well of the Holy Spirit. It is to his great work, *On the Holy Spirit*, that we now turn.

Basil's *On the Holy Spirit*

At first glance Basil's *On the Holy Spirit* can easily daunt or discourage a modern reader. Basil spends page after page, for example, in a detailed, fairly dry examination of Greek prepositions. Most will wonder what possible relationship Greek prepositions might have to do with the person and work of the Holy Spirit.

We can frame the basic problem Basil addresses as a controversy over doxologies, a disagreement that at first glance seems to be theological nitpicking but that, on closer examination, reveals key theological presuppositions about the nature of Christ *and* the Spirit.

Two different doxologies. Basil found himself in hot water with at least some Christians because in the church at Caesarea he used two different doxologies. The first, "Glory to the Father with [*meta*] the Son together with [*syn*] the Holy Spirit," had a distinguished history in non-Greek speaking churches but struck Greek Christians as nontraditional and innovative.[7] The second, "Glory to the Father through [*dia*] the Son in [*en*] the Holy Spirit," was much more familiar to Greek ears. So why the commotion? Did not early Christians have more important matters to argue about than the grammar of Greek prepositions? Any student who has ever tried to conquer the nuances of Greek prepositions can readily sympathize with the frustration of both ancient and modern readers over the relevance and fruitfulness of grammatical warfare.

Basil would respond, however, that it is often in the small, seemingly insignificant steps of exegetical and theological reasoning—steps often built on key grammatical distinctions—that we frame the issues and determine the outcomes. He warns against the intellectual laziness that would attempt to bypass the hard and, yes, occasionally boring work involved in sound exegesis and theological reasoning.

> Those who are idle in the pursuit of righteousness count theological terminology as secondary, together with attempts to search out the hidden meaning in this phrase or that syllable, but those conscious of the goal of our calling realize that we are to become like God, as far as this is possible for human nature. But we cannot become like God unless we have knowledge of Him, and without lessons there will be no knowledge. Instruction begins with the proper use of speech, and syllables and words are the elements of speech. Therefore to scrutinize syllables is not a superfluous task. Just because certain questions seem insignificant is no reason to ignore them. Hunting truth is no easy task; we must look everywhere for its tracks. Learning truth is like learning a trade; apprentices grow in experience little by little, provided they do not despise any opportunity to increase their knowledge. If a man spurns fundamental elements as insignificant trifles, he will never embrace the fullness of wisdom.[8]

Consequently, at least if Basil is right, the prepositions used in doxologies might have much more to teach us than we would believe at first glance. Basil soon directs his reader's attention to the objections of his opponents. Take a look again at the doxology under dispute: "Glory to the Father with the Son together with the Holy Spirit." Why did Basil's opponents insist that those who used such a doxology were "innovators, revolutionaries, phrase-coiners, and who knows how many other insults"?[9]

For his part, Basil is convinced that his opponents' grammatical scruples mask deeper objections. Behind the epithets thrown at Basil lies a more fundamental theological opposition: "These are the reasons for their vexation: they say that the Son is not equal with the Father, but comes after the Father. Therefore it follows that glory should be ascribed to the Father *through* Him, but not *with* Him," precisely because the preposition *with* "expresses equality but *through* . . . indicates subordination."[10]

> Even more important for our discussion of the Holy Spirit, the implications of this prepositional hesitation quickly become apparent. If the Son ends up subordinate to the Father, Basil observes, his opponents place the Spirit on an even lower level. "They insist that the Spirit must not be ranked with the Father or the Son, but

under the Father and the Son, not in the same order of things as they are, but beneath them, not numbered with them."[11]

In response, Basil asks a key question: In what way does the Son come *after* the Father? Is this *after* related to time, or perhaps to rank or dignity? An *after* related to time makes little sense, for how could "the Maker of the ages" hold "a second place; no interval could possibly divide the natural union of the Father and Son."[12]

Even limited human thought demonstrates that it is impossible for the Son to be younger than the Father; . . . we cannot conceive of either apart from their relationship with each other. . . . In addition to being impious, is it really not the height of folly to measure the life of Him who transcends all times and ages, whose existence is incalculably remote from the present? Things subject to birth and corruption are described as prior to one another; are we therefore to compare God the Father as superior to God the Son, who exists before the ages?[13]

As we have already seen in Athanasius's treatment of the begetting of the Son, whatever "begetting" means, it cannot mean a begetting involving procreation, separation or creation. As Basil puts it, "the supreme *eminence* of the Father is inconceivable; thought and reflection are utterly unable to penetrate the begetting of the Lord."[14]

Instead, Basil teaches, the wise person will maintain the concept of the Son's begetting within the "tangible boundaries" laid out in the first verse of John's Gospel: "In the beginning was the Word." Basil explains, "No matter how far your thoughts travel backward, you cannot get beyond the *was*. No matter how hard you strain to see what is beyond the Son, you will find it impossible to pass outside the confines of the *beginning*."[15] If John is correct, Basil insists, how could one possibly object to the preposition *with* in a doxology of the church? Thus prepositions prove to mean more than we had perhaps thought at first glance.

Well, Basil asks, maybe his opponents mean that the Son is subordinate in terms of place? This makes little sense, though, for how could one imagine the Father separated from the Son spatially? After all, the Father "fills all things." Further, both the Father and Son are incorporeal beings who by definition do not occupy space in the same manner as corporeal beings.[16]

Here, Basil believes, the central problem concerns his opponents' misunderstanding of biblical metaphor. They are interpreting biblical passages in a "fleshly sense" in their "attempt to confine God within prescribed boundaries. Form, shape, and bodily position cannot be invented for God; these factors are alien to the absolute, the infinite, the incorporeal."[17] When Hebrews speaks of the Son as sitting down at the right hand of the Father (Heb 1:3), does the writer intend his readers to understand "a lower place" spatially? Hardly. Rather, sitting at the Father's right hand "emphasizes the magnificence of the Son's great dignity."[18]

Bad exegesis and bad theology. Bad exegesis, in this case seen in an inability to interpret either prepositions or metaphor well, has led to bad theology. Basil scolds his opponents for their failure to read Scripture well, but he does not stop there. While they have accused him of being a theological innovator, it is actually they who have produced a new, idiosyncratic interpretation in their insistence that *with* is innovative, while *through* is biblical. The church, Basil notes, recognizes both phrases. Both make good theological sense. Basil explains:

> Whenever we reflect on the majesty of the nature of the Only-Begotten, and the excellence of His dignity, we ascribe glory to Him *with* the Father. On the other hand, when we consider the abundant blessings He has given us, and how He has admitted us as co-heirs into God's household, we acknowledge that this grace works for us *through* him and *in* him. Therefore the best phrase when giving him glory is *with whom* and the most appropriate for giving thanks is *through whom*.[19]

A better knowledge of both Scripture and tradition would serve Basil's critics well. The tradition of the church supported the use of "with whom." Indeed, Basil notes, "Everyone who steadfastly values the old ways above these novelties, and who has preserved unchanged the tradition of the fathers both in the city and in the country, is familiar with this phrase."[20] Tradition in itself, however, is not enough for Basil: "But we are not content simply because this is the tradition of the Fathers. What is important is that the Fathers followed the meaning of Scripture, beginning with the evidence which I have just extracted from the Scriptures and presented to you."[21]

Up to this point in his treatise Basil has remained relatively silent regarding the Spirit. After examining the Son's relationship with the Father in his rich introductory chapters, Basil is prepared to discuss the Spirit, but always within the stance of deep reverence and adoration. Again, as in his treatment of the Son,

Basil will look closely at Scripture and at how it has been interpreted in the history of the church.

Implications of the Spirit's titles. Basil begins by listing the different titles used for the Spirit in the Bible:

> He is called the Spirit of God [Mt 3:16], the Spirit of truth who proceeds from the Father [Jn 15:26], right Spirit, willing Spirit. His first and most proper title is Holy Spirit, a name most especially appropriate to everything which is incorporeal, purely immaterial, and indivisible.[22]

Why this listing of attributes? While Basil does not explicitly state, either here or anywhere in his treatise on the Spirit, that the Spirit is God, he wants to push his readers to this conclusion by helping them to see the implications of the prevalent biblical language for the Spirit. Basil contends, for instance, that the nature of an incorporeal being "cannot be circumscribed. When we hear the word 'spirit' it is impossible for us to conceive of something whose nature can be circumscribed or is subject to change or variation, or is like a creature in any way."[23]

Basil seems to be arguing that if we can rightly say these kinds of things about the Spirit, we will be led to the proper conclusion about the Spirit's nature. Consider the following:

> All things thirsting for holiness turn to Him; everything living in virtue never turns away from Him. He waters them with His life-giving breath and helps them reach their proper fulfillment. He gives life to all things, and is never depleted. He does not increase by additions, but is always complete, self-established, and present everywhere. He is the source of sanctification, spiritual light, who gives illumination to everyone using His powers to search for the truth—and the illumination He gives is Himself. His nature is unapproachable; only through His goodness are we able to draw near it. He fills all things with His power. . . . He is distributed but does not change. He is shared, yet remains whole. Consider the analogy of the sunbeam: each person upon whom its kindly light falls rejoices as if the sun existed for him alone, yet it illumines land and sea, and is master of the atmosphere.[24]

Has Basil actually written the words, "the Holy Spirit is God"? No. But he is clearly constructing a picture of the Spirit whose contours and colors are divine. Basil's approach is basically to ask: If the Spirit acts like this, if we draw near to the Spirit through repentance and confession, if the Spirit brings to us divine gifts for ministry, what can we conclude?

For example, Basil writes that "the Spirit comes to us when we withdraw ourselves from evil passions."[25] Clearly, then, the Spirit is a holy being who can have no contact or communion with evil. It is only when a person "has been cleansed from the shame of his evil" that he can "approach the Paraclete." After this cleansing has occurred, however, "He will show you in Himself the image of the invisible, and with purified eyes you will see in this blessed image the unspeakable beauty of its prototype."[26]

Indeed, one of the principal roles of the Spirit, "the image of the invisible," is to create spiritual people who faithfully reflect "the Royal Image." How so? By bringing human beings into "fellowship with Himself." Basil writes, "When a sunbeam falls on a transparent substance, the substance itself becomes brilliant, and radiates light from itself. So too Spirit-bearing souls, illumined by Him, finally become spiritual themselves, and their grace is sent forth to others."[27]

The result is wonderful privileges and effective ministry, for when the Spirit restores the "Royal Image" he also distributes exuberant grace and a variety of gifts.

> From this comes knowledge of the future, understanding of mysteries, apprehension of hidden things, distribution of wonderful gifts, heavenly citizenship, a place in the choir of angels, endless joy in the presence of God, becoming like God, and, the highest of all desires, becoming God.[28]

The implications of such wonders for the "greatness, dignity, and working of the Holy Spirit" would seem to be self-evident, but Basil is only getting started. He is convinced that his opponents have committed serious theological errors, errors that can deeply harm them and the church if they are not addressed and corrected. Are these teachers correct, for example, in their refusal to "rank the Holy Spirit with the Father and the Son"?

To answer this question, Basil returns to the words of the apostles contained in Scripture. Are not people baptized "in the name of the Father, and of the Son, and of the Holy Spirit"? If so, how can we legitimately drive a wedge between the persons of the Trinity in a misguided attempt to place the Spirit on a lower level in terms of rank, dignity and nature? It was the Lord himself who did not "disdain His fellowship with the Holy Spirit" when he commanded the disciples to baptize in the name of all three persons of the Trinity.[29]

Not only does the witness of apostolic testimony in Scripture attest to the Spirit's unity with the Father and Son, but the church's own practice in worship and teaching affirms this same truth. Yet it is this apostolic tradition that many teachers are attempting to overthrow. In response, Basil insists that "the Lord has delivered to us a necessary and saving dogma: the Holy Spirit is to be ranked with the Father." To set this testimony aside is to make one's own interpretation, in this case a blasphemous one, "more authoritative than the law of the Lord."[30]

A seemingly arid discussion of doxologies and baptismal confessions has soon demonstrated itself to be centered on foundational issues and questions. Basil reminds both his readers and his opponents of the words they pronounced on the day they were regenerated by the power of the Spirit, a day Basil, like all church fathers, connected with the day of baptism. "What makes us Christians?" Basil asks. "Our faith," all would respond. "How are we saved? Obviously through the regenerating grace of baptism. How else could we be?"[31] So what is Basil's conclusion? The standard of teaching affirmed at baptism was baptism in the name of the Father, Son and Holy Spirit. To deny this confession is to deny the faith, the very faith those baptized confirmed in their own handwriting.

Basil viewed faith and baptism as inseparable "means of salvation." He explains, "Faith is perfected through baptism; the foundation of baptism is faith. . . . The profession of faith leads us to salvation, and then baptism follows, sealing our salvation."[32] Though some Protestant readers might disagree with Basil's understanding of the relationship between faith, baptism and salvation, surely they can affirm his argument that all baptisms must be in the name of the Father, Son and Holy Spirit, for behind any baptism lies the persons and work of the entire Trinity, as Jesus himself affirmed shortly before his ascension (see Mt 28:19; Acts 1:5). Basil writes:

> I swear to every man who confesses Christ but denies the Father: Christ will profit him nothing. If a man calls upon God, but rejects the Son, his faith is empty. If someone rejects the Spirit, his faith in the Father and the Son is made useless; it is impossible to believe in the Father and the Son without the presence of the Spirit. He who rejects the Spirit rejects the Son, and he who rejects the Son rejects the Father. . . . Such a person has no part in true worship. It is impossible to worship the Son except in the Holy Spirit; it is impossible to call upon the Father except in the Spirit of adoption.[33]

Common Objections

Basil, like any gifted debater, knew the objections his opponents were likely to raise to his position. Did, for example, the grouping of Father, Son and Spirit together in the baptismal formula necessarily teach that all three persons were of equal rank, dignity and nature? What of other significant groupings in Scripture? Did not the apostle Paul group together the Father, Son and angels in his charge to Timothy? Paul writes: "In the presence of God and of Christ Jesus and of the elect angels, I warn you" (1 Tim 5:21).

Did such a grouping indicate that Paul considered angels to be divine beings? If not, Basil's opponents were likely to ask why they should understand the Spirit any differently. Basil contends that such thinking betrays a basic category error, particularly when we remember what salvation itself entails. That is to say, an angel might be able to testify on the behalf of sinful people, but an angel could hardly free them from sin and its corresponding judgment. Basil explains:

> If a slave is to be made free, and called a son of God, and brought from death into life, it can only be accomplished by Him who shares our nature and delivers it from slavery. How could we be joined to God's household by someone who does not share our nature? How could we be freed by someone who bears the yoke of a servant? One does not speak of the Spirit and of angels as if they were equals; the Spirit is the Lord of life and the angels are our helpers, our fellow-servants, faithful witnesses of the truth.[34]

Unlike angels, the Spirit "is organically united with God . . . through communion in the divine nature."[35]

Other texts still seemed to pose problems for Basil's perspective. Did baptism in the name of the Spirit or "in the Spirit" *necessarily* demonstrate that the Spirit was divine? Did not Paul write that the Jewish people "all were baptized into Moses in the cloud and in the sea" (1 Cor 10:2)? Basil's opponents argue that, if Basil remains consistent in his argument, the logical outcome is that Moses, too, must have been divine.

Such a conclusion can only be reached, Basil responds, if one ignores the nature of biblical typology.

> What is said concerning Moses and the cloud is a shadow or type. Surely you realize that just because divine things are foreshadowed by finite, human beings, we

cannot conclude that the divine nature is finite. Divine things are very often prefigured by means of shadowy types. Typology points out what is to be expected, indicating through imitation what is to happen before it happens.[36]

Basil then points his readers to a number of typological examples employed by biblical writers: Paul writes that Adam was a type of the coming Messiah (Rom 5:14). The rock in the wilderness was a type of Christ (1 Cor 10:4) and "a type of the living power of the Word."[37] The manna in the wilderness represented "the living bread which came down from heaven."[38] The serpent hung on a pole by Moses "was a type of the saving passion accomplished on the cross, since the life of every one who looked at the serpent was preserved."[39] Basil is convinced his opponents are straying into error regarding the Spirit because they are not reading the Scripture well. By misreading its typologies, metaphors and similes they, in turn, are misinterpreting the person and work of the Spirit.

Moreover, Basil's opponents err because they still possess "an infantile mind," a mind that by this time should have matured, manifesting its maturity through an ability to discern the fundamental direction of key Old Testament typologies. God had gradually and progressively taught the Jews, beginning with elementary concepts and principles concerning his person and work, and gradually leading them to a richer, more complete understanding of his person and purposes. The identical principle—elementary truths leading to more complex, complete ones—was true for the Christian and the church.

> He knows our eyes are accustomed to dim shadows, so He uses these at first. Then He shows us the sun's reflection in water, so as to spare us from being blinded by its pure light. The law was a shadow of things to come, and the teachings of the prophets were a reflection of truth. He devised them to train the eyes of our hearts, so that we could make an easy transition to the secret and hidden wisdom of God, which God decreed before the ages for our glorification.[40]

Basil proceeds to mount a scriptural barrage. Again, rather than simply asserting the deity of the Spirit, he directs his audience to passage after passage in Scripture and develops the implications of the biblical texts. Whatever theology Basil constructs concerning the Spirit is fundamentally rooted in this biblical foundation.

Think, for example, of Paul's teaching concerning the gift of tongues in 1 Corinthians. Paul writes: "But if all prophesy, an unbeliever or outsider who

enters is reproved by all and called to account by all. After the secrets of the unbeliever's heart are disclosed, that person will bow down before God and worship
him, declaring, 'God is really among you' " (1 Cor 14:24-25). Basil then draws out
the implications of Paul's teaching for our understanding of the Holy Spirit: "If
God is recognized to be present among prophets because their prophesying is a
gift of the Spirit, let our opponents determine what place they will give to the
Holy Spirit. Will they rank Him with God, or will they push Him down to a
creature's place?"[41]

Or consider, Basil writes, the situation of Ananias and Sapphira. When they
lied to the apostles concerning a gift of money, to whom were they actually lying?
Peter says they were tempting the Holy Spirit by lying against God (Acts 5:4, 9).
Basil draws out the implication clearly: "This shows that to sin against the Holy
Spirit is to sin against God. Understand from this that in every operation, the
Holy Spirit is indivisibly united with the Father and the Son."[42]

Think, Basil teaches, of the spiritual gifts present in the Corinthian congregation. How were they distributed? Paul explains: "Now there are varieties of
gifts, but the same Spirit; and there are varieties of services, but the same Lord;
and there are varieties of activities, but it is the same God who activates all of
them in everyone. . . . All these are activated by one and the same Spirit, who
allots to each one individually just as the Spirit chooses" (1 Cor 12:4-6, 11).
Basil comments:

> God works in various ways, and the Lord serves in various capacities, but the Holy
> Spirit is also present of His own will, dispensing gifts to everyone according to
> each man's worth. . . . Notice that he [Paul] is speaking the same way we do when
> we receive gifts: first we thank the messenger who brought the gift; next we
> remember him who sent it, and finally we raise our thoughts to the fountain and
> source of all gifts.[43]

The Divine Communion of Father, Son and Spirit

Basil's ruminations on the intimate communion between the Father, Son and
Holy Spirit draw him to ponder how that communion is illustrated through the
creation of angels, whom he describes as "pure, spiritual, and transcendent powers."[44] As with human beings, the angels receive their holiness from the Holy
Spirit. Basil observes that Scripture has not described the creation of angels but

argues that from analogy, that is, by reasoning from the creation of the world to the creation of the invisible "bodiless hosts in heaven," much can be learned.

For example, "When you consider creation I advise you to first think of Him who is the first cause of everything that exists: namely the Father, and then of the Son, who is the creator, and then the Holy Spirit, the perfector."[45] The created world came into being because of the will of the Father and through the agency of the Son, and it is perfected through the Spirit. So it is with the angelic realm: "The ministering spirits exist by the will of the Father, are brought into being by the work of the Son, and are perfected by the presence of the Spirit, since angels are perfected by perseverance in holiness."[46]

In creation, Basil believes, we can observe a willed cooperation between the persons of the Trinity. For example, to speak of the Spirit perfecting creation or angelic beings might lead one to understand that the work of the Father or the Son is somehow deficient. However, there is actually no *need* for the Father to create through the Son or for the Son's work to be perfected through the Spirit. The divine economy in creation, rather, is an apt picture of the divine community's deep and loving communion. Basil explains, "The Father creates through His will alone and does not *need* the Son, yet chooses to work through the Son. Likewise the Son works as the Father's likeness, and needs no other cooperation, but chooses to have His work completed through the Spirit."[47]

Basil encourages his readers to meditate deeply on this divine communion, describing the Spirit as proceeding from the Father and as strengthening the work of Father and Son in creation, whether this is the creation of earthly or heavenly creatures. What kind of strengthening does the Spirit provide? "Perfection in holiness, which expresses itself in an unyielding, unchangeable commitment to goodness. Such holiness is impossible without the Spirit."[48] If so, even the holy angels are dependent upon the Spirit for their holiness. "The angelic powers are not by their own nature holy; otherwise there would be no difference between them and the Holy Spirit. Rather, they are sanctified by the Holy Spirit in proportion to their excellence."[49] Unlike human beings, however, angels are "created beings which are not gradually perfected, but are immediately perfect from the moment of their creation." This perfection, however, is a graced perfection. That is, "He gives them His own grace, that their nature might be maintained in perfection."[50] *angelology is a reality in Scripture*

Take a close look at a branding-iron, Basil assures his readers, and the angels' nature and holiness will become plainer.

> When we consider a branding-iron we also immediately remember that fire is required to heat it, yet we would not claim that the iron and the fire are the same substance. The angels are a similar case; they are essentially aerial spirits, composed of immaterial fire, as it is written, "He makes His angels spirits, and His ministers a flaming fire" [Ps 103:4 LXX = 104:4]. They exist in space, and when they are seen by those who are worthy, they assume an appropriate physical form. Holiness is not part of their essence; it is accomplished in them through communion with the Spirit. They keep their rank by persevering in goodness, by freely choosing to never abandon serving Him, who is good by nature.[51]

What, then, are the demons? Angels who have chosen to exercise their free will in an evil manner by rejecting the aid that comes from the Spirit. Both the holiness and ministry of the angels is rooted in the Spirit. Angels such as Gabriel can announce the future to key individuals only as the Spirit reveals it to them, for "it is the unique function of the Spirit to reveal mysteries."[52]

Not only does the Spirit perfect creation, sanctify angels and humans, empower ministries in heaven and on earth and reveal the mystery of God's plan for the future, but the angels even see the face of the Father in heaven (Mt 18:10). How so? Through the Spirit. "One cannot see the Father without the Spirit! It would be like living in a house at night when the lamps are extinguished; one's eyes would be darkened and could not exercise their function."[53] The grace of the Spirit enables the angels to see and worship worthily the Father.

As for God's plan and action to save humanity, "who would deny that it was all made possible through the grace of the Spirit?"[54] Basil is insistent that virtually every aspect of the Old or New Testament narrative can be linked to the work of the Holy Spirit.

> Whether you wish to examine the Old Testament—the blessings of the patriarchs, the help given through the law, the types, the prophecies, the victories in battle, the miracles performed through righteous men—or everything that happened since the Lord's coming in the flesh, it all comes to pass through the Spirit.[55]

Think of Jesus' own life. Jesus was anointed with the Spirit at his baptism in the Jordan (see Mt 3:17; Jn 1:33). Indeed, Basil argues, "the Holy Spirit was

anti-mentories
words
covenant

Cov.
of
Creation

present in every action He performed."[56] Jesus' temptation in the wilderness, his miracles and his exorcisms were all accomplished successfully through the power of the Spirit. Even after Jesus' resurrection from the dead, the Spirit remained with him. Shortly before Jesus' ascension he breathed upon the disciples and "renewed mankind, [thus] restoring the grace which Adam had lost, which God had breathed into him at the beginning."[57] As the apostles, the foundation stones of the church, receive the Spirit, they are empowered for the ministry Christ has given them. In addition, the church as a whole is "set in order by the Holy Spirit," as the Spirit appoints apostles, prophets, teachers, workers of miracles, healers, helpers, administrators and gifts of tongues.[58]

Basil envisions a glorious future in which the work of the Spirit will continue. Rather than the Spirit's work ceasing when the Lord returns a second time in glory, "the Holy Spirit will be present with Him on the day of His revelation, when he will judge the universe in righteousness as its only Ruler."[59] Further, "the crown of the righteous man is precisely the grace of the Spirit." When Christ returns "glory shall be distributed in perfect abundance," a distribution proportionally based on faithfulness and fidelity of life in this present age. As some Christians have lived lives of greater faithfulness, so they will be rewarded accordingly. "In the Father's house are many mansions, meaning that some saints are of greater radiance and dignity than others."[60]

Broader Trinitarian Considerations

Basil proceeds to deal with broader trinitarian considerations, reflections that again have specific implications for our understanding of the Spirit's nature and work. Some of Basil's opponents, for instance, argued that the Spirit must be inferior to the Father and Son because he was mentioned third in doxological formulations. Did not this number three indicate the subordination or, more crassly, the inferiority of the Spirit?

Basil responds with a firm no by stressing the common nature shared by the Father, Son and Holy Spirit. Whatever the number three may mean, he teaches, it cannot mean that the divine nature is something one can divide into separate parts, with certain parts possessing a superior quality and others less so. If the Spirit shares in the divine essence, he cannot be less than divine, although named third. "Pieces of a whole cannot escape sharing the nature of the whole. . . . It would be like using a sword to cut through butter!"[61]

How could the Spirit be a *subordinate* (inferior, lesser) being if Christ himself mentioned the Spirit in the same breath with the Father and the Son? In Basil's words, "if you limit subordination to the Spirit alone, you must learn once and for all that the Lord speaks of the Spirit and the Father in exactly the same way: 'In the name of the Father, and of the Son, and of the Holy Spirit.' "[62]

> The words of baptism are the same, and they declare that the relation of the Spirit to the Son equals that of the Son with the Father. If the Spirit is ranked with the Son, and the Son with the Father, then the Spirit is obviously ranked with the Father also. Their names are mentioned in one and the same series. . . . Can numerical ranking ever change the nature of anything? . . . No amount of weighing, measuring, or counting can ever change a thing's nature. We can weigh gold or tin, but we would not claim that the *nature* of one is subordinate to the other on the basis of weight, and the same holds true for measure. Therefore we will use numbers as practical tools, and not claim that the very nature of a thing can be expressed with higher or lower ones! [63]

While Basil's discussion of divine arithmetic might at first glance seem highly esoteric and irrelevant, is this actually the case? For example, when Christians baptize in the name of the Father, Son and Holy Spirit, are they baptizing in the name of three separate gods? If so, the Christian faith is actually polytheistic.

> Those who teach subordination, and talk about first, second, and third, ought to realize that they are introducing erroneous Greek polytheism into pure Christian theology. This evil invention of subordinationism can result in nothing except a first, second, and third God. We will be content with the order established by the Lord. . . . Subordination cannot be used to describe persons who share the same nature. [64]

Hence, Christian arithmetic, at least regarding the Trinity, always adds up to one. That is, Father plus Son plus Spirit equals one, not three. Christians worship and baptize in the name of one, and only one, God. As Basil puts it:

> If we count, we do *not* add, increasing from one to many. We do not say, "one, two, three," or "first, second, and third." . . . We have never to this present day heard of a second God. We worship God from God, confessing the uniqueness of the persons. . . . As unique Persons, they are one and one; as sharing a common nature,

both are one. How does one and one not equal two Gods? Because we speak of the emperor, and the emperor's image—but not two emperors. The power is not divided, nor the glory separated.[65]

In the same way, the Spirit is unique in the Spirit's own person, but one in essence with the Father and Son. Basil explains, "The Holy Spirit is one, and we speak of Him as unique, since through the one Son He is joined to the Father. He completes the all-praised and blessed Trinity."[66]

If the Spirit shares the same divine essence as the Father and the Son, it should not surprise us that Basil insists that the Spirit in turn should be accorded the same praise, honor and glory. Basil makes his point by turning the reader to the names given to the Spirit in Scripture, to "the greatness of his deeds" and to the many blessings the Spirit bestows. For example, the Spirit's name reminds Basil that "God is spirit" [Jn 4:24]. The Spirit is called "Holy," just "as the Father is holy and the Son is holy." He is called "upright—the Lord my God is upright [Ps 92:15]—because He is truth and righteousness personified." And what of the name "Paraclete" (Jn 14:16), a name the Spirit shares with the Only Begotten? Basil contends that the implications of these names are inescapable: "The Spirit shares titles held in common by the Father and the Son; He receives these titles due to His natural and intimate relationship with them. Where else would they come from? . . . Titles like these are great and lofty, but they do not exhaust His glory."[67]

The Work of the Spirit

Not only the Spirit's names, but the Spirit's works attest to his intimacy and communion with the Father and the Son. "What does the Spirit do?" Basil asks. "His works are ineffable in majesty, and innumerable in quantity."[68] Basil speculates on the work of the Spirit "before creation began." "He existed; He preexisted; He co-existed with the Father and the Son before the ages. Even if you can imagine anything beyond the ages, you will discover that the Spirit is even further beyond."[69]

In creation, the Spirit establishes "the heavenly powers." With Christ's coming, the Spirit "prepares his way." In Christ's ministry, "the Spirit is never separated from Him. Working of miracles and gifts of healing come from the Holy Spirit. Demons are driven out by the Spirit of God. The presence of the Spirit despoils the devil. Remission of sins is given through the gift of the Spirit."[70] The Spirit nurtures intimacy with God. Through the Spirit, as Paul writes, we cry out "Abba" to God.[71] The resurrection of the dead itself is accomplished through the power of the Spirit, as is "the conversion of sinners to a better way of life."[72]

How can we not honor the Spirit, Basil asks, in light of all the Spirit's great works and gifts?

> We should instead fear that even though we ascribe to Him the highest titles we can devise or our tongues pronounce, our ideas about Him might still fall short. . . . Do not deprive Him of the faith and praise He is due. He has been within you; have you expelled Him? . . . Do not repay your benefactor's love for man with ingratitude; that would be the height of baseness. Do not grieve the Holy Spirit of God.[73]

The Limits of Human Reason

Basil remains convinced that human reason and its attendant categories simply cannot comprehend or describe adequately the person and work of the Holy Spirit. Actually, our inability to grasp the Spirit is a sign that the Spirit is to be honored and worshiped with the Father and Son. We observe the loftiness of the Spirit not only in the elevated titles the Spirit shares with the Father and Son, "but also because He, like them, cannot be grasped by our thoughts."[74] As John's Gospel expresses it, "the world cannot receive [the Spirit] because it neither sees him nor knows him" (Jn 14:17). Basil comments:

> A carnal man's mind is not trained in contemplation, but remains buried in the mud of fleshly lusts, powerless to look up and see the spiritual light of the truth. So the "world"—life enslaved by carnal passions—can no more receive the grace of the Spirit than a weak eye can look at the light of a sunbeam.[75]

The disciples themselves were first cleansed by the Lord's teaching; only then did they receive "the ability to both see and contemplate the Spirit."[76] For Basil, holiness of life is inextricably linked to theological vision and comprehension. Indeed, "the world cannot receive Him, and only holy men can contemplate Him through purity of heart."[77]

Basil refuses to give his opponents the option of honoring, glorifying or worshiping the Spirit while they simultaneously assign the Spirit a lower place than the Father or the Son. This reluctance, at best seen as a misplaced desire to honor the Father and the Son, simply cannot do adequate justice to the biblical and creedal testimony regarding the Spirit. The Spirit, Basil contends, "is always described as united with the Godhead; why should he be deprived of His glory?"

> We hear His name in the creed, at saving baptism, in the working of miracles. He takes up His abode in the saints; He bestows grace on the obedient. No gift can be bestowed on creation unless the Holy Spirit gives it; not even a single word can be spoken in defense of Christ unless the Holy Spirit inspires it—as we have learned in the Gospels from our Lord and Savior [Mt 10:19-20]. How could anyone who has partaken of the Holy Spirit be willing to forget or disregard that He is united to the Father and the Son in every way and try to tear Him away from them? Where will you take Him to be ranked? Among creatures? But all creation is in bondage and the Spirit frees it; "where the Spirit of the Lord is, there is freedom" [2 Cor 3:17].[78]

As Basil heads into the backstretch of his treatise, he lists characteristic after characteristic that demonstrate the Spirit's deity and thus the Spirit's unquestionable place with the Father and Son within the Trinity itself. The Spirit "is good by nature, as the Father and the Son are good." While a creature receives enlightenment through the Spirit, the Spirit "searches even the depths of God." The Spirit "gives life together with the Father who enlivens all things, and with the life-giving Son." What is the implication? "How can we separate the Spirit from His life-giving power and associate Him with things which by nature are lifeless? Who is so perverse . . . that he would separate the Spirit from the Godhead, and number Him among creatures?"[79]

If we rank the Spirit with the Father and Son, we acknowledge that the Spirit *coexists* with them. Why is this important? "Truly precise *co-existence* can only be predicated of things which are mutually inseparable." Thus, Basil's insistence that to use the preposition *with* in a doxology is more than appropriate, for it pictures well the inseparable coexistence of the Spirit with the Father and the Son. Basil explains this more fully by way of analogy:

> For example, we would say that heat exists *in* red-hot iron, but co-exists *with* fire, or that health is present *in* the body, but life co-exists *with* the soul. Whenever the union between things is intimate, natural, and inseparable, it is more appropriate to use *with* since this word suggests an indivisible union. . . . Therefore, when we

consider the Spirit's *rank*, we think of Him as present *with* the Father and the Son, but when we consider the working of His grace on its recipients, we say that the Spirit is *in* us.[80]

Prepositions, then, turn out to be more significant than we might have thought at first glance. Behind prepositions such as *in* and *with* lies a much greater reality, a reality and wonder that grammar and conception can never adequately capture. For when the church employs *with*, stating that the church worships the Father and Son with the Holy Spirit, the church celebrates the ineffable wonder of God's nature and the inseparable union of the persons who share that nature in inexpressible love.[81] As Basil explains:

> Light cannot be separated from what it makes visible, and it is impossible for you to recognize Christ, the Image of the invisible God, unless the Spirit enlightens you. Once you see the Image, you cannot ignore the light; you see the Light and the Image simultaneously. It is fitting that when we see Christ, the Brightness of God's glory, it is always through the illumination of the Spirit. Through Christ the Image may we be led to the Father, for He bears the seal of the Father's very likeness.[82]

Basil's words, enlightening and encouraging as they are, direct us to a new set of questions. How can Christ the Image lead us to the Father? What must be done on our behalf to enable such intimacy with an infinitely holy, righteous and loving God? What are the means God employs in restoring the ruptured relationship between God and humanity? Only by analyzing carefully the effect of sin upon human nature can we hope to understand the depth of God's sacrifice on humanity's behalf in the person and work of the Son.

"He [Christ] redeems us righteously from [the apostasy] by His own blood;
but as regards those of us who have been redeemed, [He does this] graciously.
For we have given nothing to Him previously.
Nor does He desire anything from us, as if He stood in need of it."

IRENAEUS
Against Heresies

"Human nature, indeed, was created at first faultless and sinless;
but that human nature in which every one is born from Adam,
now needs the physician, because it is not sound.
All good qualities, no doubt, which it still possesses in its constitution, life, senses,
and intellect, it has from the Most High God, its Creator and Maker.
But the flaw, which darkens and weakens all those natural goods,
so that it has need of illumination and healing,
it has not contracted from its blameless Creator,
but from that original sin, which it committed by free will."

AUGUSTINE
On Nature and Grace

SIX

SIN, GRACE AND THE HUMAN CONDITION

Key Questions to Ponder

The question of the means and the purpose of human salvation deeply interested, concerned and amazed the church fathers. As they pondered the ministry, cross and resurrection of Jesus and meditated on the apostolic testimony of Paul, Peter, John, James, Jude and the writer of Hebrews regarding the significance of these saving events, the fathers attempted to make exegetical and theological sense of a great mystery. For example, exactly what was sin? How had it entered God's good creation? How did sin manifest itself in human behavior? Even more important, in what way had it affected, even infected, the human soul, will and body? How had Jesus' ministry, and most particularly his cross, made possible human redemption from sin? How had God redeemed and reconciled humanity through this horrific yet blessed event? What might people expect as they came into a relationship with Christ and enjoyed the saving benefits of that relationship? Would they continue to struggle with sin? Was perfection possible? The fathers pondered, studied and debated these issues for hundreds of years.

In this chapter we are going to examine these questions by first visiting with Irenaeus, a bishop and theologian writing in the second half of the second century. Then we will journey forward roughly two and a half centuries to listen in on the heated debate between Augustine and the British layman Pelagius. What were Pelagius's concerns? Why did the church come to consider Pelagius's ideas so dangerous? What was the church father Augustine's role in responding to Pelagius and in clarifying the issues surrounding sin, salvation and the grace of God? But first, Irenaeus beckons us for an interesting evening's discussion.

Irenaeus on Sin and Salvation

Irenaeus draws our attention to Jesus' words in Matthew 23:37, in which he sadly laments over Jerusalem: "How often have I desired to gather your children together as a hen gathers her brood under her wings, and you were not willing." Here, Irenaeus believes, we have presented to us "the ancient law of human liberty." That is, "from the beginning" God created human beings as possessing their own power, a power to choose freely to obey or disobey God. God will not, Irenaeus insists, compel us to believe or obey. "There is no coercion with God, but a good will [towards us] is present with Him continually."[1]

God "has placed the power of choice" in both human beings as well as angels, "so that those who had yielded obedience might justly possess what is good, given indeed by God, but preserved by themselves."[2] Those who have willingly disobeyed God will experience divine judgment and have no excuse for their unwillingness to obey. Why? "God did kindly bestow on them what was good; but they themselves did not diligently keep it, nor deem it something precious, but poured contempt upon His super-eminent goodness."

Had not Paul, Irenaeus asks, said much the same in Romans 2, where he speaks of "glory and honor" being given by God to all those that do good (Rom 2:4-5, 7)? Those who receive this honor from God could only rightly receive it, Irenaeus reasons, if they had the power not to obey. Irenaeus then asks how could human beings choose to obey freely if they were "made by nature bad."

> But if some had been made by nature bad, and others good, these latter would not be deserving of praise for being good, for such were they created; nor would the former be reprehensible, for thus they were made [originally]. But since all men are of the same nature, able both to hold fast and to do what is good; and, on the other hand, having also the power to cast it from them and not to do it,— some do justly receive praise even among men who are under the control of good laws (and much more from God), and obtain deserved testimony of their choice of good in general, and of persevering therein. . . . And therefore the prophets

used to exhort men to what was good, to act justly and to work righteousness . . . *because it is in our power to do so.*[3]

Irenaeus's confidence in human ability and freedom might well shock many readers—at least if we view matters from a post-Augustinian perspective. Had not Pelagius said much the same thing? But we are getting ahead of ourselves. Irenaeus is insistent, though, that Jesus' exhortations to obedience, love and goodness make little sense if we do not possess the ability to respond freely to him. "All such passages demonstrate the independent human will, and at the same time the counsel that God conveys to humanity by which He exhorts us to submit ourselves to Him, and seeks to turn us away from [the sin of] unbelief against Him, without, however, in any way coercing us."[4] In fact, it is God who preserves human freedom's ability to choose to obey or disobey, to believe or disbelieve.

Irenaeus is clear that when human beings choose to disobey God, they "forfeit what is good, [with] no small amount of injury and mischief" the sad result. Still, a human being "is in his own power with respect to faith."[5]

It is important to realize, however, that we would misinterpret Irenaeus if we read him against the background of the Pelagian controversy. He is not concerned with Pelagius, who had yet to be born, but with Gnostic teachers who claimed that humanity's physical or material nature cripples a person's ability to respond to God in faith or good works. The Gnostics are attacking the idea of creation itself as a good thing, and *it is the goodness of creation*, even after the fall of humanity into sin, that Irenaeus takes great pains to defend.

Indeed, part of God's good creative plan is that human beings be given the opportunity to recognize and pursue goodness freely. If humans had been created good by nature, Irenaeus teaches, "their being good would be of no consequence, because they were so by nature rather than by will, and are possessors of good spontaneously, not by choice." As a result, humans would fail to recognize the beauty of goodness, a recognition that can only occur when one freely chooses to embrace the good in response to its inherent attractiveness.

Irenaeus turns again to the apostle Paul to buttress his argument. Why would Paul exhort the Corinthians to run their race in such a way as to gain the prize (1 Cor 9:24-27), if goodness itself was something we possess by nature? No, Irenaeus insists, Paul's athletic metaphor points in a different direction: "This able wrestler, therefore, exhorts us to the struggle for immortality, that we may be crowned, and may deem the crown precious, namely, that which is acquired by our struggle, but which does not encircle us of its own accord."[6] We gain the crown through a strenuous exertion empowered by the intentional choice of a will exercised freely, apart from all coercion. Indeed, the harder the contest, the greater the Christian athlete appreciates the crown.

Irenaeus is uncomfortable with the idea of a created, natural goodness in human beings because he is convinced natural goodness and intentional, willed goodness are two different things. If one is naturally good, how can one be praised for one's good actions? If one is intentionally good, such praise appears more than warranted. In addition, as Paul's athletic metaphor indicates, moral exertion leads to an appreciation of a life well lived that natural goodness fails to elicit. "Things are not esteemed so highly," Irenaeus writes, "which come spontaneously, as those which are reached by much anxious care." Just as we appreciate sight if we understand blindness, health if we have battled disease, and light if we have encountered darkness, so we rejoice over the "heavenly kingdom" more fervently if our own exertion and willing is involved in its attainment.[7]

What, then, of creation? If humanity was not created perfect by God, how should we understand God's creation of human beings? Irenaeus admits that God could have created perfect humans, but he finds this unlikely, for all creation, simply by virtue of being created rather than uncreated, falls short of God's perfection. He writes, "But created things must be inferior to Him who created them," if for no other reason than their later origin. For "it was not possible for things recently created to have been uncreated," and since they are created, "for this very reason do they come short of the perfect."[8]

Thus, the first humans were more like infants whom God would call to maturity and perfection, rather than perfect creatures from the very moment of their creation. As Irenaeus explains, "Because, as these things are of later date, so are they infantile; so are they unaccustomed to, and unexercised in, perfect discipline."[9] Consequently, God must wisely nourish his infants, feeding them first with milk rather than solid food. To have created humans perfect from the beginning, Irenaeus argues, would have been too much for creatures to bear. It would have been like force-feeding babies raw steak.

Similarly, does not the incarnation of the Son indicate God's willingness to descend to our level rather than to overwhelm us with the divine glory? "He might easily have come to us in His immortal glory, but in that case we could never have endured the greatness of the glory; and therefore it was that He, who was the perfect bread of the Father, offered himself to us as milk, [because we were] infants."[10]

Only by the Son actually entering the world as one of us, offering his breast to us as "a course of milk-nourishment," could we become "accustomed to eat and drink the Word of God [and] to contain in ourselves the Bread of immortality, which is the Spirit of the Father." The Corinthians, in their frequent strife and dissensions, manifested their continuance in an infantile state. In fact, Irenaeus believes that the Spirit "was not yet with them," an absence manifested by "their imperfection and shortcomings of their walk in life."[11]

What was the basic problem? What Irenaeus calls "the sentient faculties of the soul" among the Corinthians were "still feeble and undisciplined in the practice of things pertaining to God." The same pattern can be seen in Adam and Eve. Though God "had power at the beginning to grant perfection to man," humanity's recent creation made the reception of perfection inconceivable. We were simply not capable of receiving it.

The incarnation itself demonstrates the rhyme and rhythm of Irenaeus's argument. Although the Son was perfect, he still "passed through the state of infancy in common with the rest of humanity, partaking of it thus not for His own benefit, but for that of the infantile state of human existence, in order that a human being might be able to receive Him."[12] It is through the incarnate Son that we learn "the things of God. . . . For no other being had the power of revealing to us the things of the Father, except His own proper Word."[13] That is to say, not only does Christ redeem fallen humanity with his blood, but he enters into our world by coming to us in a manner that we can understand and assimilate.

> Again, we could have learned in no other way than by seeing our Teacher, and hearing His voice with our own ears, that, having become imitators of His works as well as doers of His words, we may have communion with Him, receiving increase from the perfect One, and from Him who is prior to all creation. We— who were but lately created by the only best and good Being, by Him also who has the gift of immortality, having been formed after His likeness (predestinated, according to the prescience of the Father, that we, who had as yet no existence, might come into being), and made the first-fruits of creation—have received, in the times known beforehand, [the blessings of salvation].[14]

How has Christ accomplished our salvation? He has redeemed "us by His own blood in a manner consonant to reason" and given "Himself as a redemption for those who had been led into captivity." Irenaeus pictures humanity's descent into sin as closely related to the devil's desire to disrupt God's creation out of envy and enmity. The temptations of the evil one were like tares sown stealthily in a field. Adam and Eve, more from immaturity than anything else, succumbed to the devil's lures from "want of care no doubt." They lacked the maturity to recognize fully the danger before them, and disaster was the result. The fault, though, seems to Irenaeus to be more the devil's than humanity's.

Redemption as Christ's victory over the devil. Irenaeus clearly portrays Christ's redemptive actions as focused on the devil and his evil dominion over humanity. The devil was "envious of God's workmanship, and took in hand to render this [workmanship] at enmity with God." The result was immediate judgment upon the devil, a banishment from God's presence because of the evil one's attempt to seduce humans to sin. The humans who succumbed to this temptation, on the other hand, God has treated with compassion.[15] In a surprising and redemptive reversal, God has turned the enmity of the devil back upon the evil one. Irenaeus writes, "He turned the enmity by which [the devil] had designed to make [humanity] the enemy of God, against the author of it, by removing His own anger from humankind, turning it in another direction, and sending it instead upon the serpent." Referring to the prediction that one day the seed of the woman would bruise the head of the serpent (Gen 3:15), Irenaeus explains that "the Lord summed up in Himself this enmity, when He was made man from a woman, and trod upon his [the serpent's] head."[16]

Both humans and angels who follow the wicked one into "apostasy" can expect only judgment from the hand of God. Irenaeus emphasizes, however, that the movement from obedience to rebellion, whether on the part of humans or the demonic hordes, is not the result of nature. "But He made neither angels nor people so by nature."[17] Irenaeus's repetition of the goodness of human nature as created by God—an emphasis that sounds quite similar to Pelagius's assertions years in the future—is surely linked to his Gnostic opponents' insistence that creation itself was the mistake of a lower deity. Irenaeus is not concerned with exhorting his readers in their quest for Christian holiness at this juncture. Rather, he is much more concerned with the Gnostic attempt to denigrate creation itself, and he responds with a loud, resounding yes to the goodness of human nature. Issues that will later surface as Christians continue to ponder the meaning of salvation, such as the effect of sin upon the will's ability to choose the good, do not occupy Irenaeus's attention. It is the devil who has led humanity into sin through envy and stealth, and it is the devil who must be overcome by Christ's blood and resurrection from the dead.

This is why Scripture designates those who "remain in a state of apostasy [as] sons of the devil." Here Irenaeus draws an important distinction between sons "in the order of nature" and sons who have been "made so." He notes, "For the first is indeed born from the person referred to; but the second is made so by him, whether as respects his creation or by the teaching of his doctrine." All human beings, then, are sons and daughters of God by reason of their creation by God, but "with respect to obedience and doctrine we are not all the sons of God: those only are so who believe in Him and do His will. And those who do not believe, and do not obey His will, are sons and angels of the devil, because they do the works of the devil."[18] That is, disobedience leads to disinheritance, and the reverse is also true: "[if] they should be converted and come to repentance, and cease from evil, they should have power to become the sons of God, and to receive the inheritance of immortality which is given by Him."[19]

The devil, then, has "tyrannized over us unjustly." Through Satan's tyranny and accompanying temptations, he has undercut creation's natural order. In Irenaeus's words, "though we were by nature the property of the omnipotent God, [the devil] has alienated us contrary to nature," with the result that we have been rendered the disciples of apostasy rather than God. However, God has not left us in this alienated, unnatural state. Rather, the "Word of God, powerful in all things, and not defective with regard to His own justice," has entered the world on behalf of humanity. He has "righteously [acted] against that apostasy," in the process redeeming from it "His own property."[20]

Irenaeus stresses, however, that the redemption of humanity does not occur "by violent means," but "by means of persuasion." Christ acted in this manner

> so that neither should justice be infringed upon, nor the ancient handiwork of God go to destruction. Since the Lord thus has redeemed us through His own blood, giving His soul for our souls, and His flesh for our flesh, and has also poured out the Spirit of the Father for the union and communion of God and humanity,

imparting indeed God to human beings by means of the Spirit, and on the other hand, attaching humanity to God by His own incarnation, and bestowing upon us at His coming immortality durably and truly, by means of communion with God,—all the doctrines of the heretics fall to ruin.[21]

Salvation and the incarnation. In the wonder of the incarnation, Irenaeus believes, the Word has genuinely come into our world, taking on all that we are, so that in Christ we might become all we were created to be. This was no apparent or halfway incarnation, an incarnation in appearance only. On the contrary, Irenaeus insists, from Mary the Word received genuine flesh and blood. If not, how could the Word have redeemed us? "For He would not have been one truly possessing flesh and blood, by which He redeemed us, unless He had summed up in Himself the ancient formation of Adam."[22] In the reality of the Word's incarnation we encounter a "new kind of generation," the generation of a "holy thing [by] the Most High God the Father of all, who effected the incarnation of this being . . . that as by the former generation we inherited death, so by this new generation we might inherit life."[23]

Those who willingly choose to remain apart from Christ and the redemption he desires to communicate "remain in that Adam who had been conquered and was expelled from Paradise." Such was surely not God's design or purpose for humanity, for God had breathed the breath of life into Adam's nostrils "at the beginning of our formation in Adam." In this divine breathing God had united Adam to himself, animating Adam, and also manifesting "him as a being endowed with reason." "So also, in [the times] of the end," in the wonder of the incarnation and its broader redemptive context and actions, "the Word of the Father and the Spirit of God, having become united with the ancient substance of Adam's formation, rendered man living and perfect, receptive of the perfect Father."

Yes, "in the natural [Adam] we all were dead, [but] in the spiritual we may all be made alive." How so? Though humanity had sinned deeply in its rebellion and apostasy, willingly and freely responding to the voice of the evil one, Adam "had never at any time" escaped "the *hands* of God," that is, the Son and the Holy Spirit. It was to the Son and the Spirit that the Father had spoken: "Let us make humankind in our image, according to our likeness" (Gen 1:26). Likewise, in these last times God has recreated humanity in Christ. "His hands formed a living man, in order that Adam might be created [again] after the image and like-ness of God."[24]

God accomplishes the entire work of salvation graciously. Irenaeus explains, "For we have given nothing to Him previously, nor does He desire anything from us, as if He stood in need of it; but we do stand in need of fellowship with Him." Because of our great need, "He graciously poured Himself out, that He might gather us into the bosom of the Father."[25] God's grace is strikingly seen in God's willingness to enter our world in the incarnation, the very act Irenaeus's Gnostic opponents regarded as illogical and unnecessary.

Apart from the incarnation of flesh and blood, salvation could not be accom-plished, particularly as Irenaeus understands the Eucharist as the locus from which salvation is communicated to all that a human being is, soul and body. If Christ had not redeemed us by means of his blood, the salvific meal offered in the Eucharist would be rendered null and void, and the communion offered there to believers emptied of its reality. Some Protestant and evangelical ears will struggle to hear Irenaeus at this juncture, but he, like other fathers, clearly believed that in the Eucharist we genuinely encounter God in Christ. By "means of the creation," through elements as ordinary as bread and wine, God comes to us. "He has acknowledged the cup (which is a part of the creation) as His own blood, from which He bedews [wettens or nourishes] our blood; and the bread (also a part of the creation) He has established as His own body, from which He gives increase to our bodies."[26]

As the "mingled cup and the manufactured bread receives the Word of God," Irenaeus writes, "the Eucharist of the blood and body of Christ is made." As the believer partakes of the Eucharist and enters into communion with Christ, the substance of "our flesh is increased and supported." Consequently, how can Gnostic teachers possibly claim to be Christian and yet deny the reality of God's incarnation in the Word? By doing so, Irenaeus insists, they undercut salvation itself and its intimate link to the Eucharist. Or, as Irenaeus asks, "How can they affirm that the flesh is incapable of receiving the gift of God, which is life eternal, which [flesh] is nourished from the body and blood of the Lord, and is a member of Him?"[27] Has not Paul himself written that "we are members of His body, of His flesh, and of His bones" (see Eph 5:30)? As the Lord became "an actual man, consisting of flesh, and nerves, and bones," this same human flesh in us "is nourished by the cup which is His blood, and receives increase from the bread which is His body."[28]

Irenaeus carries his argument further, seeing implications in the Eucharist for the future resurrection of the believer. The Word of God has entered our world in the incarnation, shed his blood on our behalf, and can now be found in the Eucharist, "which is the body and blood of Christ." As such, the bodies of Christians that the Eucharist has nourished are assured of resurrection, though "they be deposited in the earth" and undergo decomposition. They "shall rise at the appointed time, the Word of God granting them resurrection to the glory of God, even the Father, who freely gives to this mortal immortality, and to this corruptible incorruption." Our natural weakness is remedied by the strength of God. We learn "by experience that we possess eternal duration from the excellent power of this Being, not from our own nature." This experiential knowledge in turn leads us to glorify God and to acknowledge our own natural ignorance and weakness; indeed, God's decision to allow humanity to decompose "into the common dust of mortality" might well be linked to God's desire to teach us what God alone can accomplish: victory over the devil, death and sin itself.[29]

Irenaeus's thoughts on the goodness of creation and the freedom of the will must be read against the background of his battle with Gnostic teaching that denied the goodness of matter and found freedom only in an escape from the natural, created world. By the time we reach the age of Augustine, the context for understanding the freedom of the will and sin's effect upon human nature has changed dramatically. As we will soon see, Pelagius has no doubts about the goodness of the created order. Indeed, Pelagius may well be overly optimistic about human nature's capabilities and potentialities, an optimism that forces Augustine to move beyond Irenaeus in analyzing the condition of humanity after the Fall.

The Pelagian Controversy

Gerald Bonner describes Pelagius as "by nature an ascetic and a moralist."[30] Pelagius, a native of the British Isles, seems to have been particularly pained by the lifestyle and habits of the Christians he encountered in Rome and by aspects of Roman culture at large. Peter Brown observes that in the Rome of Pelagius's day Christian and Roman ideals and conventions had gradually accommodated to each other, with Roman conventions not infrequently gaining the upper hand. Many Roman families had "lapsed gradually into Christianity by mixed-marriages and politic conformity."[31] He adds, the "conventional 'good man' of pagan Rome had quite unthinkingly become the conventional 'good Christian' of the fifth century."

> The flamboyant courtesies of Late Roman etiquette could pass as "Christian humility"; the generosity traditionally expected of an aristocrat, as "Christian almsgiving". "It is better to give than to receive" was a popular tag; but, like all Biblical citations used to ease the conscience, no one could quite remember where it came from! Yet these "good Christians", "true believers," were still members of a ruling class committed to maintaining the Imperial laws by administering brutal punishments. They were prepared to fight tooth and nail to protect their vast properties, and were capable of discussing at the dinner-table both the latest theological opinion, on which they prided themselves as experts, and the kind of judicial torture they had just inflicted on some poor wretch.[32]

Pelagius was by nature "endowed with a temperament singularly free from the storms and stresses of temptation" and had little tolerance for those who referred to the "frailty of human nature" as an explanation for human sinfulness.[33] His clash with Augustine, then, over the nature of sin and divine grace appears inescapable, especially when one remembers the young Augustine's struggles with deeply ingrained patterns of sin. In fact, it is a section from Augustine's *Confessions* that drew Pelagius's ire. It reads as follows:

> My whole hope is in your exceeding great mercy and that alone. Give what you command and command what you will. You command continence from us, and when I knew, as it is said, that no one could be continent unless God gave it to him, even this was a point of wisdom, to know whose gift it was. For by continence we are bound up and brought back together in the One, whereas before we were scattered abroad among the many. For he loves you too little who loves along with you anything else which he does not love for your sake, O Love, who does burn forever and is never quenched. O Love, O my God, inkindle me! You command continence; give what you command, and command what you will.[34]

While many readers, indeed, thousands over the years, have identified closely with Augustine's cry for the enabling power of the grace of God, Pelagius could see in these words only an invitation to license and laxity. In addition, Bonner points out that Augustine had much more experience than Pelagius dealing with the daily struggles of his flock. Augustine knew what it was to be a pastor and to deal frequently with his parishioners' struggles with the dynamics of temptation and sin.[35] Augustine's keen insights are reflected in his comments to a widow struggling to maintain sexual purity: "I have, however, observed this fact of human behavior that, with certain people, when sexuality is repressed avarice seems to grow in its place."[36] Brown observes that "the Pelagian writings can offer nothing so shrewd."[37]

What can we know of the nature and content of Pelagius's teaching? First, Pelagius desired to combat any tendency within the Christian community to excuse their sinful actions *because of a defect in human nature itself.* Pelagius thought it highly improbable that God would ask human beings to obey divine commandments, if all along God knew such an obedience to be impossible because of a fundamental flaw in human nature. If we ought to do something, namely, obey God's commandments, surely we should be able to do so. If not, how could God rightly hold us accountable for our disobedience?

To assert, then, that human nature was tainted by its connection with Adam and Adam's sin would necessarily undercut the goodness of God's creation. Why should subsequent humans be held accountable or guilty for Adam's poor choices? Julian of Eclanum, Pelagius's brilliant disciple, expressed sharply his objections to the idea of a fundamental taint in human nature connected to Adam's sin:

> You ask me why I would not consent to the idea that there is a sin that is part of human nature? I answer: it is improbable, it is untrue; it is unjust and impious; it makes it seem as if the Devil were the maker of men. It violates and destroys the freedom of the will . . . by saying that men are so incapable of virtue, that in the very wombs of their mothers they are filled with bygone sins. You imagine so great a power in such a sin, that not only can it blot out the new-born innocence of nature, but, forever afterwards, will force a man throughout his life into every form of viciousness. . . . (And) what is as disgusting as it is blasphemous, this view of yours fastens, as its most conclusive proof, on the common decency by which we cover our genitals.[38]

Pelagius taught that "in any moral action, three elements are to be seen."[39] They can be summarized as follows: (1) We must be able to perform the action *(posse).* Pelagius assigns *posse*, the ability to perform a certain action, to human nature as created by God. (2) We must be willing or desire to do the action *(velle)*. (3) The action must actually be performed *(esse)*. Both *velle* and *esse*, unlike *posse*, "are to be referred to the human agent, since they have their source in his will."[40]

Augustine summarizes Pelagius's teaching with the three words *possibility, will* and *action*.[41] We have the possibility of performing a moral action because God has created human beings as moral beings with the ability to reason morally and to will to obey God. Whether we choose to obey God, however, is dependent upon our willingness to exercise our free will to obey God in our actions. Hence, we can praise both God and human nature when moral actions occur. In Pelagius's words,

> in the Will and in good work there is praise for man or, rather, for man and God, who has given the possibility of will and work, and who always assists that possibility with the help of His grace. For it certainly is of God alone that man is able to will a good thing and bring it to completion; and this one quality, possibility, is able to exist without the other two, will and action; but these two latter cannot exist without the former.[42]

Pelagius, then, cannot be accused of denying God's role in helping us to obey, but he largely limits this helping role to those innate abilities God created in human nature with the creation of Adam and Eve. The choice remains for each human being as to whether he or she will choose to exercise these divinely given abilities in obedience to God and God's commandments.

Freedom, the ability to choose to obey or disobey, was a basic given for Pelagius. As Brown explains, "it was simply part of a common-sense description of a human being. He was assumed to be responsible (or how could his sins be called sinful?); he was conscious of exercising choice; therefore . . . he was free to determine his actions."[43]

In addition, Pelagius insists that the moral capabilities created within humanity by God cannot be lost. Pelagius uses the example of physical capabilities such as eyesight to illustrate this fundamental principle. Bonner comments:

> That I can see is not under my control; but the use I make of my sight is. And what is true of sight is true of our other endowments. God has given us the power to act, to speak, and to think, and helps us to do so; but whether we act, speak, or think

rightly depends upon ourselves. We can turn these gifts to evil uses; but this does not alter the fact that the original endowment was of God. Possibility depends on Him, and on Him alone.[44]

Pelagius's argument appears strikingly optimistic, as Augustine was quick to point out. Yet is the exercise of divinely created endowments—either mental or physical—as simple or straightforward as Pelagius believes? Simply think back to the last time your eyes wandered in the wrong direction. The question of the health of the human will is inescapable, and if the will is infected or distorted by sin, then Pelagius's faith in the power of innate, divinely created endowments is significantly jeopardized.

The Question of the Will

How healthy is the human will? Does the human will retain, as Pelagius argues, its created, inherent capabilities even after the Fall? Or has the sin of Adam and Eve deeply compromised the will's ability to love and to choose the good? Pelagius contends that each person is born with a will capable of obeying God's commandments. That is, newly born human beings find themselves in basically the same situation as Adam and Eve before the Fall. In creating us, God has provided all that human beings need to live a moral life of obedience: a soul, mind, will and body. Hence, all humans can freely choose to obey or to disobey God. To use a modern illustration, the cards are stacked against no one. What has come before—in this case, the sin of the original human pair—has not crippled or infected human nature itself. We can be *influenced* by what has happened in the case of Adam and Eve, but it is the example of their sin, rather than a taint passed on through human nature itself, that poses a danger to us.

Augustine quotes Pelagius as arguing that "the primary sin was injurious not only to the first man, but to the whole human race not by transmission, but by example." While Augustine will argue that infants themselves are infected with Adam's sin, Pelagius insists that Adam's situation was drastically different from that of a baby. Infants, for example, "are not yet able to receive the commandment, whereas he was able; and further because they do not yet make use of that choice of rational will which he certainly made use of, since otherwise no commandment would have been given him."[45] What seems to face us is a simple choice: Will we choose to obey or not?

Augustine argues that Adam and Eve had originally possessed a will free from sin's infection, but since the entrance of sin into the world through humanity's original disobedience, all descendants of Adam and Eve have inherited a crippled, distorted, bent will. We know the right, affirm the right, but desire or will to do the very thing we know to be wrong. *Why* this is the tragic state of affairs for humanity will remain at the center of the debate between Pelagius and Augustine. Bonner comments:

> The besetting sin need not be incontinence, it may be any one of the other six deadly sins; but whatever it is, there is a struggle between a sincere desire to be rid of it and the lurking feeling that the sacrifice is too great, that we need a little longer, just a few days more, before making the effort lest having God we may have naught beside.[46]

Augustine argues that we can "reach the goal" if we have the will to do so. The problem is that, left to ourselves, our will is "changeable, twisting, fluctuating." We will to do something, but not entirely.

> The mind commands the mind to will, and yet though it be itself it does not obey itself. Whence this strange anomaly and why should it be? I repeat: The will commands itself to will, and could not give the command unless it wills; yet what is commanded is not done. But actually the will does not will entirely; therefore it does not command entirely. For as far as it wills, it commands. And as far as it does not will, the thing commanded is not done. For the will commands that there be an act of will—not another, but itself. But it does not happen entirely. Therefore, what is commanded does not happen; for if the will were *whole and entire*, it would not even command it to be, because it would already be.[47]

Here we have the crux of the problem and a central disagreement between Pelagius and Augustine. For Pelagius, the will is whole and entire. It has not been infected or crippled by the sin of Adam. One must simply choose to obey. Augustine disagrees. One might wish that such is the case, but neither Scripture nor human experience backs up Pelagius's assertion. In order for human beings to exercise their will in obedience to God, they need help outside themselves and their own capabilities, divine help, the grace of God.

A Struggle with Words

Part of the difficulty in understanding the debate between Augustine and

Pelagius is that they frequently use the same words but define them differently. For example, Pelagius agrees with Augustine that we need the grace of God to fulfill God's commandments. Pelagius, however, defines grace as *the natural, created abilities God has given human beings for living a moral, obedient life.* He sees no need for an additional divine power, external to ourselves, to enable us to do the right. That is, since we have been created in the image of God, God has freely given us everything required or necessitated for living a life pleasing to God. We have a mind that can comprehend God's commandments, a will that can freely choose to obey them and a body through which the divine life can be lived. What more could we possibly need?

Here we find the source of Pelagius's anger and frustration with Augustine and his theology. When he hears Augustine praying, "Give what you command and order what you will," Pelagius can only shake his head. He cannot help but believe that Augustine is praying foolishly. Augustine is asking for what he already possesses. God has already given him all that he needs to obey God. There is nothing more to give. He has a mind, a will, a soul and a body. All Augustine must do is to exercise his will in choosing to obey. As Caelestius writes: "it is the easiest thing in the world to change our will by an act of the will."[48] Pelagius and his followers simply beckon Christ's disciples to exercise their God-given will. What more could we need to do the good?

"Much more," Augustine will reply. Why? Something has happened since humanity's original creation that has crippled our ability to live a consistently faithful and obedient life. Sin has entered the world, originally through the transgression of Adam and Eve. As their children we continue to be plagued with the same disease. Most significantly, this sin—contracted from Adam and Eve—has deeply wounded the human will. The will does not exist in the free, unblemished state imagined by Pelagius. In fact, it has been warped in such a fashion that it never wills *entirely* to obey God and cannot do so unless God empowers it to obey *through a grace external to itself.* It is this fundamental disagreement over the present state of the human will and God's grace that lies at the heart of the controversy between Augustine and Pelagius.

The Problem of Choice

A basic problem of the fallen will is that it does not love the good. In other words, more is involved in the choice to obey than choice itself. I will exercise my will to choose *in line with* my feelings, loves and desires, and if I love the wrong things, I will consistently choose the wrong things. Peter Brown explains that "an act of choice is not just a matter of knowing what to choose: it is a matter in which loving and feeling are involved. And in men, this capacity to know and to feel in a single, involved whole has been intimately dislocated."[49] As Augustine puts it, "The understanding flies on ahead, and there follows, oh, so slowly, and sometimes not at all, our weakened human capacity for feeling."[50] Brown observes:

> Men choose because they love; but Augustine had been certain for some twenty years, that they could not, of themselves, choose to love. The vital capacity to unite feeling and knowledge comes from an area outside man's powers of self-determination. "From a depth that we do not see, comes everything that you can see."[51]

It should not surprise us that Augustine frequently employs the language of healing to describe God's graceful response to humanity's fall into sin. For it is only through the healing power of God's grace, a grace external to us that comes to us and heals us in our fallen state, that we begin to *love* what is good. As Brown explains, in this healing process, "love and knowledge are reintegrated."[52] This "is made possible by an inseparable connection between growing self-determination and a dependence on a source of life that always escapes self-determination. The healed man enjoys a more acute sense of responsibility, clearer knowledge, a greater ease of choice."[53] Consequently, rather than the will operating autonomously, solely on the basis of its created abilities, God heals the will and continues to empower it in a relationship of continuing interdependence. Thanksgiving, rather than self-congratulation, should be the happy result. Yet Augustine observes, "Some men try hard to discover in our will what good is particularly due to ourselves, that owes nothing to God: how they can find this out, I just do not know."[54]

Augustine, in fact, argues that a grace external to Adam and Eve was necessary even before their fall into sin. Why would sinless, created human nature still need such external aid? This question is hard to answer. It is even more difficult to understand why a sinless, free will should ever turn away from God in disobedience. Gerald Bonner speculates that Augustine may have felt that all created things, even before the Fall, possessed an "inevitable imperfection . . . inevitable from the very fact of their being created, which makes them tend to not-being unless they are conserved by the power of God."[55] It is difficult, though, to understand how a creation that God identifies as good could still possess an inevitable imperfection, though Irenaeus also spoke of the weakness of the created order left to itself.

Though the original choice of Eve and Adam to disobey God remains a deep mystery, history amply demonstrates that something has gone wildly wrong with humanity and that we remain incapable of freeing ourselves from our own deep propensities toward evil. We need help beyond ourselves, divine help, and Augustine describes this divine aid as a divine grace surpassing what Adam and Eve originally possessed. It is a grace specifically designed to help us in our weakness.[56] As Bonner describes it, "Grace is not only the endowment given to us as created beings made in the image of God, but it is the ministration of the Holy Spirit, assisting our wills and actions."[57] Or as Augustine expresses it in prayer: "The house of my soul is too narrow for Thee to come in to me; let it be enlarged by Thee. It is in ruins; do Thou restore it."[58] Clearly, Augustine views grace as enabling the will to choose the good, something the will could not do if left to itself because of its disordered loves.

Pelagius could not disagree more. His argument, based upon a highly optimistic view of the Fall, contends that God would not ask us to do something that we are incapable of doing. If we ought to do something, surely we can do it. This is not to say that obedience is easy, but it is possible.

> We say: "It is hard! It is difficult! We cannot, we are but men, compassed about by the fragile flesh!" Blind folly and holy rashness! We accuse the God of knowledge of a twofold ignorance, so that He seems to be ignorant of what He has done or what He has commanded—as if, unmindful of human frailty, whose author He Himself is, He has imposed commands upon man which man is not able to bear.[59]

Peter Brown describes the teaching of Pelagius as "simple and terrifying."[60] Here was a man who genuinely believed human perfection was possible, indeed, obligatory. Brown writes, "Pelagius never doubted for a moment that perfection was obligatory; his God was, above all, a God who commanded unquestioning obedience. He had made men to execute his demands; and He would condemn to hell-fire anyone who failed to perform a single one of them."[61]

In the modern world, Pelagius's position seems almost incomprehensible. Yet his argument possesses its own rhyme and rhythm if we accept his fundamental assertion that human nature was designed for moral perfection and remains capable of attaining it. Pelagius desires to teach others not only about the commands and prohibitions of the Christian life, but more importantly, about the strength and characteristics of human nature. According to Pelagius, a Christian can lead a virtuous life once he or she understands clearly what human nature is capable of doing.

To devalue human nature, Pelagius argues, is to undercut all motivation to lead a moral life.

> Where a more perfect form of life is to be established, the explanation of nature's goodness should be correspondingly fuller. If the soul has a lower estimation of its capacity, it will be less diligent and insistent in pursuing virtue. Not realizing its inner power, it will assume that it lacks the capacity. We must therefore reflect fully on the power that is to be exercised, and *explain clearly the good of which nature is capable.*[62]

The first step, then, toward Christian virtue is to realize that human nature can obey God's commandments. Pelagius wonders how anyone could think otherwise. Could God justly ask for our obedience while already knowing that we could never obey? Pelagius thinks not: "To ask a person to do something he considers impossible does him no good."[63] Exactly how should we view human nature, at least from a Pelagian perspective? First of all, Pelagius reminds his reader, we must remember "the goodness of human nature . . . as created by God."

> He made the whole world and all the good things in it. How much more excellent, then, did he fashion human beings, for whose sake he made everything else. The goodness of humanity was indicated even before it was created when God prepared to form it in his image and likeness.[64]

Pelagius stresses that humanity possesses an "armament" that is interior in nature. These "interior weapons . . . reason and judgment," demonstrate the superiority of human beings to other "animals." Humans, for example, can use these faculties "to dominate the beasts and to serve God." Pelagius particularly emphasizes that God wishes for humanity to use these created gifts "voluntarily rather than by coercion" and thus gave humans the ability freely to choose to obey or disobey. Only "ignorant people" such as the Manichaeans would believe that created human nature was evil. Pelagius explains, "You must not think that human nature was not created truly good because it is capable of evil and because it is not, on account of its impetuosity, bound by necessity to immutable good." Rather, humans can choose to commit evil deeds, and this capability of freely choosing is actually "the glory of a reasonable soul." Pelagius summarizes, "In this, I submit, lies the dignity of our nature; this is the source of honor, reward, and praise merited by the best people. If a person could not choose evil, he would not practice virtue in persevering to the good."[65]

Humans are, indeed, set off from other forms of animal life by their ability rationally to choose the good. As Pelagius explains, "Our souls possess, as it were, a natural integrity which resides in their depths and passes judgments of good and evil." The question of the natural integrity of the soul, however, will remain at the heart of the debate between Augustine and Pelagius. Augustine agrees that the soul as created by God possesses a natural integrity but parts from Pelagius in believing that the fall of Adam and Eve into sin has severely compromised human nature's ability to love and choose the good. Pelagius, on the other hand, will continue to "reject the notion that nature's inadequacy inevitably leads us to do evil. We do either good or evil only by our own will; since we always remain capable of both, we are always free to do either."[66]

Not a few were attracted to Pelagius's ideas. Many were concerned by perceived laxness in Christian commitment and morals, and Pelagius's teaching seemed to offer a road back to fervor, sacrifice and obedience. Letters from followers of Pelagius clearly demonstrate the sense of excitement and commitment his teaching could evoke:

> When I lived at home, I thought that I was being a worshipper of God. . . . Now for the first time, I have begun to know how I can be a true Christian. . . . It is easy to say: I know God, I believe in God, I fear God, I serve God. But you do not know God, if you do not believe in Him; and you do not believe in Him, unless you love Him; and you cannot say you love Him, unless you fear Him; you cannot say you fear Him, unless you serve Him; and you cannot be said to serve Him if you disobey Him in any single point. . . . *Who believes in God, attends to His commandments. This is the love of God; that we do what He commands.*[67]

Caelestius, one of the young leaders of the Pelagian movement, was deeply impressed by Pelagius's teaching as a young man and made his way to Carthage to present confidently his understanding of his master's teaching.[68] Caelestius questioned the justice, for example, of the entire human race being condemned for the sin of Adam and Eve. In a word, is it just for you or me to inherit both the damaged nature and moral guilt of our forebears? Would a just God allow this to occur?

Pelagius was confident that God would help the person who chose freely to exercise his or her will in obedience. The problem, of course, at least if Augustine is reading Scripture correctly, is that, left to oneself, no one will choose freely to obey God. Why? The effect of sin on the will has crippled its ability freely to choose the good.

Why was Pelagius so insistent on the continuing, inherent goodness of human nature in its entirety? Why was he reluctant to adopt the more pessimistic attitude of Augustine, at least regarding human capabilities and possibilities after the Fall? Modern Christians might too quickly condemn Pelagius as simply a moral rigorist, exaggeratedly optimistic about the moral capabilities and strengths of human nature, and nothing more. We have, however, already seen that he was deeply concerned about the moral decay crippling the Roman world and seeping into the Christian community. In addition, Pelagius might well have been combating ideas that Augustine also fought against, those of the Manichaeans. Bonner notes:

> In his approach to human nature, Pelagius was dominated by the sense of the need to refute the Manichaean doctrine of the two souls in man, the one good and the other evil, and their belief that matter and the human body are evil. In consequence, he emphasized the anhypostatic conception of evil: evil is not a substance but a privation, and all that exists is good. Accordingly, he found it impossible to believe that something non-material could have any real effect upon human nature, something essentially good and created by God.[69]

Thus, Pelagius's understanding of grace as situated in creation itself becomes more comprehensible, since nature itself is a good gift from God and a source of God's grace. Furthermore, Pelagius argues, God created in human nature the very means, themselves very good, to live a life pleasing to God: "For if I said: a man can argue, a bird can fly, or a hare can run, and should not mention the means whereby these actions are performed (namely tongue, wings and feet) should I have denied the means of these actions, when I have admitted the actions themselves."[70]

Augustine responds, however, that Pelagius is only mentioning "such things as are by nature efficient, for the members of the bodily structure which are here mentioned are created with natures of such a kind—the tongue, the wings, the legs." The problem, at least as Augustine views matters, is that Pelagius is confusing natural functions and means with grace and its constellation of issues and concerns. Pelagius "has not here pointed [to] any such thing as we wish to have understood by *grace*, without which no human person can be justified; for this is a topic which is concerned about the cure, not the constitution, of natural functions."[71]

Pelagius sees grace not only present in the natural, created character of humanity but also present in the mind's ability to learn, what Bonner calls "enlightenment." Thus, though Pelagius understood the will to be sound, the "mind is clouded and needs to be shown what to do."[72] Both Old and New Testaments could supply the believer with the guidance needed to live a righteous life, though one can see quickly how Pelagius and followers such as Caelestius left themselves open to the charge of confusing the Old Testament law with the gospel of the kingdom.

A Further Look at the Grace of God

Pelagius's doctrine of grace can be broken down into three aspects, two of which we have already touched upon. First, we have the grace found in human nature as created by God. Second, Pelagius refers to the grace obtained through enlightenment, as the law and gospel inform and educate the mind. Third, Pelagius speaks of the "remission of sins through baptism."[73] In baptism, past sins are forgiven, but Pelagius pictures the Christian's continuing ability to lead a holy life as a result of enlightenment or "illumination"[74] rather than "the indwelling of the Holy Spirit." As Bonner comments, Pelagius's "conception of Grace was simply the formula: redemption from sin by Christ followed by the inspiration of the example of Christ stirring us to perfection of justice."[75]

Grace, then, for Pelagius appears to illuminate the mind more than to aid or empower the will.[76] Pelagius writes:

God helps us through His doctrine and revelation, while He opens the eyes of our heart; while He shows us future things, lest we should be concerned with present matters; while He reveals the snares of the devil; and while He *illuminates us* with the multiform and ineffable gift of heavenly Grace. Does the man who says this seem to you to deny Grace? Or does he not, rather, confess the free will of man and the Grace of God?[77]

Thus, a central difference between Pelagius and Augustine concerning grace is its role or function. Does grace serve, as Augustine feels Pelagius to be arguing, primarily to enlighten the mind concerning matters of law and doctrine, or does it play a much wider role in the salvation of the believer?

Questions Concerning the Fall

Pelagius's understanding of grace clearly influenced his understanding of the Fall, and vice versa. Indeed, as Bonner is quick to point out, the Pelagians "never formulated any doctrine of the Fall as Augustine and later theologians understood the term."[78] Pelagius understands the Fall to be an event that affected only two individuals, Adam and Eve. The descendants of this original pair could well learn from the example of their fall into sin, but each subsequent human being's nature was identical to that of Adam and Eve before the Fall. We can imitate Adam's mistake by succumbing to temptation, since the possibility always exists of exercising our free will in a willfully sinful fashion. But if we choose to do so, our own sinful choice is due to our free decision to sin and not to a defect in nature inherited from Adam and Eve after the Fall. Bonner explains, "Since their system of morality was one based upon the unfettered exercise of the will and because they insisted that it was always possible for a man to discharge his moral obligations, they were compelled to deny that Adam's sin had in any way affected his descendants except by evil example."[79]

Pelagius believes that the idea of original sin contains within itself the seeds of its own destruction. He poses at least four major objections to the idea that the sin and guilt of Adam and Eve was passed on to or inherited by all their descendants:

1. The doctrine of original sin seemed to contain within itself the seeds of universalism: "If Adam's sin injured even those who do not sin, Christ's righteousness ought likewise profit even those who do not believe."[80]

2. If baptism cleanses from sin, how can baptized parents pass sin on to their chil-

dren? "No one can transmit what he has not; and hence, if baptism cleanses
from sin, the children of baptized parents ought to be free from sin."[81]

3. If God creates each human soul individually, why should this sinless soul
inherit a sin committed in Adam's flesh? "If the soul is not inherited, but only
the flesh, then only the latter inherits the sin, and it alone deserves punishment; it would be unjust for the soul, which is now created and does not come
out of the lump of Adam, to bear the burden of so old a sin committed by
another person." [82]

4. Is it right for God to condemn one person for the sins of another? "It cannot be
admitted that God, who remits to a person his own sins, should impute to him
another's."[83]

In fact, Pelagians such as Julian of Eclanum consider the sin of Adam less
grave than that of Cain's murder of Abel or the evils of Sodom and Gomor-
rah.[84] If so, Julian argues, why would God punish Adam's sin "with a quite dis-
proportionate penalty?" On the contrary, the Pelagians contend, we have not
inherited a skewed, sinful nature from Adam. Rather, each individual receives
from God a nature similar to that of Adam's before his sin. "Everyone 'starts
fair.' "[85]

If such is the true state of affairs, one would surely expect there to have been
individuals in the biblical narrative who did not make Adam's bad choice and
who led lives of sinless perfection. Abel, Enoch, Melchizedek, Abraham, Isaac,
Jacob, Joshua, Phinehas, Samuel, Nathan, Elijah, Joseph, Elisha, Micaiah,
Daniel, Hananiah, Azariah, Mishael, Mordecai, Simeon, Deborah, Judith and
Esther are among the worthies Pelagius contends "not only lived without sin, but
are described as having led holy lives."[86] Augustine wryly responds that if

> we could only assemble together all the forementioned holy men and women, and
> ask them whether they lived without sin whilst they were in this life, what can we
> suppose would be their answer? Would it be the language of our author, or in the
> words of the Apostle John? I put it to you, whether, on having such a question sub-
> mitted to them, however excellent might have been their sanctity in this body, they
> would not have exclaimed with one voice: "If we say we have no sin, we deceive
> ourselves, and the truth is not in us" [1 Jn 1:8].[87]

The logic of Pelagius's position drives him to seek examples of human perfection, for surely, if Pelagius's understanding of sin and grace is correct, such exam-

ples should be readily forthcoming. If sin is only an action, the unfortunate result of a bad choice rather than a defect in human nature itself, why is it so difficult to find convincing examples of people who always made good choices in obedience to God?

The Pelagians respond that human beings are deeply affected by the bad examples of those around them. That is, if you watch enough people doing the wrong thing, sooner or later you are apt to follow their example. The sad result is "a darkening of the minds of men, both as a race and as individuals, by repeated sins."[88] Humanity's problem is basically intellectual. The human mind is "darkened and needed the 'file of the Law' to remove the rust. The grace of Christ illuminated the dark mind and showed what should be done." Once the mind comprehends the truth, Pelagius contends, the "will was adequate for the task."[89]

Human history and experience, viewed on a wide scale or on an individual basis, fails to demonstrate Pelagius's fundamental thesis. Pelagius, Augustine is convinced, had not gone deep enough in his analysis of human nature. The problem of human sinfulness is not primarily one of ignorance, since even humans who know what they should do often do the very opposite thing. The deeper dilemma of sin and salvation is that humans do not love the good. Something is gravely wrong with human nature itself, a defect in the affections and will that Augustine links to the original sin of Adam and Eve.

Augustine responds to Pelagius that his definition of grace is much too narrow. Grace might well communicate to us the knowledge of what we must do, but it also must empower us to "do what we have discovered—not only that we believe what ought to be loved, but also that we love what we have believed." If grace is to be called enlightenment, Augustine argues, "let it at any rate be so called in such wise that God may be believed to infuse it, along with an ineffable sweetness, more deeply and internally . . . in such a way, that He not only exhibits truth, but likewise imparts love."[90]

Because humanity's sinfulness extends to human nature, whatever effects, teaching or enlightenment God imparts in grace must extend to the healing of that same nature. Augustine writes, "For it is thus that God teaches those who have been called according to His purpose, giving them simultaneously both to know what they ought to do, and to do what they know."[91]

Augustine posits the necessity of a more drastic healing of human nature because he understands the Fall to be drastic in its consequences. While Pelagius sees the sin of Adam and Eve affecting only themselves, Augustine understands their act as having fatal consequences for all of humanity. Not only has death entered the world and human life because of Adam's sin—death of both the body and the soul—but human nature itself has been damaged, infected with sin's contagion. As a result, as Bonner puts it, "a clouding and weakening of all man's faculties" has occurred.

> His body becomes liable to disease in a regrettable and familiar way; but, in a far more distressing way, he loses control over his body so that, even when he is well, his will cannot fully control it and has to confess its impotence to rule the body which, the philosophers are all agreed, should be subservient to the soul. But even this is not enough. The body has not only become a rebel, but the mind has become darkened and weakened by sin. The power of the will of vitiated nature is inadequate to avoid sin, unless it has a special aid—the Grace of Christ.[92]

Augustine is willing to agree with Pelagius that "human nature, indeed, was created at first faultless and sinless." Human nature "born from Adam," however, "now needs the physician, because it is not sound." Those "good qualities" that human nature still retains find their source in God. But human nature itself, at its heart and core, is flawed. This "flaw . . . darkens and weakens all those natural goods, so that it has need of illumination and healing."[93] Thus, all humans possess the need of grace, a grace that comes to them from outside their own condition, grace they cannot earn or deserve.

> This grace of Christ, without which neither infants nor adults can be saved, is not, however, rendered for any merits, but is given *gratis*, on account of which it is also called *grace*. "We are justified freely through his blood," says the Apostle [Rom 3:24]. Whence, they are indeed justly condemned who are not liberated through grace, either because they are not yet able to hear, or because they are unwilling to obey, or again because they did not receive, at the time when they were unable to hear on account of their youth, that bath of regeneration, which they might have received and through which they might have been saved. The reason is that they are not without sin, either that which they have inherited from their birth, or that which they have added from their own misconduct. . . . The entire mass, therefore, incurs penalty; and if the deserved punishment of condemnation were rendered to all, it would without doubt be rightly rendered. They, therefore, who are delivered

from it by grace are called, not vessels of their own merits, but "vessels of mercy" [Rom 9:23]. But of whose mercy, if not of him who sent Christ Jesus into the world to save sinners, whom he foreknew, and foreordained, and called, and justified, and glorified? [Rom 8:29-30]. Now, who could be so madly insane as to fail to give ineffable thanks to the mercy which liberates whom it would? The person who correctly appreciates the whole subject cannot possibly blame the justice of God in wholly condemning all whatsoever.[94]

We need to take a closer look at Augustine's understanding of original sin and its effect upon humanity. Bonner suggests three specific interpretations of the way in which Adam's sin has affected his descendants. *~ eastern church*

First, we have the *medical* interpretation. Sin is here pictured as a "hereditary disease," one that "weakens and enfeebles our nature, making us spiritually sick and in need of the Divine Physician, by whose stripes we are healed."[95] Bonner adds that the medical illustration of original sin was particularly popular in the Christian East. Second, we have the *juridical* interpretation. This understanding of Adam's sin focuses upon its legal aspects and is "characteristically western and Latin." Viewed from this perspective, "in his sin, Adam involved the whole human race which, in some fashion, shared his guilt."[96] In the third principal interpretation of original sin the first two views are combined "so that we think of Original Sin both as an inherited disease and as inherited guilt." Augustine supports this third interpretation. A major task for Augustine, then, is to explain how the guilt of Adam could also justly be the guilt of individuals living thousands of years later. After all, it was Adam who sinned, not me! What kind of strange reckoning is this? Why am I considered guilty for his sin and, if guilty, worthy to be punished in the same manner as Adam?

Augustine responds that we are guilty of Adam's sin because "in that one man were we all, when we were all that one man."[97] This strange and mysterious concept will require some unpacking. Augustine bases his understanding of original sin on a "seminal" relationship between Adam and his descendants. In a word, Adam's descendants, that is, his seed, were present in his loins at the time he sinned. Hence, Augustine argues, when Adam sinned we sinned with him.

While a strange argument to modern ears, the idea of a seminal connection between a patriarchal figure and his descendants would have been significantly less foreign to ancient writers and readers. The writer of Hebrews, for example, speaks of Levi as mysteriously paying a tithe to Melchizedek, even though Levi would not be born for hundreds of years. How could Levi pay such a tithe? He was present in the loins of Abraham when Abraham paid a tithe to Melchizedek. Thus we read, "One might even say that Levi himself, who receives tithes, paid tithes through Abraham, *for he was still in the loins of his ancestor* when Melchizedek met him" (Heb 7:9-10; emphasis added). Augustine believes Paul is making the same type of seminal connection in Romans 5:12.

Augustine, reading Paul's words in Latin translation, heard Paul saying: "Therefore, just as sin entered this world by one man and through sin, death; so death passed into all men, in whom all sinned." This last phrase, "in whom all sinned [*in quo omnes peccaverunt*]," led Augustine to believe that Paul was saying that all people had actually sinned in Adam when Adam sinned. A strange idea, Augustine might think, but not entirely foreign to Scripture. One had only to think of Hebrews 7:9-10. As Bonner rightly asks, however, does Augustine's Latin translation correctly render Paul's thought? Sadly, no. Paul's Greek text reads *eph hō pantes hēmarton*, not *en hō*, "which Augustine's interpretation requires."

For example, the New International Version translation of Romans 5:12 reads: "Therefore, just as sin entered the world through one man, and death through sin, and in this way death came to all men, *because all sinned*" (emphasis added). The New Revised Standard Version reads: "Therefore, just as sin came into the world through one man, and death came through sin, and so death spread to all *because all have sinned*" (emphasis added).

It is difficult to understand why Augustine chooses to rely on a defective Latin translation of Paul's Greek text, unless his commitment to a seminal understanding of original sin blurs his better judgment.[98] As Bonner points out, Augustine could defend the idea of a seminal interpretation without relying on a faulty translation of Romans 5:12. Moses, for example, had spoken of the sins of parents being visited upon their children to the third and fourth generation (cf. Deut 5:9). Moreover, as we have seen, the idea of seminal identity also occurs in the New Testament (Heb 7).

How does humanity's link with Adam manifest itself? Both in the guilt of humanity before God (because of our seminal identity with Adam) and in the diseased character of human nature after the Fall, an infection Augustine specifically terms "concupiscence." Bonner writes that "this weakness both dominates our lives and determines the way in which we inherit the guilt of Adam."[99] If so, it is wise for us to take a closer look at its specific character.

Augustine's understanding of concupiscence is closely related to his analysis of Adam's life before and after his fall into sin. Augustine pictures Adam before the Fall as living in "perfect health and freedom from passion." His body was free from disease, and his will exercised perfect control over his body's created desires and natural actions. Adam's ability to control his body's desires and passions, however, was conditional. He could do so only as long as he continued to obey God. When Adam chose to disobey God, the previous control he had exercised over the natural impulses of his body was lost, a loss Augustine especially portrays as affecting his sexuality. Bonner explains:

> Our sexual appetite and ability are not directly under our will at all, and with this weakness—perhaps because of it—there exists a sense of shame, the sense of sexual shame which came upon Adam and Eve after the Fall, when their eyes were opened and they perceived their nakedness. This shame Augustine associates with the loss of control which he regards as the punishment of the disobedience of the Fall, and in so doing he is probably right; but the conclusion which he drew from this, that in Paradise man had the same control over his sexual organs that he has today over his hand or foot, is based upon a defective knowledge of physiology.[100]

While we might fault Augustine for his understanding of human physiology, his understanding of human shame and its connection to alienated human relationships and sexual functioning and desire is quite insightful. Augustine's own past continually reminds him that there is something disordered in human sexual desire, a disability in human nature that particularly manifests itself in how humans relate to one another sexually. Augustine connects this disability, brokenness and lack of control over our bodies' sexual responses to Adam's fall into sin and labels it "concupiscence" or "lust."[101] Indeed, Augustine believes that even within marriage our sexuality remains tainted by the Fall, an element of his thought that continues to arouse debate.

How are Augustine's ideas concerning concupiscence and sex related to the larger question of sin and grace? On the one hand, Augustine argues that the desire to procreate within the boundaries of marriage is a good thing. On the

other hand, the procreation of children inevitably entails the evil of concupiscence. Bonner writes, "Thus two things are simultaneously propagated: nature,
which is good; and the vice of nature, which is evil. It is from, and by, concupiscence that the guilt of Original Sin is conveyed from the parents to the child."[102]
He adds:

> Concupiscence itself is not Original Sin; it is a wound and a vice of human nature,
> making it a slave to the devil; can be the occasion of sin, even in the baptized; and is
> the means whereby Original Sin is transmitted. It is an infection which conveys a
> legal liability. It is cleansed by baptism, but its effects are not removed, and it is for
> that reason that the children of baptized parents are themselves in need of the laver
> of regeneration.[103]

The results of Augustine's reasoning could not be further from those of
Pelagius. Whereas Pelagius understands the sin of Adam and Eve to be theirs
and theirs alone, Augustine sees the guilt of their sin passed on to all humans,
together with a twisting in human nature manifested in the human sexual
response itself. All humans are born in this woeful state, Augustine argues, and
apart from the regeneration of baptism will die separated from God. Hence, for
Augustine, infant baptism is an absolute necessity, for any babies who die unbaptized must unhappily experience damnation because of their connection with
Adam and Eve.[104]

Though the prospect of infant damnation is a horrible one, it proceeds
directly from Augustine's understanding of the Fall and its effect upon human
nature. If human nature is fallen and this fallen state is related to more than simply the choice to follow others' bad example, all humans are infected with sin,
whatever their age. Augustine relentlessly follows the logic of his theological
model to its difficult conclusion. It includes the following steps: (1) The sin of
Adam and Eve has affected, indeed, infected, all human beings. (2) All humans,
regardless of their age, have inherited both the guilt of Adam's sin and a sin
nature that is distorted or skewed. This distortion is primarily seen in our distorted loves. (3) God must sovereignly act through grace's empowerment in
Christ to overcome human nature's slavery to the devil and to heal human nature
from its inherited infection. Until the empowering of grace, humans will consistently, inevitably choose to exercise their will in a fallen fashion. That is to say, we

might freely choose to act in a given manner, but we will never choose to love or obey God—if left to ourselves. Our wills are bent and must be healed. (4) Not all humans are saved. (5) Consequently, God sovereignly elects some from sinful humanity to salvation, but not all. Why God would choose to elect one person to salvation and to leave another in his sin is an "inscrutable" judgment. The fact that God chooses to save anyone is an act of divine grace. God owes nothing to fallen humanity.

> There was one lump of perdition out of Adam to which only punishment was due; thence are made *vessels unto honour* [Rom 9:21] out of the same lump. For *the potter hath power over the clay of the same lump* [Rom 9:21]—of what lump? For it had already perished, just damnation was assuredly already due to that lump. Give grateful thanks that you have escaped. . . . But, you say, why has He made me to honour and another to dishonour? . . . Two little children are born. If you ask what is due, they both cleave to the lump of perdition. But why does its mother carry the one to grace, while the other is suffocated by its mother in her sleep? Will you tell me what that one was deserved which was borne to grace, and what that one whom its sleeping mother suffocated? Both have deserved nothing of good but *the potter hath power over the clay, of the same lump to make one vessel unto honour, and another unto dishonour.* Do you wish to dispute with me? Nay rather, do you wonder with me and exclaim with me: *O the depth of the riches!* [Rom 11:33]. Let us be filled with dread, let us both cry: *O the depth of the riches!* Let us agree together in fear, lest we perish in error. *O the depth of the riches of the wisdom and knowledge of God! How unsearchable are His judgements, and His ways past finding out!*[105]

Conclusions

The church in the West widely affirmed Augustine's conclusions concerning sin and grace. The sixteenth council of Carthage, for example, produced eight canons regarding principle points developed by Augustine: the original state of Adam, the nature of original sin, infant baptism and justifying grace.[106] Whereas Pelagius had argued that Adam would have died apart from any decision to sin, the council condemned this view. In addition, it affirmed that all infants had contracted the taint of original sin from Adam, a "trace of original sin that must be expiated by the bath of regeneration."[107]

As for grace, the council disagreed with Pelagius's attempt to limit grace's justifying role to sins already committed. "Whoever says that the grace by which we are justified through Jesus Christ our Lord serves only for the remission of sins already committed, and is not also a help not to commit them, *anathema sit* [let such a one be condemned]."[108] Grace, the council taught, does much more than enlighten or instruct the mind in the commandments of God. Not only does the grace of God instruct, but it enables or strengthens the human will to both love and obey the commandments. In the words of the council:

> Likewise it has been decided: Whoever says that this same grace of God through our Lord Jesus Christ solely helps us not to sin because through it an understanding of the commandments is revealed and opened to us that we may know what we should seek and what we should avoid, but not because through it is given to us the love and strength to do what we have recognized to be in our duty, *anathema sit*.[109]

The council rightly noted that knowledge divorced from love was likely to produce pride, as Paul taught: "Knowledge puffs up, but love builds up" (1 Cor 8:1). Thus, the council wrote that "it would be very wrong to believe that we have the grace of Christ for knowledge which puffs up and not for love which builds up; for both are the gift of God: the knowledge of what we should do and the love to do it, so that, built up by love, we may not be puffed up by knowledge."[110]

The council insisted that God's grace, a grace separate from all natural endowments, lies behind and empowers *all* our good actions. Grace is not something tacked on to whatever we can accomplish based on our innate capabilities but is an absolute necessity if we are to exercise our will in obedience. Jesus did not say, for example, "that apart from Him we could do things with greater difficulty, but rather: 'Apart from me you can do nothing.' "[111]

As for the possibility that a Christian could lead a sinless life, the council piled text upon text that indicated that only self-deceived persons could believe they had reached a state of sinlessness. John, for example, taught that we deceive ourselves "if we say we that have no sin" (1 Jn 1:8). Moreover, what of the Lord's Prayer? Pelagians had argued that those who had not sinned could still pray the clause "forgive us our debts" (Mt 6:12), but when they prayed this petition, they were actually praying for others in the church. The council responded with a resounding no. Had not James taught that we "all offend in

many things" (Jas 3:2, Vulgate)? The universal nature of sin, both in human
nature and action, is reiterated in a number of texts (2 Chron 6:36; Ps 143:2;
Dan 9:5, 15, 20). Indeed, the council asked, "who could tolerate that a person
who prays be lying not to other persons but to the Lord Himself, by saying
with his lips that he wishes to be forgiven while in his heart he denies that he
has any debts to be forgiven?"[112]

Augustine remained convinced that in his response to Pelagius he had not
overthrown the freedom of the will and the heart of the gospel. Whether such is
the case remains to be seen. Bonner comments, however, that Augustine "tends
to regard 'to will' as an equivalent for 'to use free will'. The fact that we have a will
is as obvious as the fact that we live; we feel ourselves will and not will. And the
testimony of consciousness is reinforced by the moral sense."[113] That is to say,
when we choose to sin or to violate our own moral compass, our conscience kicks
in and condemns us for doing so. Why would it function in this manner, Augustine asks, if we are not free moral agents?[114]

Thus, human beings freely choose to act. The problem, though, is that
because of the corrupted nature we have inherited from our ancient parents,
when we choose, that choice is motivated and shaped by our skewed and corrupted loves. We freely choose to love the wrong things. Hence, at least for
Augustine, "to have free will is not the same as to be free."[115] That is, "The man
who chooses evil is a slave to his vices; but his free will was given him by God, and
once he has thrown it away by choosing vice, it cannot be recovered except
through the action of God."[116]

Such a conclusion, of course, is light years from the position of Pelagius, who
defined free will as "nothing other than the possibility of sinning or not sinning,"[117] a definition related to Pelagius's much more optimistic understanding of
human nature. Augustine rightly perceived the more realistic biblical awareness
of human nature's inherent sinfulness, a perception derived from his reading of
the Scripture and verified by his own life experience. Thus, Augustine clearly
understood that grace must be a power for change and healing external to a
human being's own created, innate qualities and powers. We need help beyond
ourselves, and left to ourselves we would only drown in the sea of our malformed
and misdirected loves.

Whether Augustine's clarion call to a biblically grounded understanding of grace necessitates the entire acceptance of his soteriology is another question. The church, for example, has not agreed with Augustine's pessimism regarding the damnation of unbaptized infants. It has affirmed, however, that Augustine's deep understanding of sin and its effect upon the will is much closer to the truth than Pelagius's more optimistic approach. In fact, sin has left its mark not only on human nature but on creation itself. Was God still in control of the created order? In what ways did God govern and control his world? The question of God's providence is a pressing one and particularly interested John Chrysostom. Chrysostom's understanding of providence will occupy us for the next two chapters.

"For God's providence is as plain as the sun and its rays.
In each situation and place, in the wilderness, in inhabited regions and uninhabited,
on earth or sea or wherever you might go,
you will observe the clear and sufficient, ancient and new, reminders of this providence."
JOHN CHRYSOSTOM
On Providence

"For those who are well-disposed, the revelation of God in and of itself,
even before the proof drawn from his works,
suffices to demonstrate not only his providence, but also his fervent love toward us.
For he does not simply watch over us, but also loves us;
he ardently loves us with an inexplicable love, with an impassible
yet fervent, vigorous, genuine, indissoluble love, a love that is impossible to extinguish."
JOHN CHRYSOSTOM
On Providence

SEVEN

GOD'S TRANSCENDENT PROVIDENCE

The Question of God's Providence

Is God truly in control of human history? People living at the beginning of the twenty-first century might well have their doubts. Theologians, pastors and laypeople continue to ponder, and at times struggle mightily with, the question of God's goodness and power as manifested in the midst of the unprecedented suffering and evil of our century. Modern horrors such as the Holocaust, the Armenian genocide, the death of millions in Cambodia, Rwanda and Kosovo, and the more recent destruction of the World Trade Center towers silence any flippant responses to the question of God's control and governance of human history.

Each one of us has at one time or another asked the question *why*. Whether we have encountered or experienced an accident, sickness, natural disaster or war with its accompanying horrors, the question wells up within us—Why? Why didn't God protect us? Why couldn't circumstances or timing have been different? If only my husband hadn't been on that plane! If only my little girl hadn't run across the road! If only I had locked the door! Moreover, where were you, God? Didn't you promise to protect and keep me? Why didn't you act to protect and preserve me? Was it because you lacked the power to do so? Or the love to motivate you to save and preserve me and those I love? Perhaps God possesses infinite power but exercises it with less than infinite mercy? Is God really good? Or perhaps God is good but lacks the power to manifest his goodness consistently? Question piles upon question as we attempt to reconcile the reality of a fallen world with the existence of an infinitely powerful, infinitely loving God.

How might the church fathers help us to deal with these significant questions? Sooner or later the sharp blade of suffering will cut into our lives. Can the fathers help us to form a response that will sustain and nurture our faith in the midst of our suffering or as we face its inevitability?

Think, for example, of John Chrysostom, bishop of Constantinople in the late fourth century. Is it possible for such an ancient voice to speak viably in the twenty-first century? Can Chrysostom help us to make sense of circumstances that seem to defy all categories of why and wherefore? He lived so long ago. How could he begin to understand our present modern situation?

The possibility exists, though, that the very fact that Chrysostom lived so long ago might serve to our advantage. The length of years that separates him from us could provide the distance and perspective we need to help us recognize modern assumptions that too easily cloud our thinking regarding providence and its relationship to human suffering.[1] Are there modern blind spots that can be illuminated by ancient wisdom? As Frances Young has observed, to see theological questions debated in a "different intellectual" and cultural setting might well be edifying and enlightening.[2] In this chapter, then, we will purposely attempt to step outside our own modern setting, our culturally conditioned presuppositions, and see whether we can view the issue of divine providence in a light that may prove clearer than our own blurred perspective.

This is not to ignore the need for constructing a hermeneutical bridge between the world of the fathers and our own. Our world is in significant ways quite different from that of John Chrysostom, and the intervening years between our time and his will color our perspective and our ability to hear what advice he might offer us. We will err if we expect Chrysostom to address all the questions a modern person might pose concerning providence and suffering or to answer them in a manner one feels is appropriate, enlightened or politically correct. Yet we would do well to remember that Chrysostom and the fathers in general inhabited a world well-acquainted with injustice, sickness, brutality, cruelty, disaster, war and murder. It was no easier to watch a child die of a crippling disease in the ancient world, nor to see one's village ravaged by a sudden incursion of military power, whether that of the Romans or the "barbarians." Soldiers were no more gentle at that time than they are today.

Chrysostom tasted firsthand the chilling draught of fear, experienced betrayal, hopes smashed, willful misinterpretation of his motives, unfair and illegal court proceedings and judgment, and finally died alone in exile, far from the church he had loved and served. Whatever thoughts John Chrysostom has to offer his reader concerning the question of divine providence and human suffering have been tried in the fire of his own experience. He is not writing from the comfort of the philosopher's easy chair.

Chrysostom's basic presuppositions about God's character, the incarnation of Jesus Christ, this present life as time lived between the ages, eschatological hope for the future in light of Christ's cross and resurrection, and the incomprehensibility of many of God's providential orderings of creation and history would have been familiar terrain to other church fathers, though his ideas will occasionally jar modern sensibilities. Many modern thinkers, for example, believe it is impossible to reconcile the reality of divine providence with the rampant human suffering of the twentieth century. In the age of Auschwitz, how can one maintain credible belief in an omnipotent and loving God?[3]

Patristic teaching recognizes the difficulty of reconciling divine providence and human suffering, but constructs an analytical prism honed from the incarnation, death and resurrection of Christ. As the murkiness of God's providence is filtered through this christological prism, the fathers believed matters would increasingly clarify themselves, though patristic writers never deny the mystery of God's being and actions. Chrysostom will contend that it is not so much events themselves, but how we view them, through what lens and with what disposition, that will make all the difference.

Christian Disposition and Divine Providence

In *On Providence*, a work composed during a painful exile at the end of his life, Chrysostom pondered the mysteries of God's providence. He often found his thoughts drifting to the great patriarch of Israel, Abraham. What could have been more inexplicable and horrific than God's command to Abraham to sacrifice his son Isaac, the very child of the promise? What, Chrysostom asked himself, enabled Abraham to respond in obedience to God's incomprehensible command? Abraham's *disposition*, cultivated and trained over the years, enabled him to willingly obey God's strange and dark command. Abraham's receptive and responsive disposition became a central focus in Chrysostom's own understanding of providence and how human beings are to respond to God's ordering of their lives.

In chapter ten of *On Providence* Chrysostom portrays the scene as God calls to Abraham to prevent the sacrifice of Isaac: "For the voice did not simply call 'Abraham,' but 'Abraham, Abraham,' through the repetition of his name restraining and arresting his intention that was focused solely on the command, so complete was his absorption on the command."[4]

Chrysostom's point is that Abraham's intention, his *proairesis*, was entirely concentrated on obeying God's command. Although God's command appeared to be diametrically opposed to the promise God had already made to Abraham and to God's character as loving and compassionate, Abraham was still prepared to obey. Why? "He didn't meddle in God's affairs."[5]

Abraham's ability to respond in obedience to God's seemingly nonsensical command did not arise in a vacuum. In fact, much of what Chrysostom says in *On Providence* concerns his understanding of how God works in human beings to produce Abraham's obedient response. A number of significant themes intertwine in Chrysostom's explanation of Abraham's willingness to sacrifice Isaac. Chief among them is Chrysostom's understanding of human disposition and how disposition inclines the human will toward good or evil. The larger question of human evil is, of course, intimately related to the choice facing Abraham. Will he obey God, or will evil evidence itself in a perverted or disobedient choice or *proairesis*?

Proairesis is an extremely rich word with an interesting constellation of meanings and nuances. Its first definition refers to the human faculty of free choice. In addition, it refers to human intention, motive and disposition.[6] Chrysostom consistently denies that human evil is the result of God's action. Nor is its source to be found in the nature of created matter or the human body. Creation itself is good, as the writer of Genesis clearly declares. The beauty and utility of creation demonstrate this inherent, created goodness. Evil erupts, as it might in Abraham's response to God's command, as human disposition and choice combine to violate God's desire.

Church fathers contend that disposition and choice (*proairesis*) are in themselves gifts from God, key properties and privileges of human nature. The problem, as Chrysostom presents matters, is that human disposition and choice are corrupted by sin. Chrysostom, however, like most Eastern fathers, does not see this corruption as completely debilitating human freedom. He is convinced, in a manner that would perhaps cause problems for a Latin father such as Augustine, that human choice remains free.

In this vein, Chrysostom writes, "We are free and masters of our own free choice."[7] He insists that his teaching concerning providence cannot be forced on anyone. "For I will not stop continually repeating this: it is not possible to force or constrain this cure on anyone who does not wish to be healed."[8] The difficult events of life, events allowed providentially by God, "can be a correction even for those who do not pay attention to the Scriptures, *provided they are willing*."[9] When Paul writes that we should assume the place of clay in the potter's hands, "he is certainly not destroying our free will by saying this." Rather, Paul is endeavoring to teach his readers to place themselves in a dispositional stance before God that facilitates the appropriate use of their free will.[10]

Our disposition and its accompanying choices, however, must be trained to respond to God's world and its accompanying structures and demands. That is, Chrysostom believes, we must train or educate the various created gifts God has given to us in creation—the soul, mind, body and will—so that the good and true choice can be made in the midst of the perplexities and turmoils of life in this present evil age. The only *true* suffering Christians will encounter occurs when they fail to exercise their choice in light of what they know to be the truth. Hence, the importance for Chrysostom of linking together judgment and human choice.

Think of the decision facing Abraham as he contemplated obeying or disobeying the command of God to sacrifice Isaac. Abraham chose and acted obediently because he had already judged correctly regarding the overall situation. He had already accomplished his obedient act in his intention or judgment. That is, he had thought things through carefully, judged well and acted accordingly. Proper judgment and appropriate action overcome the apparent stumbling block posed by God's command. Abraham chose to act obediently on the basis of what he did know, though that knowledge was incomplete and in significant ways incomprehensible. Abraham's willingness to respond obediently on the basis of limited knowledge actually expanded his understanding.

Chrysostom considers human disposition and choice themselves to be the essence of humanness and is critical of any attempt to posit a "substance" or "nature" that determines or undercuts the ability of a human being to make correct moral decisions. In his sermons on Colossians, for example, Chrysostom states that the "moral choice demonstrates one's humanity rather than a [human] substance, and characterizes humanness rather than substance. For [a person's] substance does not cast him into hell, nor lead him into the kingdom, but human beings themselves."[11]

Chrysostom appears to come perilously close to overlooking the need for divine grace to empower the fallen *proairesis* to function well as created by God. Thankfully, throughout his work Chrysostom affirms the believer's constant need for the grace of God. He can sometimes be misinterpreted, though, because he refuses to drive a wedge between grace and the concrete means God provides for the nurturing and training of human disposition and choice. Chrysostom is convinced that the underlying disposition that shapes judgment and choice can be trained to respond in a godly and healthy manner—that is, to judge things correctly and not simply on the basis of appearances. If Abraham had judged on the basis of appearances, disaster would have occurred. Chrysostom argues that much human suffering—one of the great problems for those who wish to affirm divine providence—can be traced to human ignorance, that is, a failure to form a proper judgment concerning the affairs and circumstances of this life. Thus he writes, "There are many things which from ignorance alone cause us sorrow, so that if we come to understand them well, we banish our grief."[12]

What, then, are the main obstacles that prevent someone from clearly seeing the true nature of things and making a clear judgment? Chrysostom points his finger at what he identifies as the "passions," an aspect of the human personality that darkens a person's understanding, prevents the cultivation of the various Christian virtues and spiritual peace and wars against prayer. Chrysostom writes:

> It is not possible to be master of one's self, being in a passion. Like a sea rolling mountains high, it is all hurly-burly: or even as a pure fountain, where mire is cast

into it, becomes muddied, and is in turmoil. . . . It is your own soul that you have
cut open; it is there that you have inflicted a wound: you have flung your own char-
ioteer from his horses, you have got him dragging along the ground upon his
back.[13]

The passions, as Chrysostom views matters, throw the faculty of reason off
balance. They cast blinders over the eyes of the mind that cripple its ability to
form a realistic and fitting opinion, judgment or conviction concerning basic
moral values—that is, what is genuinely good and genuinely evil—and prevent
people from accepting, appreciating and praising God's providential actions in
the world. Again we must emphasize, the passions are intimately linked to
human sin and the distortions it causes throughout the human personality.

Chrysostom is convinced that we will never understand the nature of God's
providence if we overlook the issue of the passions and their distorting influence
on a person's ability to perceive God at work. That is, Chrysostom's goal is to
release his readers from the influence of passions that prevent them from thinking and perceiving clearly. If they continue to allow their passions to govern them,
their ability to reason well about providence and life in general will be drastically
undercut. Chrysostom's flock will lack the eyes to truly discern what God is up to
in the world. Not only will human beings fail to recognize God's providential
activity, but they will judge according to appearances. Things that are genuinely
good will be branded as evil, evils will be proclaimed as goods, and indifferent
things will end up either praised or condemned. The ultimate outcome will be
that God's providence is blasphemed.

A number of telling passages in Chrysostom's *On Providence* illustrate how disordered passions interfere with our ability to discern God's goodness in providence and Chrysostom's remedy for this spiritual sickness. For example, in the
midst of an extended discourse on the role of nature in demonstrating God's
providence, Chrysostom digresses into a discussion of the beneficial aspects of
death.

Death, surely, is a genuine evil, yet Chrysostom argues that death can be a
benefit for both the believer who has died and for those who remain behind.
How so? Those who continue to live in this world after the death of a loved one
have received a powerful lesson on the transitoriness of life and the danger of
thinking and acting as though life will never end. One is "humbled, learns to act

in a more level-headed fashion, is taught to think in a more spiritual manner, and introduces into his mind the mother of all goods, humility."[14] The one who has died is in no way wronged, "for he will receive this same body pure and incorruptible." Thus, death actually becomes "a teacher of the spiritual life, instructing the understanding, bridling the passions of the soul, quelling its billows and creating calm."[15]

If we judge solely according to appearances, we will view death only as an evil. Hence, Chrysostom insists, the danger of an inexperienced and foolish person "immediately expressing at the outset a premature opinion."[16] If we analyze death in the wider light of the gospel, though, Chrysostom believes it can be seen as a genuine good.

Chrysostom also enjoys illustrating the goodness of providence and the dangers of the passions from the story of Joseph. Joseph represents for Chrysostom the true Christian philosopher, that is, the genuine Christian who bridles one's passions, refuses to judge by appearances and waits for the final outcome of events before passing judgment on God's providence. Chrysostom portrays other characters in the story, such as Joseph's brothers and Potiphar's wife, as prime examples of the folly and ruin that occur when the passions run out of control.

The responses of Joseph's brothers to his dream that he would one day rule over them are a veritable litany of disordered passions. They became, Chrysostom writes, "more savage than wolves toward their brother."[17] How so? "The father of this war was *irrational envy and unjust malice. Seething with anger . . . envy kindling this furnace and stirring up the fire.*"[18] When Rueben prevented them from actually carrying out Joseph's murder "their anger boiled anew, their wrath reached its zenith, and their passions raged out of control like a storm at sea."[19] A "madness" consumed them that finally led to the sale of Joseph into slavery.

Joseph's trials, however, were only beginning. In a sense, he left one insane asylum only to enter another, that inhabited by Potiphar's wife. Once Potiphar's wife placed her eyes on Joseph, her passions exploded in heated desire. She was, Chrysostom argues, "beside herself over the beauty of the young man."[20] Each day she went out in search of her prey, "*incited by her passion and unbridled love.*"[21] Still, despite "her appearance and frenzied passion," Joseph withstood her temptations. When Joseph refused her advances and fled the scene naked, she was overtaken by anger, "another even more grievous passion, joined in with extreme savagery."[22]

Both Joseph's brothers and Potiphar's wife serve as apt foils for Joseph's own response to his difficulties. For Chrysostom, both *what* God in his providence allowed to occur in Joseph's life and *how* Joseph responded are of central importance. First, God made a great promise to Joseph in a dream that he would rule over his brothers. Second, God allowed events to occur that according to all appearances would prevent God's promise from reaching fulfillment. Chrysostom notes, "the events which were occurring after the visions were contrary to the dreams."[23]

As for Joseph, when his brothers plotted against him "he exhibited the disposition of a brother."[24] When they sold him into slavery Joseph maintained an even keel. Despite his tremendous suffering and difficult circumstances, matters Chrysostom makes no attempt to disguise or downplay, Joseph was neither baffled nor shocked.

> Nevertheless, he was not baffled by any of these things. . . . He was not at all troubled there, nor was he shocked by the occurrence of these events, for he reminded himself of the dreams that announced contrary things. Neither was he unduly concerned about these matters, asking himself, "How could these things have ever happened."[25]

Joseph overcame the allurements of Potiphar's wife, not because the temptations were not genuine—Chrysostom paints a vivid picture of their reality—but because Joseph's disposition in these circumstances shaped a response governed by a specific understanding of God's providence. Joseph clearly understood what God had promised, yet he realized that a full comprehension of God's actions or seeming failure to act would have to wait "the final outcome of events." Joseph recognized "full well the resourcefulness of God and the ingenuity of his wisdom."[26]

Chrysostom emphasizes that Joseph's ability to respond wisely to God's providence and his own suffering was framed by a specific *interpretive stance* before God and his providential acts. That is to say, how Joseph chose to respond in his circumstances, his *proairesis*, was molded significantly by his willingness to shape his judgment of affairs within certain specific guidelines. These hermeneutical boundaries—the nature of God's character, the inherent incomprehensibility of his providence and the guarantee of final deliverance in the future—enabled Joseph to respond faithfully to God's providential ordering of his life. He would see clearly as long as he remained within this interpretive framework.

Other biblical characters such as Abraham and David, Chrysostom believes, also consistently demonstrated the same hermeneutical perspective. Chrysostom views them as the true Christian philosophers, a concept we need to understand clearly if we are to appreciate Chrysostom's ideas on providence and suffering.

The Christian Philosopher

What are the characteristics of the Christian philosopher or genuine Christian? The authentic Christian possesses the ability to make proper distinctions between good, bad and indifferent realities. The genuine good consists of the basic virtues, such as temperance and generosity. Chrysostom categorizes bad things (*kaka*) as any sinful acts or attitudes (luxury, lust). Indifferent things (*adiaphora*) become good or bad according to how one uses them. For example, wealth can lead to avarice or generosity, while poverty can lead to blasphemy or true philosophy.[27]

Good things (the virtues) can never become bad. Truly bad things (sins) can never become good. All other things, such as sickness, death, insults, riches, dishonor, freedom and slavery, become good or bad according to how they are understood and utilized by the person experiencing them. That is, the moral value of *adiaphora* or indifferent things is determined by the individual's chosen response (*proairesis*) to them. Chrysostom writes:

> Life itself belongs to that middle class of indifferent things, while to live well or poorly is in ourselves. We do not hate life, for we may live well, too. So even if we live poorly, we do not even then cast the blame on life itself. And why not? Because it is not life, but the free choice of those who live it poorly that is to blame.[28]

The relationship, then, between a correct judgment and the question of human suffering is immediate. The Christian will suffer only by classifying an indifferent thing as an evil or by actually sinning. These are the only two possibilities envisaged by Chrysostom. He unrelentingly argues that the mistake most people make in their understanding of suffering and providence is a mistake in moral discernment. Indifferent things are classified as evils, and unnecessary and avoidable suffering results.

How can we avoid this error in moral discernment? Chrysostom advises immersing the mind in sound Christian doctrine so that the Christian can form wise judgments. Thus, for Chrysostom "Christian philosophy" is the art of learning to think and to live like a disciple of Jesus Christ. Christian *philosophia* is Christian thinking and living as opposed to the life and thought of the pagan world. It is a way of life founded on the basic tenets of the Christian faith.[29] Christian philosophy for Chrysostom, as Edward Nowak explains, is not simply a way of thinking, a set of ideas, but the incarnation of the Christian faith in all its various aspects. It is a philosophy of practical living, a strenuous effort toward virtue and Christian perfection.[30]

Christian disposition, then, a personality nurtured and shaped by both Christian doctrine and disciplined discipleship, is for Chrysostom the key element in helping the believer to make sense out of God's providence. Christians who behave in a Christian manner—Chrysostom's description of the Christian philosopher—will more often than not possess the skill and discernment to make correct judgments about their circumstances and God's relationship to them. They will maintain a hermeneutical stance before God that is formed by the realities of the gospel and will not be thrown off their feet when circumstances take on an apparently dark cast.

Chrysostom directs us to the example of the apostle Paul to illustrate his argument. Think, Chrysostom asks, of Paul's attitude behind bars: "Do you see the courage? Do you recognize the boldness? Do you discern his soul's perseverance? *Do you perceive the spiritual perspective of a Christian?*"[31] Paul's perspective on life had been deeply shaped by his relationship with Christ, with courage, boldness and perseverance as the result. His imprisonment itself was an indifferent thing. If Paul's disposition had not matured over the years, he might well have suffered much in prison. But, Chrysostom insists, because he had a Christian disposition an indifferent matter was turned to the good.

Chrysostom believes that the death of the believing thief on the cross demonstrates the same dynamic. He deliberately juxtaposes the response of the crowd of mockers surrounding the cross and that of the thief. The crowd stumbled over the event of the cross. The thief *witnessed the very same event and yet responded in an entirely different manner.* Chrysostom explains, "Indeed, the thief on the cross condemns these kinds of people; for he saw Christ crucified and not only did not stumble in his faith, but in the event of the crucifixion received a greater reason to think like a Christian."[32]

What were the significant elements that framed the thief's appropriate and faithful response to the cross? First, Chrysostom writes, the thief had "moved beyond all human speculations."[33] His perception of Christ's suffering was shaped by his interpretive stance, part of which involved a willingness to bridle a speculative curiosity.

Second, the thief's faith lifted him beyond the immediate situation. Broader considerations, such as his hope for the future with Christ, determined his present response to the apparent defeat and death of the Son of God. In Chrysostom's words, "he was lifted up by the wings of faith, and meditated on the things of the future."[34] Finally, the thief "pondered the resurrection."[35] His attentive and submissive disposition before God enabled him to perceive the situation correctly. The crowd, on the other hand, remained "senseless and negligent," missing the wonder and benefit the cross offered them.[36] All they perceived, Chrysostom contends, was based on appearances. They were unable to see beneath the surface.

For Chrysostom, the thief is an apt example of those "who have a right disposition and are vigilant," thereby deriving "a tremendous profit from those things which scandalize others."[37] Perhaps surprisingly, Chrysostom sees the cross as an indifferent event, in the sense that it can be viewed as either evil or good, depending on one's disposition. It is not the event, but rather the disposition of those who observe it, that determines how they will respond and whether benefit or stumbling will result. Only senseless people are scandalized by the cross, which when viewed from a Christian perspective becomes the "foremost good, that is to say, the cross through which the world was saved."[38] Therefore, Chrysostom continually exhorts his readers: "Learn to think and live like a Christian, and you will not only not be harmed by any of these events, but will reap the greatest benefits."[39]

To summarize, the one who has learned to think like a Christian, the one whose thinking has been shaped by the gospel and the realities it represents, will not judge God's providence by appearances. Instead, genuine believers will remain sensible and vigilant, wary of making a premature judgment concerning

God's actions or permission. They will understand that the events of this life *in themselves* are indifferent matters and take on the character of good or evil *according to our response to them*. Chrysostom unfailingly insists that it is the human response—a response governed by a disposition formed by the Holy Spirit as individuals accept the truths of the gospel and incorporate them into their lives—that is the central determinant in making one's way safely through the world of God's providence.

By way of contrast, those who are "worldly, difficult to lead, self-willed, and utterly carnal" will continually misread God's providence because they lack the eyes to see him at work, a vision that only comes to those who are actively exercising faith, that is, allowing their perspective to be shaped by the gospel and acting accordingly.[40]

The believer who possesses a deeply grounded Christian disposition will experience pain and grief on his journey home, but never harm. As Chrysostom puts it, "no other person is able to harm the one who does not harm himself."[41] What could Chrysostom mean by such a seemingly extravagant, naive and unrealistic statement? Again, Chrysostom turns our eyes to the biblical narrative itself to defend his position.

Think, Chrysostom suggests, of the great saints of the faith and their intense suffering. Abel was murdered by his brother. Jacob lived in hunger as an exile. Joseph suffered as a slave and prisoner, the victim of terrible slander. Moses endured the continual rebellion and rejection of Israel. Job was attacked by the myriad devices of the devil. Shadrach, Meshach, Abednego and Daniel were exposed to countless dangers in Babylon. Elijah lived in dire poverty as a fugitive and wanderer. David suffered at the hand of his own son, Absalom. John the Baptist was beheaded by Herod.[42] Yet in the case of each of these key biblical characters, Chrysostom asks in what way they were *harmed* by their sufferings. Suffering occurred, but harm was avoided. How so? Evidently in Chrysostom's thinking, suffering and harm are two entirely different things. For example, in speaking of the martyrs Chrysostom writes:

> In what way were the martyrs harmed, whose souls were broken by the most severe tortures? Didn't they all shine most brightly at the very moment they were being abused, at the time others set traps for them, when they nobly stood firm while suffering the worst agonies?[43]

Chrysostom clearly differentiates pain, suffering and harm. Harm as a contin-uous, unjust, unrighteous reality, a permanent source of lasting damage to the Christian, is thoroughly conquered through the realities introduced into human history through Christ. In a striking paradox, suffering overcomes harm through the cross of Christ.

Whether we experience harm in our sufferings in this present age is largely dependent *upon our chosen and proper response* in light of two principal factors: *what* Christ has accomplished on our behalf and *how* he conducted and completed his work. As Chrysostom writes in his homilies on the Pastoral Epistles: "For it rests with us either to profit, or to be injured, by afflictions. *It depends not upon the nature of the affliction, but upon the disposition of our own minds.*"[44]

We would misinterpret Chrysostom's thought and life itself if we viewed him as removed from human suffering, spouting unrealistic ideas out of touch with the reality of sorrow, sickness and death. Chrysostom himself was an extremely sensitive individual. He knew that suffering entailed genuine pain and sorrow and never tried to disguise that fact. In his letters to Olympias, for example, Chrysostom writes movingly of his own trials in exile.[45]

> For the winter, which has become more than commonly severe, brought on a storm of internal disorder even more distressing, and during the last two months I have been no better than one dead, nay worse. . . . I spent all my time closely con-fined to my bed, and in spite of endless contrivances I could not shake off the per-nicious effects of the cold; but although I kept a fire burning, and endured a most unpleasant amount of smoke, and remained cooped up in one chamber, covered with any quantity of wraps, and not daring to set a foot outside the threshold I underwent extreme sufferings, perpetual vomiting supervening on headache, loss of appetite, and constant sleeplessness.[46]

Not only is Chrysostom fully cognizant of the very real nature of his own suf-ferings, but he is diligent to counsel Olympias to take care of her own health because of the oppressive nature of sickness and his awareness of how illness can sap spiritual strength.

> Wherefore I beseech you dear lady, and entreat you as a very great favor to pay great attention to the restoration of your bodily health. For dejection causes sick-ness; and when the body is exhausted and enfeebled, and remains in a neglected condition, deprived of the assistance of physicians, and of a wholesome climate,

and an abundant supply of the necessities of life, consider how greatly this aggravates our distress.[47]

Chrysostom's correspondence with Olympias demonstrates well his awareness of the frailty of the human condition and his sensitivity to the intimate relationship between physical and spiritual well-being. We see the same insight in his counsel to those who are grieving. One the one hand, Chrysostom does not hesitate to speak of the valuable lessons that can be learned from death and the attitude of faith a Christian should exercise when death occurs. In his homilies on John's Gospel Chrysostom writes:

> You were born human, and mortal; why then do you grieve that what is natural has come to pass? Do you grieve when you are nourished by eating? Do you try to live without this? Act in the same way in the case of death. If you are mortal, do not yet seek for immortality. Once for all this thing has been appointed. Therefore, do not grieve, or play the role of the mourner, but submit to laws laid on all alike.[48]

At first we cringe at the seeming harshness of Chrysostom's words, yet he was deeply aware of the pain that the separation of death produces for those left behind. He knew that sorrow is a fitting response.

In Chrysostom's homilies on 1 Corinthians, for example, he aptly balances both sides of the Christian's response in his discussion of Job's grief over the loss of his children. Job was "a father and a loving father; and it was right that . . . the compassion of his nature should be shown." If Job had exercised self-command apart from a demonstration of genuine compassion and grief over the loss of his children, his self-control could easily have been interpreted as "mere insensibility." "Therefore," Chrysostom writes, "Job indicates both his natural affection and the exactness of his piety, and in his grief he was not overthrown."[49]

Chrysostom rightly reasons that even in our grief our minds should attempt to recall the truths of the gospel to carry us through the valley of death. "But if you will trust sound reason with this grief, and will consider with yourself who has taken him away, and that by nobly bearing it you offer your mind to our God, even this wave will not be too strong for you to stem."[50]

He also acknowledges that tears are appropriate, both for those who have suffered loss and for those who rightly identify with them in their grief. Thus he writes, "There is nothing that ties love so firmly as sharing both joy and pain one with another. Do not then, because you are far from difficulties yourself, remain aloof from sympathizing too."[51] In a homily from Chrysostom's series on Acts he comments: "Let us have a soul apt to sympathize, let us have a heart that knows how to feel with others in their sorrows: no unmerciful temper, no inhumanity. Though you are able to offer no relief, yet weep, groan, grieve over what has happened, even if this is to no purpose."[52] "I am neither brutal nor cruel," Chrysostom assures his audience. "I know that our nature asks and seeks for its friends and daily companions; it cannot but be grieved."[53]

We must remember, however, the important distinction Chrysostom draws between *suffering* and *harmful suffering*. All Christians can expect to suffer. In fact, Christianity and suffering go hand in hand. But the harmful effects of suffering, at least as Chrysostom understands the word *harmful*, are erased through a Christian disposition and response that has absorbed and reflects the gospel's depths.

> This is our life. That is, the natural consequence of an apostolic way of life is to suffer countless evils. . . . So the apostolic life is purposely designed to suffer abuse, to suffer evils, to never have a respite, to never have a cessation of hostilities. And for however many are vigilant, they are not only not harmed by these events, but instead profit from them. . . . Learn to think and live like a Christian, and you will not only not be harmed by any of these events, but will reap the greatest benefits.[54]

Harmful suffering only occurs in the lives of those who consider indifferent matters as true evils or who willfully transgress God's moral order. That is to say, for Chrysostom, sin and harm are intrinsically connected. A key example of this dynamic is the life of Herod Antipas. Even though John the Baptist was beheaded, it was Herod who reaped the bitter harvest of sin.

Chrysostom invites his reader to "contemplate what it is likely Herod suffered" as John, a convicted prisoner, reproved him for his sins.[55] Immediately after John's execution Herod's conscience was troubled "to such an extent that he believed John had been raised from the dead and was performing miracles."[56] The final outcome of events was that Herod was reproved for all time, while John was crowned for his faithfulness. "Therefore, do not say: 'Why was John allowed to die?' For what occurred was not a death, but a crown, not an end, but the beginning of a greater life."[57]

If the main contours of Chrysostom's argument concerning the centrality of Christian disposition prove persuasive, a further question immediately presents itself. How is a Christian disposition formed? In addition, what other elements or constituents embody a Christian understanding of providence? For example, how much can we rightly expect to understand of God's providential control and ordering of the world and of the universe? What are the limits of our understanding of providence? What aspects of providence will remain incomprehensible? It is to these latter questions that we now turn.

The Incomprehensibility of God's Providence

Our discussion thus far has stressed the importance of maintaining a proper hermeneutical stance before God's providence if we are to discern clearly what God is up to in his world. A Christian disposition, much like ears trained to discern and appreciate the tonal qualities of the gospel, is an absolute necessity if God's providence is to be adequately perceived and interpreted. In a sense, Chrysostom argues, *the manner in which we approach the problem of providence* will ultimately determine whether we reaches the goal of comprehending how God is at work in history.

Indeed, Chrysostom clearly believes there is a helpful and harmful way to seek for an understanding of providence. He describes some attempts to understand providence as "sick," diagnosing their disease as rooted in a failure to understand and submit to the limitations and boundaries imposed by the nature of human reason and the character of God's providence.

> What, therefore, is the cause of such a sickness? A curious mind preoccupied with vain questions, one that wants to understand all the causes of everything that comes to pass and to strive contentiously with the incomprehensible and ineffable providence of God. It shamelessly scrutinizes and concerns itself with a subject which, in its very nature, is infinite and untraceable.[58]

There are two poles, then, to the problem Chrysostom wishes to address. The first pole is human reason itself. Chrysostom insists reason possesses a propensity for overstepping its limits, for asking the wrong questions, for prying into areas it is unequipped to understand adequately. The second pole is the character of God's providence, a providence that remains essentially "infinite and untraceable."

Chrysostom employs three principal word groups to describe the danger and futility of unbridled human reason, and we would do well to look at them in greater detail. Chrysostom usually links the first two word groups (*periergazō–polypragmoneō*) together, and when coupled in this fashion they most often have a negative connotation. Chrysostom enjoys using this word group to describe the disposition of those who want to understand God's providence, but on their own terms.[59] He warns: "It is precarious and absolutely insane to be unduly inquisitive [*polypragmonein*] and curious [*periergazesthai*] about the unutterable wisdom of God."[60] He condemns a curious mind that "shamelessly scrutinizes [*periergazesthai*] and concerns itself [*polypragmonein*] with the incomprehensible and ineffable providence of God."[61]

Instead of prying into things, the one seeking after a knowledge of God's providence should be like clay in the potter's hands, "following wherever the artist leads, not resisting, not prying into things [*mēde periergazomenon*]."[62] Again and again Chrysostom derides an exaggerated, inquisitive attitude as audacious, insane, obstinate, foolish, improper, mad, impudent, shameless, bold, inappropriate, ignorant, indiscrete, arrogant, ridiculous and curious.

A third word group that Chrysostom employs is derived from the root *skandal* and encompasses the verb *skandalizō* and the noun *skandalon*. It is the sense of *skandalizō–skandalon* as a shock, hindrance, stumbling-block or difficulty that is in the forefront of Chrysostom's thinking. Chrysostom specifically writes *On Providence* "to those troubled [*tous skandalizomenous*] by the lawless deeds of recent days."[63] His aim as a physician of souls is "is to heal not only one or two sick people, but all who are appalled [*skandalizomenous*] by the events occurring in the world."[64] In fact, the goal of *On Providence* is "to state the cause from which the scandal is generated" and to provide a framework for viewing God's providence that effectively overcomes the stumbling block providence presents at first glance. That is to say, Chrysostom aims to provide his readers with epistemological eyeglasses that enhance their ability to see and comprehend how God is at work in the world in this present age. He firmly believes that if he can get his audience thinking the right way, the stumbling block (*skandalon*) will be eliminated, even if the difficult events that caused his readers to stumble in the first place still occur.

The heart of humanity's struggle with God's providence, then, is found in the improper use of human reason. Chrysostom would not hesitate to say that reason's misuse is what creates the problem in the first place. In the realm of human suffering, providence and the incomprehensible nature of God, human reason must be employed, *but only in an appropriate, wise, humble and reverential manner.* Both because of reason's inherent limitations and weaknesses and because of the infinite and incomprehensible nature of God and his working throughout the created order, definite boundaries exist for the exercise of human reason. When these limits are transgressed, whether by refusing to accept the limitations of human reason or by ignoring or rejecting what God has revealed about his character and activity in Scripture or nature, the stumbling block of human suffering will again present itself.

Chrysostom preached a series of sermons against the Anomoean heresy in Antioch during the first year of his priesthood that illustrate well his later thoughts on the incomprehensibility of God's providence. The teaching Chrysostom opposed in Antioch appeared to be both simple and entirely logical. As Paul Harkins explains, the argument of the Anomoeans went something like this: (1) God is essentially simple and one, unbegotten and not produced. (2) Therefore, no being can be God who is begotten or produced. (3) The conclusion? The Son cannot be of the same, or of a similar, or even of a like substance with the Father, "but must be dissimilar and unlike *(anomoios)* God."[65]

The gist of Chrysostom's response to the Anomoeans is built on a series of biblical texts that emphasize the necessarily limited range and ability of human reason in its efforts to understand the divine nature and God's providence. Harkins summarizes the first homily as an apt description of "how meager and mediocre human knowledge is and what madness it is for men to pretend they possess the fullness of the knowledge of God since God is incomprehensible to both men and angels."[66]

The second homily in the series insists that the Anomoeans' quest for a complete knowledge of God betrays a lack of trust in God and an inquisitive, curious nature. In an argument similar to one we find in *On Providence,* Chrysostom calls on the listener to imitate the attitude of the apostle Paul in his unwillingness to pry into God's providence. Other homilies in the series emphasize God's condescension in accommodating himself to human nature as he reveals himself and note that, while such revelation is true, it is also incomplete.[67] Chrysostom minces no words:

When you hear this, do you not weep for yourself, do you not bury yourself in the earth because you have lifted yourself to such a pitch of madness that you are playing the busybody and striving to meddle with God? . . . Paul was a man filled with abundant wisdom. When he looked at the incomparable excellence of God and the worthlessness of human nature, he grew vexed with those who were meddling with the way God was governing the world and he was so deeply displeased that he said: "Man, who are you to answer God back?" Who are you? Ponder first your nature. In no way can anyone find a name which can express your nothingness.[68]

It is this clash between finite human reason and an infinite, incomprehensible God that we must examine in greater detail. In chapter two of *On Providence*, Chrysostom commences his attack against unbridled human reason, that is, "a curious mind preoccupied with vain questions, one that wants to understand all the causes of everything that comes to pass and to strive contentiously with the incomprehensible and ineffable providence of God."[69] Undisciplined human reason refuses to acknowledge that it is dealing "with a subject which in its very nature is infinite and untraceable."

Chrysostom presents the apostle Paul, by way of contrast, as an illustrious example of one who retreated before the incomprehensible.[70] Paul, too, desired to investigate the depth and wonder of God's providence but was "overcome by a kind of dizziness before the impossibility of ever explaining it."[71] Why? Chrysostom responds that we "lack the capability of reaching their end," the final end of God's purposes and actions. God's knowledge is "boundless," his judgments are "unsearchable," his ways are "inscrutable," his gift is "indescribable," and his peace "surpasses all understanding."[72]

Chrysostom does not sidestep or ignore reason. He does assert, however, that the quest for complete or full knowledge is "madness and folly," precisely because human reason is finite and inherently weak. It is not created with the ability to encompass or comprehend knowledge of an infinite nature.

For the prophets continually evoke all these figures of speech to illustrate the difference between human nature and the divine nature. They compete with one another in demonstrating the inferiority of our nature. But the one you expose to your insatiable curiosity is indestructible, unchanging, always exists and exists in the same manner, without beginning, without end, unfathomable, surpassing human thought, challenging false ideas, inexpressible, indescribable, incomprehensible, not only to me, you, prophets and apostles, but even to the powers above, who are pure, invisible, incorporeal, and dwell continuously in heaven.[73]

Once we acknowledge the finiteness and weakness of human reason, though, the door is opened for a greater receptivity to what God has chosen to reveal about himself. *God reveals himself to human reason, as human reason responds in faith.* Chrysostom explains, "Rather, you have received the greater part of the knowledge of these matters from above, because this knowledge is too immense to be grasped by your understanding."[74]

We see this same emphasis on a humble stance of faith before God's providence as the path to understanding in a sermon Chrysostom delivered at Antioch during the episcopate of Flavian, more than twenty years before he penned *On Providence*. As we respond in faith to the little we can comprehend, Chrysostom preaches, we gain a greater insight into the larger whole.

> And if any of the events which happen surpass our understanding, let us not from this consider that our affairs are not governed by providence, but perceiving His providence in part, in things incomprehensible let us yield to the unsearchableness of His wisdom. For if it is not possible for one not conversant with it to understand a man's art, much rather is it impossible for the human understanding to comprehend the infinity of the providence of God. . . . But nevertheless from small portions we gain a clear and manifest faith about the whole, we give thanks to him for all that happens.[75]

Chrysostom's reasoning and illustration is quite similar to the example of the physician he employs in chapter eight of *On Providence*. There he argues that his readers are willing to submit to the surgeon's knife and bitter prescriptions because they have a keen awareness of their own ignorance and inexperience in medical matters and of the surgeon's training and knowledge. Chrysostom's point is that if it is ridiculous for ignorant and inexperienced people to question the physician or artisan, it is even more foolish and arrogant "to seek after the why and wherefore of what has come to be, recognizing clearly that this wisdom is infallible, that his goodness is boundless, that his providence is inexpressible . . . and not to await the final outcome of all that comes to pass."[76] This key link between God's present activity and the final outcome of God's providence demands further exploration.

Understand the Present in Light of the Future

Our understanding of the present, Chrysostom argues, must always be coupled to our hope in Christ for the future. Instead of exercising our reason beyond its created limits in a futile attempt to probe the depths of God's providential actions, Chrysostom invites us to "await their final outcome."[77] He employs a number of illustrations to exhort his audience to "wait for the final outcome and consider how things will turn out. Don't be troubled or disturbed at the outset."[78]

> If people uninformed about the purification of metals should observe a goldsmith at work, would they not think the artisan was destroying his gold by mixing it with ashes and chaff? If someone born and raised on the ocean were suddenly transported to land and saw a farmer cultivating his land, casting seed into the muddy earth, wouldn't he think the wheat was soon to be destroyed? Wouldn't he pass judgment on the farmer for treating it in this way?[79]

The observer's reservations and misgivings, though, arise from "inexperience and folly," not "from the nature of what had been done." The inexperienced observer has issued "a premature opinion," without waiting for the final outcome of events. Chrysostom's conclusion is straightforward: "above all, stop meddling in the affairs of our common Master of all things. But if you are so contentious and bold as to act in such an insane fashion, *wait for the outcome of events*."[80]

If the farmer can wait an entire winter, focusing attention on the coming harvest and not on what the seed is suffering in the ground, so can believers learn to focus on the final outcome of their own time of cultivation in this present life. It is the final objective of glory in heaven that will provide the needed perspective toward God's work in our lives while we are on earth.

> That is to say, the plan of God has reference to the single outcome of each of these two lives, our salvation and our glory. If it is divided in two by time, it is united by the final objective. Therefore, when you see the Church scattered, suffering the most terrible trials, her most illustrious members persecuted and flogged, her leader carried away into exile, don't only consider these events, but also the things which have resulted: the rewards, the recompense, the awards for the athlete who wins in the games and the prizes won in the contest.[81]

Hence, Chrysostom's insistence on the qualitative difference between the infinite and finite reason is buttressed by his firm belief in God's love and goodness.

In addition, in the future God will resolve all unanswered questions and apparent or real injustices. Indeed, we can confidently submit to the framework God has created for reason's exercise because we know that God is infinitely loving and good and thus can be trusted. This trust, Chrysostom insists, must be exercised in the areas of life that at present remain blurred and inexplicable.

The boundaries for theological reflection on God's providence, then, are founded on God's character, a human response of trust to what God has already accomplished in nature and history and a continuing trust in what God promises to consummate in the future. Because we know that God loves us and acts in infinite goodness toward us, we can trust God in this present in-between time, between Christ's first and second coming.

We must also remember that God often acts providentially in light of long-term goals, goals often not discernible or apparent in the context of this life alone. In light of what we do know of God's character and future, we can bear our sufferings nobly and faithfully. As Chrysostom states in his exegesis of the story of the paralytic let down through the roof:

Knowing therefore that God is more tenderly loving than all physicians, do not inquire too curiously concerning His treatment nor demand an account of it from Him, but whether He is pleased to let us go free or whether He punishes, let us offer ourselves for either alike; for He seeks by means of each to lead us back to health, and to communion with Himself, and He knows our several needs, and what is expedient for each one, and who and in what manner we ought to be saved, and along what path He leads us. Let us then follow wherever He bids us, and let us not too carefully consider whether He commands us to go by a smooth and easy path, or by a difficult and rugged one.[82]

Hope for the future is for Chrysostom firmly grounded in God's love, a theme we must explore in some detail in our next chapter.

"It is a contest, this present life: if so, to fight is our business. It is war and battle.
In war one does not seek to have rest,
in war one does not seek to have dainty living, one is not anxious about riches,
one's care is not for a wife then. One thing only he looks at, how he may overcome his foes.
Be this our care likewise. If we overcome, and return with the victory,
God will give us all things. Let this alone be our study, how we may overcome the devil.
Yet after all, though we study, it is God's grace that does the whole business."

JOHN CHRYSOSTOM
Homilies on Acts

EIGHT

GOD'S WISE AND LOVING PROVIDENCE

God's Providence and the Love and Goodness of God

Perhaps some readers are bristling at the direction Chrysostom's thoughts on divine providence have taken us. Do Chrysostom's arguments and reflections really make the best sense out of the world's reality? Do they cogently provide a viable epistemological framework strong enough to lead us through the mystery of suffering and evil? Many modern discussions of the problem of providence and suffering follow an inductive approach. That is, we first inductively weigh the evidence—apart from prior presuppositions about what we should or should not encounter—and then make philosophical and theological decisions about the viability of traditional understandings of God's character and God's governance over creation and history. Modern realities and events such as Auschwitz seem *ipso facto* to refute an understanding of God as omnipotent and loving.

Chrysostom's approach takes the opposite methodological tack. It is deductive rather than inductive. He accepts by faith certain revelatory truths, whether found in nature, Scripture or history, as fundamental presuppositions for a correct understanding of providence. Among these fundamentals is God's love for humanity. Chrysostom contends that well-disposed people, that is, those who willingly place themselves within the context God has framed for understanding how God works, will recognize "not only his providence, but also his fervent love toward us" as they enter into the world of scriptural testimony.[1]

Chrysostom teaches that God's providence is neither mechanistic nor distant. "For he does not simply watch over us, but also loves us; he ardently loves us with an inexplicable love, with an impassible yet fervent, vigorous, genuine, indissoluble love, a love that is impossible to extinguish."[2]

God's impassibility and fervent love are not mutually exclusive. Rather, as G. L. Prestige explains, impassibility guarantees the consistency of all God's attitudes and actions toward humanity. While the passions that plague fallen people cause their love to weaken or disappear as circumstances change, God's transcendent, impassible nature remains above "the forces and passions such as commonly hold sway in the creation and among mankind."[3] Prestige writes:

> It is clear that impassibility means not that God is inactive or uninterested, not that He surveys existence with Epicurean impassivity from the shelter of a metaphysical insulation, but that His will is determined from within instead of being swayed from without. It safeguards the truth that the impulse alike in providential order and in redemption and sanctification comes from the will of God.[4]

Hence, Chrysostom readily describes God's love as both impassible and fervent. God has committed himself to act toward us in consistent, unchanging love. God longs for us to realize that whatever he does or allows to happen occurs within love's broader framework and that God's own changeless character makes it impossible for God to act in an unloving manner.

In Chrysostom's *Exhortation to Theodore After His Fall*, he highlights the pastoral implications of the distinction between changeable human passions and God's unchangeable tenderness. He writes:

> For if the wrath of God were a passion, one might well despair as being unable to quench the flame that he had kindled by so many evil doings; but since the Divine nature is passionless, even if He punishes, even if He takes vengeance, he does this not with wrath, but with *tender care, and much lovingkindness;* wherefore it behooves us to be of much good courage, and to trust in the power of repentance. . . . He acts with a view to our advantage, and to prevent our perverseness becoming worse by our making a practice of despising and neglecting Him.[5]

Chrysostom employs the example of parental love to make his point. He knows his readers, especially in the time of persecution they and he are now experiencing, will be tempted to feel abandoned by God. Could this actually be the case? Chrysostom notes that the prophets have already shown this to be an impossible scenario. For example, Isaiah wrote: "Can a woman forget her nursing child, or show no compassion for the child of her womb?" (Is 49:15). According to Chrysostom, the lesson to be learned is clear: "The prophet says this to make the point that just as a woman would not forget her own children, so neither would God forget humankind."[6]

Chrysostom exhorts his readers, however, not to limit their reflection to the level of the comparison. The interface between the human comparison and the love of God is insufficient in itself to communicate the incomparable reality of the divine love. We must immediately exercise our reason to move beyond. Thus he exhorts, "I have given these examples so that when I introduce other illustrations you wouldn't limit your thinking to the measure of what is spoken by the prophets, *but having this rule you should use your reason to go even further and see the unspeakable excess of the love of God.*"[7]

> Do you see how the degree of God's love exceeds that of a mother? In order that you might see how God's love super abundantly transcends the warm affection of a mother and the love of a father for their children. . . . As great as is the difference between light and darkness, between evil and goodness, so great is the difference between the goodness and providence of God in comparison to the tender love of a father.[8]

One senses Chrysostom's own frustration with the limitations of human language to express the divine reality. He knows the issue at hand is a strategic one. If he can convince his readers of God's love for them despite their painful and tragic circumstances, he will have paved the road for a clear and broad understanding of providence. If Chrysostom fails at this juncture, the other planks in his presentation will be irreparably damaged. To further make his case, Chrysostom refers to other illustrations drawn from Scripture.

David, for example, compares God's love to the distance between heaven and earth.[9] Hosea speaks of the care with which God communicates his distress over Israel's spiritual adultery, fearing that in some way he would grieve his beloved.[10] Jonah's distress over the gourd that withered in the sun is overshadowed by the depth of God's concern with the plight of the Ninevites.[11] Isaiah rebukes those who would question God's loving control of history.[12]

Chrysostom's purpose in referring to these key texts is to focus on one central affirmation: God loves humanity with an infinite, unchanging love, a love that "differs from all these [illustrations] as much as evil differs from goodness."[13] That is, "He speaks this way, not so you would think his love to be something human—I will not stop saying the same things over again—but that through these images you might discern the warmth, genuineness, excess, and fire of his love."[14]

We can derive a number of implications from Chrysostom's presentation for our understanding of God's providence, particularly in its relationship to suffering and evil. First and foremost, the love of God for us must be a primary interpretive grid for making sense of the empirical data of our lives. God allows sickness to strike or an accident to take place. Does this occurrence indicate that God does not love us, does not possess knowledge of the future or has lost control of history? No, Chrysostom insists. Because Chrysostom accepts by faith God's love as a fundamental datum for interpreting human experience, any interpretation we give to the data of our lives, no matter how inexplicable or harsh our circumstances might be, must be framed within the context dictated by divine love.

It is at this juncture, however, that confusion reigns supreme. Why? Largely because *our conception and judgment of how love and goodness would or should act in a given instance* is limited both by our scanty knowledge of the broader circumstances involved in any given event and by our general conception of love and goodness itself. The incomprehensibility of God's providence demands a humble epistemological disposition, as we have already seen. The events of our lives will always possess a certain inexplicable character because our knowledge of broader contexts, issues, events and personalities is extremely restricted.

A faulty conception of God's love and goodness poses a serious roadblock to our acceptance and praise of God's providence. To use a modern illustration quite similar to Chrysostom's perspective, C. S. Lewis warns against attaching a trivial conception to the word *love*. We do so, for example, when we equate love and kindness. Lewis explains:

> By Love, in this context, most of us mean kindness—the desire to see others than the self happy; not happy in this way or in that, but just happy. What would really

satisfy us would be a God who said of anything we happened to like doing, "What does it matter so long as they are contented?" We want, in fact, not so much a Father in heaven as a grandfather in heaven—a senile benevolence who, as they say, "liked to see young people enjoying themselves," and whose plan for the universe was simply that it might be truly said at the end of each day, "a good time was had by all."[15]

Much the same could be said of a misconceived notion of God's goodness. Frequently we ask the question in the midst of our suffering, How could a good God allow this to happen? Chrysostom would encourage us to answer our question in light of two further considerations: (1) *God has embraced our suffering in the incarnation of his Son,* an idea we will soon develop; and (2) the *final goal* God has in mind for his creation governs how divine goodness and mercy manifest themselves in corporate human history and in the narrative of individual lives.

If, as both Chrysostom and Lewis point out, all God's purposes and actions for humanity could be summed up in the phrase "human contentment," most of us would remain happy indeed. We long for a God who will meet our needs as we define them but who will also leave us alone, to ourselves and our own devices.

But this is exactly what the divine love refuses to do. God discerns our illness even though we believe we are healthy and will take whatever steps necessary to restore us to full health. These steps often involve pain, just as the lance of the surgeon's knife and the aftermath of the surgery entail suffering. The ultimate outcome of the pain suffered is the restoration of health with the eradication of sin's infection, the very goal God pursues in history through his providential actions.

Divine love, then, will often be a painful love, one Chrysostom describes as fiery, precisely because the disease love is acting to heal can only be conquered through pain and death. Hence, the incarnation and cross serve as fundamental paradigms for interpreting how God's love and goodness are presently operative in history.[16]

Because he was not satisfied with the instruction from nature which brings the knowledge of God—since many people out of their own ignorance derived no benefit from this—he opened up other pathways to this knowledge; at last he accomplished the foremost of his kindnesses. He sent his own Son.[17]

The Incarnation, the Cross and God's Providence

What are the significant components of Chrysostom's understanding of the incarnation and cross of Christ *as they relate to his overall comprehension of providence and human suffering?* Chrysostom emphasizes that God in Christ has willingly and deliberately identified with humanity in our sufferings and *has experienced these sufferings as his own.* Thus he writes "The one who is of the same nature as God becomes what I am."[18] He adds, "For he himself passed through all these things and shared in them with you."[19] Chrysostom plainly considers this to be a foundational truth and emphasizes it in his attack against such groups as the Manichaeans, who undercut the reality of the incarnation.

> Just as He hungered, as He slept, as He felt fatigue, as He ate and drank, so also did He deprecate death, thereby *manifesting his humanity, and that infirmity of human nature which does not submit without pain to be torn from this present life.* For had He not uttered any of these things, it might have been said that if He were a man He ought to have experienced human feelings. And what are these? In the case of one about to be crucified, fear and agony, and pain in being torn from the present life: for a sense of the charm which surrounds present things is implanted in human nature: on this account wishing to prove the reality of the fleshly clothing, and to give assurance of the incarnation He manifests the actual feelings of man with full demonstration.[20]

We should be careful to note that Chrysostom realizes that a fear of death is a natural and fitting human response. He points to Christ's suffering in Gethsemane, observing that this

> greatly shows His humanity, and a nature unwilling to die, but clinging to this present life, and proving that He was not exempt from human feelings. For as it is no blame to be hungry, or to sleep, so neither is it to desire the present life; and Christ indeed had a body pure from sin, yet not free from natural wants, for then it would not have been a body.[21]

Two immediate implications can be drawn. First, Christ will never ask his disciples to endure something he has not first undergone himself. Indeed, because Christ has already walked this path, we can know we will finish the journey ourselves. Second, fellowship with Christ and suffering with Christ are mutually intertwined. For the Christian, Chrysostom avers, suffering is not a sign of God's rejection but rather an invitation to fellowship as God refines our character.

> But whoso is in affliction and temptation, this man stands near to Him, whoso is journeying on the narrow way. *For He Himself trode this; whence too He says, "the* Son of Man has no where to lay His head." *So then grieve not when you are in affliction; considering with Whom you have fellowship, and how you are purified by trials, and what great gain is yours.*[22]

Augustine likewise emphasizes the interconnection between Christ's sufferings and our own, focusing on the reality of the mystical fellowship between Christ and his body. In his commentary on Psalm 62 Augustine writes:

> For whatever he has suffered we too have suffered with him and what we suffer he too suffers with us. If the head suffers in any way, how can the hand assert that it does not suffer? If the hand suffers, how can the head say that it does not suffer? If the foot feels something, how can the head say that it does not feel it too? . . . Whatever his Church suffers by way of this life's tribulations, temptations, constrictions and deprivations (for we must be schooled to be purified like gold in the fire), this he also suffers.[23]

Fellowship with Christ in our sufferings not only leads to encouragement but also trains us how to respond to adverse circumstances, especially as we imitate Christ's own responses. Thus Chrysostom writes, "For he himself passed through all these things and shared in them with you . . . *training and teaching you* not to be anxious about any of these trials."[24] Again, Christ died on the cross "that you might learn endurance, that you might be trained in patience, that none of the things of the present life might distress you."[25]

The apostle Paul's life demonstrates the same pattern of suffering, fellowship, imitation and courage. Chrysostom writes:

> Do you see the courage? Do you recognize the boldness? Do you perceive the spiritual perspective of a Christian? The Philippians saw their teacher in prison, wrapped in chains, throttled, hit hard, and suffering a thousand hardships; not only were they not shocked or troubled, but they acquired an even greater zeal. The sufferings of their teacher fueled their own progress in the conflict.[26]

A great reversal occurs in the light of Christ's incarnation and cross. Circumstances and actions his disciples might normally scorn and reject are instead welcomed, patterned and emulated. Chrysostom develops this theme in his *Homilies on the Statues* when he states that though Paul's chains were made of iron "they contained the grace of the Spirit." Though objects such as chains and crosses were once thought to be abominations, they have now become "symbols of salvation." Those means which were thought to be vehicles of death and destruction turn out to be avenues by which the grace of God is "kindled."[27] In his commentary on Philippians 1:18, Chrysostom adds, "For not so splendid does the diadem make a royal head, as the chain his hands; not owing to their proper nature, but owing to the grace that darted brightness on them."[28]

Chrysostom delights in the way the cross and incarnation have turned the world upside down. At first glance, the cross seems to offer and communicate nothing but disaster: "for the Cross has not merely no appearance of being a sign sought out by reasoning, but even the very annihilation of a sign;—is not merely deemed no proof of power, but a conviction of weakness;—not merely no display of wisdom, but a suggestion of foolishness."[29]

Yet, as Chrysostom teaches in his homilies on 2 Timothy, *the cause* of our suffering and its ultimate goal play a key role in the value reversal the Christian's suffering represents. When the Christian's suffering is viewed through the prism of the cross, our perspective is dramatically altered.

> For in themselves death and imprisonment and chains are matters of shame and reproach. *But when the cause is added before us, and the mystery viewed aright*, they will appear full of dignity, and matter for boasting. For it was [Christ's] death which saved the world, when it was perishing. That death connected earth with heaven, that death destroyed the power of the devil and made men angels, and sons of God: that death raised our nature to the kingly throne.[30]

Out of seeming defeat, disgrace, suffering and the reality of death comes unimaginable victory. In chapter eight of *On Providence*, a key chapter in Chrysostom's teaching on the great reversal of the incarnation and cross, he develops first the suffering Christ endured on our behalf and then the surprising and unexpected fruit his suffering and death produced.

Christ was "nailed to a high cross, bound, thrashed with sticks, struck on the face, ridiculed, buried through kindness, and seals were placed upon his tomb."[31] The story seems over—yet through what had appeared to be unmitigated tragedy and injustice humanity and creation itself are healed. The sovereignty of sin is broken, the citadel of the devil demolished, the cords of death cut, heaven's gates opened, the curse overturned, the Holy Spirit sent, apostles chosen and commissioned and an entirely new way of life introduced on earth.[32]

It is essential that we grasp the centrality of the cross in Chrysostom's thought as a fundamental interpretive paradigm for understanding God's broader work in providence.[33] In the cross all the major themes of Chrysostom's presentation intersect. For example, Chrysostom's stress on the role of disposition in discerning God's providence is illustrated in the different responses of people to the crucifixion of Jesus. On the one hand, "How many stumbled over the cross of our Master—a cross shared by all of us—and became even more lawless and insolent?"[34] The crowd surrounding the cross judged by appearances. Only if Christ delivered himself from these sufferings would they believe. *Because they lacked the disposition to see God at work, they misinterpreted his greatest act on their behalf.*

The believing thief, on the other hand, was lifted beyond mere human speculations "by the winds of faith." He meditated "on the things of the future," confessed his sin and pondered the resurrection. This broader perspective, Chrysostom contends, was the fruit of a teachable and humble disposition formed by the thief's response to the grace of God. God's grace gave him eyes to see and ears to hear the message represented in the cross as he himself died an excruciating death.

> You see, then, that the senseless and negligent gain nothing from the things which are beneficial. Those, however, who have a right disposition and are vigilant derive a tremendous profit from those things which scandalize others.[35]

A vigilant and humble disposition is intimately linked to an awareness that nothing in this world can harm the person who is joined to the realities Christ has introduced into history through his death and resurrection. The stumbling block of the cross "does not arise from the nature of the cross, but rather from the folly of those who are scandalized."[36]

What *appeared* to be the greatest tragedy in the history of the world *was actually* the most blessed event. If so, Christians can view the circumstances of their lives, however painful, in a new light. For Chrysostom, reality rather than appearance is the heart of the matter. Thus the cross is "the foremost good, . . . a proof of

God's great providence, goodness, and love."[37] The paradigm of the cross becomes the pattern according to which Christians are called to mold their own understanding of God's providence at work in their lives. In addition, only life lived in the shadow of the cross will enable us to see God's love and goodness in this present evil age.

The Hope of the Future and the Life of the Present

Chrysostom would be quick to add, however, that we must interpret our present situation in light of God's ultimate goal for human history. We must view the *present* in light of the *final end*. Consequently, premature opinions and judgments must be avoided.

Chrysostom's understanding of providence is unashamedly founded on the principle that the purpose and goal of human life surpasses our present experience. In fact, he speaks of God's plan as having reference to "each of these two lives, our salvation and our glory. If it is divided in two by time, it is united by the final objective."[38] Chrysostom believes this division between the present and the future provides an essential grid for any adequate understanding of providence and its relationship to human affairs.

First, Chrysostom contends that human knowledge *in its present state* is drastically limited. At present, as Paul writes, "Anyone who claims to know something does not yet have the necessary knowledge" (1 Cor 8:2). Chrysostom explains that Paul "goes on to demonstrate that our present knowledge is grossly deficient and that complete knowledge is reserved for the age to come. Only a very small amount has been given to us at the present time."[39] Granted, when "the complete comes, the partial will come to an end" (1 Cor 13:10), but until that time "the distance between this present knowledge and that of the future" will remain great. Much is still to be revealed.[40]

God, however, has not left humanity in the lurch. What he has already accomplished in history and what he promises to consummate in the future provide us with a sufficient, though incomplete, knowledge that should both assuage our fears and curb our inquisitiveness. Chrysostom advises, "Therefore, recognizing all the things through which he has revealed himself, *through which he has acted and will act*, don't indiscreetly inquire into things, nor be unduly concerned."[41]

On the one hand, we have the inscrutable side of God's wisdom and providence, an aspect Chrysostom describes as "indescribable," "ineffable, inexpressible, and incomprehensible."[42] On the other hand, the incomprehensibility of God's providence does not cloud either its wonder or its promise for the future. God's character and promise are the guarantee "that in every circumstance all things that come to us from him have a favorable outcome—provided that our own activities don't get in the way."[43] The prudent and wise course is to await the final outcome of events.

> Above all, one should not inquire too inquisitively, neither at the beginning of events nor at their conclusion. But if you are so curious and unduly inquisitive, wait for the final outcome and consider how things will turn out. Don't be troubled or disturbed at the outset.[44]

The Example of Abraham and Joseph

Chrysostom argues that both Abraham and Joseph illustrate wisdom's response to God's providence. The connection between Abraham and Joseph is their perspective on *both the resourcefulness of God and the time framework for his work.* Abraham "understood the nature of the promise of God, its resourcefulness and richness, that it is not hindered by the laws of nature, nor the inherent difficulty of circumstances."[45] Abraham's humble and receptive disposition, vibrant faith and broad perspective enabled him to see God at work, even when adverse events occurred or God gave commands that appeared contrary to earlier promises. He glorified God by not worrying unduly "about the how and wherefore of the promise" and instead yielded "to the incomprehensibility of his providence."[46]

Abraham knew that God possesses the power to fulfill the promise in the future, even if present circumstances seemed dark and inexplicable. Chrysostom writes:

> Instead, [Abraham] again fled for refuge to the power of the one who made the promise—a power that is indescribable, resourceful, ingenious, a power that manifests itself in contrary circumstances, is mightier than any opposition, is not limited by the laws of nature, and admits no obstacle.[47]

If Abraham had been unable to wait for the final outcome of events, if he had insisted on curiously demanding an explanation from God whenever he could not figure out the rationale for God's actions, "his faith would soon have been crippled."[48] Instead, Abraham "regarded 'invisible things' as much more clear than 'visible things' because of the promise of God. This was evidence of a fully devoted faith."[49]

Joseph reflects the same pattern. Again, "the events which were occurring after the visions were contrary to the dreams" Joseph had experienced, dreams predicting his future elevation over his brothers.[50] Joseph, however, waited in faith for the fulfillment of the promise. He awaited "the final outcome of events, knowing full well the resourcefulness of God and the ingenuity of his wisdom."[51]

The continuity of Chrysostom's thought concerning providence and hope for the future is remarkable. In his *Homilies on the Statues*, composed while Chrysostom was still a resident of Antioch, he writes: "For this too is a thing in which it behooves the Christian to differ from the unbelievers, the bearing all things nobly, and *through hope of the future*, soaring above the attack of human evils."[52] "He who is nourished with good hopes," Chrysostom insists, "*and is confident respecting things to come*, has already tasted of the kingdom! For nothing ordinarily so repairs the soul, and makes a person better, as a good hope of things to come."[53]

Chrysostom does more, however, than simply link epistemology to eschatology. He is utterly convinced of the reality of future rewards and punishment and freely incorporates the actuality of heaven and hell into his understanding of providence. Faithfulness in this life, especially in the midst of adverse circumstances, will be richly rewarded. Even though God's providence remains in many ways incomprehensible and inexpressible, so too is the blessedness in store for the future. He explains, "For your sake, Friend, he prepared a kingdom; for your sake indescribable good things, that portion which is in heaven, distinctive and manifold dwelling places, that blessedness which cannot be adequately spelled out by any human expression."[54]

One cannot express too strongly that Chrysostom's overall argument will remain inexplicable to his audience unless his conviction regarding the hope of the future is treated with seriousness. As a pastor Chrysostom has witnessed the scattering of his flock and experienced tremendous personal suffering. His life is drawing to a close. Soon he will die in exile. He is not writing about suffering from the secure enclosure of an ivory tower. It is in the midst of these crucial junctures of life's testing, in Chrysostom's case, junctures laced with deep personal suffering, that an individual's bedrock convictions become apparent. Hence, Chrysostom's insistence on the future as an integral aspect of making sense of providence and suffering becomes even more significant. Against this backdrop he writes:

> Therefore, when you see the church scattered, suffering the most terrible trials, her most illustrious members persecuted and flogged, her leader [Chrysostom] carried away into exile, *don't only consider these events, but also the things which have resulted: the rewards, the recompense, the awards of the athlete who wins in the games and the prizes won in the contest.*[55]

In many ways Chrysostom is echoing Paul's words in 1 Corinthians 15. There Paul contends that "If for this life only we have hoped in Christ, we are of all people most to be pitied" (1 Cor 15:19).[56] Indeed, "If the dead are not raised, 'Let us eat and drink, for tomorrow we die' " (1 Cor 15:32). Chrysostom makes much the same point in his homilies on 1 Thessalonians:

> Unless future things had somewhat excited us, unless we had been persuaded that there is a good hope, our suffering would have produced little liveliness in us. For who would have chosen for the sake of what we have to endure in this present life so many sufferings, a life of anxiety, one full of dangers?[57]

Our perception of God's providence will remain clouded, though, as long as we live as though this present life encompasses all of reality and believe that final fulfillment and deliverance from suffering must come now if it is to come at all. "There is nothing we refuse to undergo" in order to obtain honor in his life, Chrysostom preaches in his homilies on Colossians. We are reluctant to invest in the future, he argues, largely because we hold it in little esteem.[58] This shrunken perspective surely turns reality upside down for the Christian. A perspective shaped by future hope, Chrysostom believes, must dictate how we interpret and respond to our present circumstances.

The Reality of Future Judgment

Rewards and the life of heaven are not the only aspects of the future that influence Chrysostom's thought. He also has a keen awareness of future judgment and punishment. While those who suffer in this life "are beloved, praised, admired, proclaimed, and crowned by those who know them and those who

don't," those guilty of persecuting and plotting against Christ's church face certain judgment. They are like wild, unreasoning beasts who, even though they
have received a death blow, continue to thrash about savagely. Their conscience,
however, remains intact, convicting them of their evil deeds and leaving them
trembling and fearful.[59] Not only does the conscience of the wicked bear witness
against them, but other people "accuse them, reproach them, convict them, dishonor them, curse them with countless imprecations, and long to see them in
punishment and retribution."[60]

Chrysostom sees this process at work in the relationship between Herod and
John the Baptist. A first glance might leave one with the impression that Herod tri-
umphed. He had beheaded John, seemingly removing his tormentor. The coast
seemed clear to marry his brother's wife, Herodias. Yet Chrysostom asks, "Who is
the one who is blessed by all? Who is the one who arouses our envy? Who is proclaimed? Who is crowned? Who is lauded? Who is praised?"[61] John, even though
his journey on earth had drawn to a close, still lives in heaven and in the praises of
the church. Indeed, "does not one shout every day in the church: 'It is not lawful for
you to have the wife of Philip your brother'?"[62] Herod, on the other hand, was
denounced in his own lifetime and in the memory of the church from that point on.
His conscience also bore constant witness against his evil actions.

> As for John, he immediately inspired fear in Herod after his murder—*for fear was
> disturbing his conscience* to such an extent that he believed John had been raised from
> the dead and was performing miracles—and in our own day and through all suc-
> ceeding time, throughout all the world John refutes him through himself and
> through others.[63]

As for John the Baptist, he escaped harm, "for what occurred was not a death,
but a crown, not an end, but the beginning of a greater life."[64] Herod, on the other
hand, met a dreary end and awaits final judgment before God's tribunal. Not
only he, but all who have struggled against God's kingdom, face a fearful future.
The lesson for Chrysostom is clear:

> But what kind of account should one present of things above? If one who has
> caused only a single person to stumble is sentenced to such a severe punishment
> that it would have been better for a millstone to be hung around his neck and cast
> into the sea, contemplate how great a punishment these will suffer before that fear-

ful tribunal, how great a retribution they will submit to—those who did everything within their power to trouble the whole world, who overturned so many churches, who warred against so great a peace, who laid countless stumbling blocks everywhere.[65]

Chrysostom takes the reality of hell seriously and minces no words in describing its horror. In his homilies on Romans, for example, he urges his listeners to make hell a frequent topic of conversation. Hell's reality, Chrysostom argues, will make the pains and evils of this present world seem a small thing and the world's problems and pleasures mere trifles. Viewed in this light, "what would you tell me was an evil? Poverty? Disease? Captivity? Maiming of the body? Why all these things are sport compared to the punishment there."[66]

Chrysostom's view of the future, then, clearly influences his attitude toward the events of this present life and God's providential control of history. He knows his readers are in danger of losing heart. The church has been scattered. Persecution is rampant. Families are breaking apart. Only a perspective that includes the future within its boundaries will be broad enough to encompass these trying times without breaking under their pressure. As Chrysostom explains:

> The true life and the trustworthy and unchanging realities await us in the future. For the circumstances and events of the present life have the character of a journey, but the realities of the future life await us in our true homeland.[67]

The Perspective of the Pilgrim

If this is indeed true, if this present life is a journey, if God's goal for us reaches fulfillment in a life we have yet to experience, what are the lessons God is trying to teach us now? The character of God's providence and of our own experience and circumstances will become clearer as we delve deeper into the nature of our present time. That is to say, *our expectations for how God's providence will manifest itself in our lives must be predicated on God's goals for this present in-between time, not on our own.* Pilgrims on a journey will view and interpret the terrain differently than settlers who are striving to set up a permanent residence. Attitudes toward trials, priorities, possessions and even time will all be affected accordingly.

Chrysostom can be devastatingly practical in his insistence that pilgrims must travel light in their journey toward home. In his homilies on Ephesians, for example, Chrysostom reflects on the foolishness of making a large house the center of one's dreams, at least if the believer is a pilgrim rather than a settler.

> But as to us, let us not be insatiable. . . . let us not be seeking out for splendid houses; for we are on our pilgrimage, not at home; so that if there be any that knows that the present life is a sort of journey, and expedition, and, as one might say, it is what they call an entrenched camp, he will not be seeking for splendid buildings. For who, tell me, be he ever so rich, would choose to build a splendid house in an encampment? . . . The present life is nothing else than a march and an encampment.[68]

Chrysostom insists that the lay of the land appears differently to a pilgrim than to a settler. The same can be said of the pilgrim's perspective toward the pain and hardship the journey homeward inevitably entails.

> We are strangers and sojourners. Let us not grieve over any of the world's painful things. For if you come from a renowned country and from illustrious ancestors, and find yourself in a distant land, known to no one, having neither servants nor wealth, and then someone insults you, would you grieve as though these things had taken place at home? The knowledge that you were in a strange and foreign land would persuade you to bear all easily, and to despise hunger, thirst, and any suffering. So consider that you are a stranger and pilgrim, and do not let anything bother you in foreign territory. You have a city whose builder and creator is God, and the journey is but for a short and little time. Let whoever wishes strike, insult, revile. We are in foreign territory, and live there in difficulty.[69]

Chrysostom echoes much the same sentiment in his *Homilies on the Statues:*

> If you are a Christian, no earthly city is yours. . . . Though we may gain possession of the whole world, we are nonetheless strangers and sojourners in it all! We are enrolled in heaven: our citizenship is there! Let us not, after the manner of little children, despise things that are great, and admire those which are little![70]

For the present time, Christ has called us to adopt the life of the traveler, but he promises to accompany us on our journey as a fellow voyager and exile. Chrysostom comments that Ignatius understood this truth better than the devil. "The Devil," Chrysostom writes, did not know that Ignatius had "Jesus with him, as a fellow traveller, and fellow exile on so long a journey, [and] he [Ignatius] rather became the stronger, and afforded more proof of the power that was with him, and to a greater degree knit the Churches together."[71]

Though we might well encounter difficulties on the road to our final destination, Chrysostom insists it is the person who tries to set up permanent residence in this present evil age who ultimately experiences disaster. Shadrach, Meshach and Abednego, for example, were carried off to a foreign land and yet "were not harmed at all," while "those who remained in their homes, enjoying all the good things of their homeland, stumbled and were condemned."[72]

The Rhyme and Reason of Our Present Trials

Chrysostom rightly insists that God's permitting of life's abundant trials will remain inexplicable *if we ignore or misunderstand God's purpose in allowing trials*. Why might God allow so many trials and apparent snares for his children? Chrysostom responds: "The present life is a wrestling school, a gymnasium, a battle, a smelting furnace, and a dyer's house of virtue."[73] Chrysostom frequently employs this group of metaphors to illustrate his fundamental conviction that God is presently at work transforming "the soul into a serviceable condition for virtue." He writes:

> Desiring to transform the soul into a serviceable condition for virtue, God works it, melts it, and delivers it over to the testing of trials, in order to strengthen those who have lost heart and who have let themselves go, in order that those who have already been tested might be even more approved and unconquered by the plots of the demons and the snares of the devil, completely worthy for the reception of the good things to come.[74]

In order to understand Chrysostom's thought, we must examine each key metaphor in greater detail. First, Chrysostom writes that the present life is a smelting furnace. How so? A smelting furnace purifies metals by burning away impurities and so leaving only the valued gold. In the same way, God is active to create "steadfast and patiently enduring people" and does so by allowing the coinage of their lives "to be tried by every means."[75]

Chrysostom specifically mentions how his own sufferings and those of his followers function as a kind of spiritual boot camp. Before these difficult times, many of his flock were addicted to the theatre, horse races and the dissolute practices that accompanied these diversions. The flame of persecution, "the fervent heat of a raging fire," purified them, bringing them to their senses and gathering "such wealth, such gain, such profit" into the church.[76]

The example of the paralytic healed by Jesus illustrates this process. God allowed the man to suffer for an extended period, not out of negligence or cruelty, but rather as "a sign of the greatest care for his welfare." As Chrysostom explains:

> For as a gold refiner having cast a piece of gold into the furnace allows it to be proved by the fire until such time as he sees it has become purer: even so God permits the souls of men to be tested by troubles until they become pure and transparent and have reaped much profit from this process of sifting; wherefore this is the greatest species of benefit.[77]

We can be assured, Chrysostom believes, that God knows how long the metal must remain in the fire to be thoroughly cleansed. He will not allow it to remain in the fire "until it is destroyed and burnt up." Hence, we can know in the midst of our trials that "when He sees that we have become more pure, He releases us from our trials so that we may not be overthrown and cast down by the multiplication of our evils."[78]

Chrysostom usually speaks of *gold* being refined in the furnace. In his *Homilies on the Statues*, however, he speaks of God burning away *rust* on the soul.

> For just as in the case of rusted implements, he that rubs them only with water, though he spend a long time on them, will not rid them of all that foulness; but he that puts them in a furnace, will make them presently brighter than even those newly fabricated: so too, a soul, stained with the rust of sin, if it cleanse itself slightly, and in a negligent way, and be every day repenting, will gain no further advantage. But if it cast itself into the furnace, as it were, of the fear of God, it will in a very short time purge all away.[79]

Chrysostom also employs the furnace/flame metaphor to illustrate two other aspects of the spiritual life. First, he pictures flames as the heat of virtue itself. Potiphar's infuriated and frustrated wife, for instance, accused, slandered and imprisoned Joseph. Her efforts to harm him, however, were futile. The trials she instigated were simply like chaff thrown on the coals of Joseph's virtue. The coals might at first be covered, but in actuality they are being kindled to an even higher intensity. As Chrysostom puts it, "so virtue, when it seems to be mistreated, later flowers to an even greater degree through the very obstacles themselves, reaching to heaven itself."[80]

Second, as a smelter's furnace purifies, it also separates. In the same way persecution and trials serve to separate the true believer from the mere pretender. Many in the church had "clothed themselves in a mask of piety." However, the sudden rush of persecution had cleansed their sham away "like water" to disclose "what they really were."

> Now this is no small thing. Rather it is of considerable importance for the utility of those who are willing to pay heed, both for the discerning of those who have skins of sheep and for avoiding the mixture of wolves who conceal themselves as sheep with those who really are such. *For this present time has become a furnace for distinguishing those pieces of money containing bronze by melting down the lead, burning up the residue, and rendering the precious material even more precious.*[81]

Chrysostom also frequently employs athletic metaphors to illustrate God's providence and the process of spiritual formation. Two of his favorites are the present life as a wrestling school and gymnasium.[82]

Through athletic metaphors Chrysostom teaches that life in this world is a training camp where the spiritual athlete is coached to respond in a virtuous manner to whatever God in his providence allows to occur, including the attack of the devil. However, a lack of preparation and training will guarantee defeat at the time of the true contest. Indeed, Chrysostom compares the thirty-day preparation period of catechumens to a wrestling school in which they are momentarily separated from the dangers of life for a time of intense training. He explains to his catechumens that their present training, difficult as it is, will prepare them for future spiritual contests and battles.

> For in the wrestling schools falls of the athletes are devoid of danger. For the wrestling is with friends, and they practice all their exercises on the persons of their teachers. . . . So then, in your case these thirty days are like some wrestling school, both for exercise and for practice: let us learn from thence already to get the better of that evil demon.[83]

The Christian does not need to fear the evil one. Rather, Chrysostom argues, the trained athlete can expect to triumph. Moreover, preventing the devil from attacking would be to rob prepared athletes of the chance to display their power and receive the victor's crown, as Chrysostom points out:

If the antagonist were taken away he who overcomes is thereby injured. For if you let the adversary remain, those who are lazy are injured, not on account of the more diligent, but by their own laziness; whereas if you take away the antagonist, the more diligent are betrayed on account of those who are lazy, and neither can display their own power, nor win crowns.[84]

The disciplines of the spiritual life are an integral part of this training process. Thus in his homilies on the Acts of the Apostles Chrysostom states:

If through study and practice we can throttle into submission even elephants and wild horses, much more the passions within us. . . . We have never practised this art: never in a time of leisure when there is no contest, talked over with ourselves what shall be useful for us. We are never to be seen in our place on the chariot, until the time for the contest is actually come. Hence the ridiculous figure we make there.[85]

To avoid unpreparedness for the trials and battles of the present age, Chrysostom recommends a discipline such as self-denial:

If now it should happen, as I pray it may not happen nor at any time fall out, that there be a war against churches, and a persecution, imagine how great will be the ridicule, how sore the reproaches. And very naturally; for when no one exercises himself in the wrestling school, how shall he be distinguished in the contests? . . . Do you not see those called Pentathletes, when they have no opponents, how they fill a sack with much sand, and hanging it up try their full strength against it? . . . Emulate these, and practice the wrestlings of self-denial. For, indeed, there are many that provoke to anger, and incite to lust, and kindle a great flame. Stand, therefore, against your passions, bear nobly the mental pangs, that you may endure also those of the body.[86]

Chrysostom's premonition of future persecution was fulfilled in the last years of his life, and it was precisely those Christians who were prepared and trained who stood firm in their sufferings. Chrysostom calls those well-trained Christians who faithfully endured prison, abuse and even execution "these extraordinary spiritual athletes" who had been coached and prepared by the master trainer.[87]

Chrysostom exhorts his readers, though, not to focus only on the recent persecutions but also on "the things which have resulted: the rewards, the recompense, *the awards for the athlete who wins in the games and the prizes won in the contest*."[88]

If God did not permit trials, such as the conflagration the spiritual athletes Shadrach, Meshach and Abednego endured, "there would not have been such a radiant recompense, nor such a brilliant crown."[89]

Another favorite metaphor Chrysostom uses is that of the spiritual life as combat or battle. He praises the martyrs because they had prepared themselves for battle and willingly died in the struggle.[90] Through their deaths they provided an example for others, "training men and women for the battles of the Christian life."[91] Chrysostom is quick to observe that not only men but also women and children are involved in this fight to the death, often showing "greater bravery than men."[92]

Athanasius makes the same point in his discussion of the inspiration Christ's victory over the devil has given to his followers:

> But when they are gone over to Christ's faith and teaching, their contempt for death is so great that they even eagerly rush upon it, and become witnesses for the Resurrection the Savior has accomplished against death. For while still tender in years they make haste to die, and not men only, but women also, exercise them-selves by bodily discipline against it.[93]

The dedicated Christian can expect conflict because of the devil's opposition to God's kingdom and its extension in this world. Satan specifically attacks those whom he sees responding to God. Just as pirates and thieves ignore "chaff and hay, or sand" but are quick to plunder "gold and pearls," so "in like manner when the devil sees the wealth of the soul gathered together and an abundance of piety increased, *it is there he gets down to work and plies his machinations*."[94]

Those who through careful training for battle have acquired an alert disposi-tion are aware of the devil's wiles and through the victory of Christ are protected from the harm the devil attempts to inflict on the unwary or unprepared. In his homilies on Acts Chrysostom states:

> It is a contest, this present life: if so, to fight is our business. It is war and battle. In war one does not seek to have rest, in war one does not seek to have dainty living, one is not anxious about riches, one's care is not for a wife then. One thing only he looks at, how he may overcome his foes. Be this our care likewise. If we overcome, and return with the victory, God will give us all things. Let this alone be our study, how we may overcome the devil. Yet after all, though we study, it is God's grace that does the whole business.[95]

As the devil's schemes are defeated, they actually become a means God uses to develop and mature the character of believers, thereby magnifying the church's ministry in the world.

> Nevertheless, though the devil had set so many traps, not only did he not shake the church, but instead he made her more brilliant. For during the period when she was not troubled she did not teach the world as effectively as she now does to be patient, to practice self-restraint, to bear trials, to demonstrate steadfast endurance, to scorn the things of the present life, to pay no regard to riches, to laugh at honor, to pay no heed to death, to think lightly of life, to abandon homeland, households, friends, and close relations, to be prepared for all kinds of wounds, to throw oneself against the swords, to consider all the illustrious things of the present life—I am speaking of honor, glories, power, and luxury—as more fragile than the flowers of springtime.[96]

This extended passage captures well Chrysostom's overall perspective on this present world as an arena God uses to shape our character. The present life is a smelting furnace, a wrestling school, a gymnasium, and a battleground, *specifically because we are unfinished products, works of art* that God is molding through the trials and various adverse circumstances he allows to enter our lives in his gracious providence.

Finally, Chrysostom compares the life of the Christian in the present time to a "dyer's house of virtue." The hides to be stained are initially unfit for the reception of the dye and must be worked vigorously by the tanners to bring out the valued color.[97] Or, Chrysostom suggests, picture this life as winter rather than summer. Wise farmers wait for winter to pass, knowing that the germination of the seed during this harsh season is absolutely necessary. The farmer focuses attention, not "on what the wheat suffers during the season of cold," but rather on what is soon to be obtained.[98]

Likewise, in speaking to the people of Antioch during the crisis of the statues, Chrysostom describes such times as a winter of the soul:

> And this may be observed, not only among human beings, but even with the very seeds; for where we expect the ear of corn to spring and flourish, there must be much rain, much gathering of the clouds, and much frost; and the time of sowing is also a rainy season. *Since therefore the winter, a winter not of the elements, but of souls, has now set in, let us too sow in this winter that we may reap in the summer; let us sow tears, that we may reap gladness.*[99]

God does not leave us alone in life's struggles and trials, however, but has willingly entered into the arena with us, in the incarnation of the Son becoming what we are, identifying with us in our suffering, providing us with an example of how to respond to our trials and supplying us with the essential supernatural power we need to triumph in the gift of the Holy Spirit.

> For he himself passed through all these things and shared in them with you; he surpassingly conquered all of these things, training and teaching you not to be anxious about any of these trials. Still, he was not satisfied only with this, but *having returned to heaven he freely gave the indescribable gift of the Holy Spirit* and sent the apostles to minister as his servants.[100]

It is the grace of the Holy Spirit that teaches us that our trials and sufferings are permitted to take place so that the truth of the gospel might shine more brightly, in our own lives and to the unbelieving world around us.[101] The Spirit is, indeed, the oil the divine trainer applies liberally to his athlete, ensuring triumph over all enemies and a lasting crown in heaven.[102]

"We have learned the plan of our salvation from no one else other than
from those through whom the gospel has come down to us.
For they did at one time proclaim the gospel in public.
And, at a later period, by the will of God, they handed the gospel down to us
in the Scriptures—to be 'the ground and pillar of our faith.'"
IRENAEUS
Against Heresies

"When, however, the Gnostics are confuted from the Scriptures,
they turn round and accuse these same Scriptures
as if they were not correct, nor of authority. They say that they are ambiguous,
and that the truth cannot be extracted from them
by those who are ignorant of tradition. . . . But, again,
when we refer them to that tradition which originates from the apostles
. . . they object to tradition."
IRENAEUS
Against Heresies

"A sound mind . . . that is devoted to piety and love of truth
will eagerly meditate upon those things that God has placed within the power of mankind
and has subjected to our knowledge. . . . Such a mind will advance in the knowledge
of those things . . . by means of daily study.
I am referring to those things that fall under our observation
and are clearly and unambiguously set forth in the sacred Scriptures in clear terms."
IRENAEUS
Against Heresies

NINE

THE SACRED
SCRIPTURES

Irenaeus, the Gnostics and the Question of Biblical Revelation and Authority

The topic of the church fathers' attitude toward the Bible and the issue of patristic biblical interpretation are extremely important ones that I have explored in some detail elsewhere.[1] In this chapter I have a more modest goal: to investigate the thought of a single father—Irenaeus—on the issue of the Bible and divine revelation as he responds to the Gnostic threat in the second century A.D. How, for example, did Irenaeus respond to the Gnostic claim that their doctrines were derived from direct, secret, divine revelation? What was the link between the apostles and authoritative revelation? How was the Bible to be interpreted wisely and reverently? What was the relationship between the Old Testament and the New Testament? How was the church itself related to the question of biblical authority and interpretation?

Irenaeus, writing in the latter half of the second century, strongly asserted the authority of the Scripture against his Gnostic opponents. Gnostic teachers claimed to possess divine authority for their particular doctrines and often taught they had received secret revelation in either written or oral form, handed down to them by the apostles. "They tell us, however," Irenaeus writes, "that this knowledge has not been openly divulged, because all are not capable of receiving it, but has been mystically revealed by the Savior through means of parables to those qualified for understanding it."[2]

In addition, the Gnostics undercut the authority of the Old Testament Scriptures by arguing that a lesser deity—the Demiurge—was responsible for inspiring the Old Testament, the same god responsible for the cosmic tragedy of creation itself. The Gnostics produced their own collections of sacred writings, sometimes incorporating aspects of the New Testament documents into their canon but drastically editing them in the process. Marcion and his followers, for instance, used the Gospel of Luke, but only in a dramatically reshaped form. In response, Irenaeus was quick to affirm the public nature of revelation, the clear continuity between the Old and New Testaments and the unique authority of the canonical documents.

Irenaeus writes that the church had not learned the gospel in a secretive, mysterious manner. How could the Gnostics claim to possess a secret gospel when the apostles had proclaimed the gospel "in public, and, at a later period, [had] by the will of God, handed [the gospel] down to us in the Scriptures, to be the ground and pillar of our faith."[3]

Apostolic Authority

While some Gnostics claimed to supplement apostolic teaching with their supposedly secret revelation, Irenaeus insists that there is no need to go beyond the apostles in a search for further revelation. Why? The apostles, personally chosen by Jesus to be his unique representatives and interpreters, possessed "perfect knowledge. . . . For, after our Lord rose from the dead, the apostles were invested with power from on high when the Holy Spirit came down upon them, were filled from all His gifts, and had perfect knowledge."[4] Apostolic revelation and interpretation, then, were intimately linked to the Holy Spirit and divinely inspired in a manner that set apostolic testimony apart as the word of God.

As Christ's chosen witnesses, the apostles traveled throughout the Mediterranean basin, bearing witness to Christ both orally and in written form. Irenaeus notes, for instance, that "Matthew issued a written Gospel among the Hebrews in their own dialect, while Peter and Paul were preaching in Rome, and laying the foundations of the Church." After the "departure" of these great apostles, "Mark, the disciple and interpreter of Peter, did also hand down to us in writing what had been preached by Peter." Additionally, Irenaeus observes, "Luke also, the companion of Paul, recorded in a book the Gospel preached by him. Afterwards, John the disciple of the Lord, who also had leaned upon His breast, did himself publish a Gospel during his residence at Ephesus in Asia."[5]

Irenaeus succinctly presents a synopsis of the faith and the inseparable, authoritative link between the apostles, Christ and God the Father. First, the apostles in their teaching "have all declared to us that there is one God, Creator of heaven and earth," rather than the Gnostic hierarchy of divine aeons ruled by a remote, supreme deity. The God of prophetic and apostolic testimony, the Lord of heaven and earth, freely chose to create. Hence, creation is good and not the cosmic mistake of a lower deity. Second, both "the law and the prophets" proclaim that there is "one God [and] one Christ, the Son of God." To disbelieve or attempt to undercut these truths is to subvert the gospel itself and its normative pattern of authority: the apostles, Christ and God the Father. Thus Irenaeus concludes, "If any one does not agree to these truths, he despises the companions of the Lord; indeed, he despises Christ Himself the Lord; yes, he despises the Father also, and stands self-condemned, resisting and opposing his own salvation, as is the case with all heretics."[6]

In an inventive interpretation, Irenaeus argues that there could be only four Gospels, because "there are four zones in the world in which we live, and four principal winds." Indeed, Irenaeus believes it was only appropriate that the church, as the "pillar and ground of the truth" (1 Tim 3:15), should have the four Gospels as its four supporting pillars. The gospel has been given to the church "under four aspects," all "bound together by one Spirit."

Irenaeus turns to the book of Revelation and finds therein support for his argument. The four living creatures of Revelation 4 become symbols of the four Gospels:

- the lion = John
- the calf or ox = Luke
- the man = Matthew
- the eagle = Mark

The Gospel of John, Irenaeus writes, brims with confidence as it portrays a high and holy picture of the Son of God. That is, "For that according to John relates His original, effectual, and glorious generation from the Father, thus declaring, 'In the beginning was the Word, and the Word was with God, and the

Word was God' " (Jn 1:1). Luke, in his presentation of Zechariah's priesthood, points to "the priest offering sacrifice to God. For now was made ready the fatted calf, about to be immolated for the finding again of the younger son." As for Matthew, he narrates the generation of the Son as a human being. Irenaeus explains, "This, then, is the Gospel of his humanity; for which reason it is, too, that the character of a humble and meek man is kept up through the whole Gospel." Finally, Mark "commences with a reference to the prophetical Spirit coming down from on high to men, saying, 'The beginning of the Gospel of Jesus Christ, as it is written in Isaiah the prophet' " (Mk 1:1-2). By beginning this way, Mark points to Jesus' character as a great prophet, who "used to converse with the pre-Mosaic patriarchs, in accordance with His divinity and glory; but for those under the law he instituted a sacerdotal and liturgical service. Afterwards, being made man for us, He sent the gift of the celestial Spirit over all the earth, protecting us with His wings."[7]

> Such, then, as was the course followed by the Son of God, so was also the form of the living creatures: and such as was the form of the living creatures, so was also the character of the Gospel. For the living creatures are quadriform, and the Gospel is quadriform, as is also the course followed by the Lord. For this reason were four principal covenants given to the human race: one, prior to the deluge, under Adam; the second, that after the deluge, under Noah; the third, the giving of the law, under Moses; the fourth, that which renovates humankind, and sums up all things in itself by means of the Gospel, raising and bearing human beings upon its wings into the heavenly kingdom.[8]

The Unity of Biblical Authority and Testimony

Irenaeus refuses to allow heretical teachers such as Marcion to drive a wedge between the God revealed in the Old Testament and the God revealed in Christ, nor to undercut the authority and unity of figures such as Luke and Paul. Marcion, for instance, appeared to elevate Paul as a supreme authority over writers such as Luke, particularly when the book of Acts or Luke's Gospel violated Marcion's interpretation of the Scripture. Such a hermeneutical strategy was a dead end, Irenaeus argues, because "Luke was inseparable from Paul, and his fellow-laborer in the Gospel." The use of the editorial "we" in the book of Acts, for instance, points to the close relationship between Paul and Luke. Thus Irenaeus concludes, "As Luke was present at all these occurrences, he carefully noted them down in writing, so that he cannot be convicted of falsehood or boastfulness, because all these particulars proved both that he was senior to all those who now teach otherwise, and that he was not ignorant of the truth."[9]

If Luke "had learned nothing different from Paul," Irenaeus asks, "how can these men, who were never attached to Paul, boast that they have learned hidden and unspeakable mysteries?"[10] To reject or set Luke's testimony against that of Paul, Irenaeus points out, is to "manifestly reject that Gospel of which he claims to be a disciple." For it is by Luke's witness itself "that we have become acquainted with very many and important parts of the Gospel," including "the generation of John, the history of Zechariah, the coming of the angel to Mary, the exclamation of Elizabeth, the descent of the angels to the shepherds, the words spoken by them," and so on.[11]

Teachers such as Marcion are guilty of an ideological hermeneutic that encourages them to embrace those sections of Luke's Gospel that fit their theology and to reject those aspects that would cast suspicion on their theological formulations. Such picking and choosing just will not do, Irenaeus insists. "It follows then . . . that these men either receive the rest of [Luke's] narrative, or else reject these parts also. For no persons of common sense can permit them to receive some things recounted by Luke as being true, and to set others aside, as if he had not known the truth."[12]

Irenaeus levels much the same critique against those teachers who would reject the authority of the apostle Paul by appealing to Luke. For it was Luke himself who tells us in the book of Acts that Jesus appeared to Paul on the road to Damascus. To reject Paul, then, whether by attempting to pit Luke against him or for other principles, is to reject the choice and command of Christ. To do so is to "despise the election of God, and separate themselves from the company of the apostles. For neither can they contend that Paul was no apostle, when he was chosen for this purpose; nor can they prove Luke guilty of falsehood, when he proclaims the truth to us with all diligence."[13]

Indeed, the unity of Luke and Paul's testimony is a striking witness to the overarching wisdom of God's purposes. Whether it be Luke's testimony in his Gospel or in his history of the Acts of the Apostles, both writings contain "the unadulterated rule of truth" by which one "may be saved." Here is no secret, mysterious, hidden testimony available to only a few teachers who have obtained true knowledge through private revelation. Rather, Luke's testimony is "true, and the doctrine of the apostles is open and steadfast, holding nothing in reserve; nor did they teach one set of doctrines in private, and another in public."[14]

Irenaeus insists that the testimony of the Old Testament is one with the authority of New Testament authorities such as Luke and Paul. Marcion, for instance, attempted to expunge all Old Testament references from his canon of New Testament documents, largely because he was convinced that the god portrayed in the Old Testament was a different deity from the God revealed in Jesus Christ. In Marcion's thinking, the Old Testament deity was a god of wrath, judgment and anger. "Marcion," Irenaeus writes, "advanced the most daring blasphemy against Him who is proclaimed as God by the law and the prophets, declaring Him to be the author of evils, to take delight in war, to be infirm of purpose, and even to be contrary to Himself."

According to Marcion, the God revealed in Christ, by way of contrast, was a God of grace, mercy and forgiveness and unrelated to the wrathful god of the Old Testament. As Irenaeus summarizes Marcion's teaching, "Jesus being derived from that father who is above the God that made the world, and coming into Judaea in the times of Pontius Pilate [abolished] the prophets and the law, and all the works of that God who made the world."[15]

Marcion's position, Irenaeus contended, simply could not be supported by the biblical testimony itself. Such a gap between the Old and New Testament Scriptures was the result of Marcion's irresponsible mutilation of the text. Irenaeus observes that Marcion mutilates Luke's Gospel, "removing all that is written respecting the generation of the Lord, and setting aside a great deal of the teaching of the Lord, in which the Lord is recorded as most clearly confessing that the Maker of this universe is His Father." Not only so, but Marcion attempted to place his own authority above that of the apostles, persuading "his disciples that he himself was more worthy of credit than are those apostles who have handed down the Gospel to us, furnishing them not with the Gospel, but merely a fragment of it."[16]

Marcion is shockingly willing to edit out apostolic teaching that does not fit his own preconceptions of the gospel. He "dismembered the Epistles of Paul," Irenaeus complains, "removing all that is said by the apostle respecting that God who made the world, to the effect that He is the Father of our Lord Jesus Christ, and also those passages from the prophetical writings which the apostle quotes, in order to teach us that they announced beforehand the coming of the Lord."[17]

Key Hermeneutical Principles

What was Marcion's problem? He was reading the Scriptures in a sloppy, negligent, inattentive fashion. Anyone, Irenaeus insists, who reads "the Scriptures with attention . . . will find in them an account of Christ, and a foreshadowing of the new calling." That is, it is foolish to eliminate the first chapters of a story that provide key plot lines for the final chapters. Foreshadowings of Christ are peppered throughout the Old Testament literature. For example, Christ is a treasure "hid in the Scriptures . . . since He was pointed out by means of types and parables." Granted, the Old Testament references to Christ are not always simple to discern, but this difficulty is to be expected, "for every prophecy, before its fulfillment, is to people full of enigmas and ambiguities. But when the time has arrived, and the prediction has come to pass, then the prophecies have a clear and certain exposition."[18]

Indeed, Irenaeus proposes as a general hermeneutical principle that ambiguous passages must be interpreted in light of passages that are clear and straightforward. Otherwise, one ambiguity will lead to another, ending in a hermeneutical dead end. He explains, "For no question can be solved by means of another which itself awaits solution; nor, in the opinion of those possessed of sense, can an ambiguity be explained by means of another ambiguity. . . . But such . . . receive their solution from those [passages] which are manifest, consistent, and clear."[19]

Irenaeus calls his readers to develop a "sound mind," one "devoted to piety and the love of truth." A key characteristic of such a mind, Irenaeus believes, is its ability to distinguish between those truths God has chosen to reveal to human understanding and those God has chosen to keep to himself. A devout or sound mind will "eagerly meditate upon those things which God has placed within the power of humankind, and has subjected to our knowledge, and will make advancement in [acquaintance with] them, rendering the knowledge of them easy to him by means of daily study."[20]

Irenaeus contends that the focus of wise and devout study is not an ambiguous mystery revealed only to a select few. Rather, we should study and meditate upon things "such as fall [plainly] under our observation, and are clearly and unambiguously in express terms set forth in the Sacred Scriptures." The Gnostic tendency to find hidden, esoteric meanings in Jesus' parables, for instance, violates a devout, sound hermeneutic. It leads to a hermeneutical free-for-all in which each individual touts the mysteries he or she alone has discovered. "For in this way," Irenaeus comments, "no one will possess the rule of truth; but in accordance with the number of persons who explain the parables will be found the various systems of truth, in mutual opposition to each other, and setting forth antagonistic doctrines."[21]

The highly idiosyncratic hermeneutic of Gnostic interpreters, highly dependent upon ambiguous passages in the Bible, can only lead to theological turmoil, indeed chaos. The Gnostics "put fetters upon themselves, and every one of them imagines, by means of their obscure interpretations of the parables, that he has found out a God of his own." Such is hardly the prudent and wise path to follow. Since "parables admit of many interpretations, what lover of truth will not acknowledge, that for [Gnostics] to assert God is to be searched out from these, while they desert what is certain, indubitable, and true, is the part of men who eagerly throw themselves into danger."[22]

Wise Christians, Irenaeus advises, will always center their attention upon the Scripture but will rebuke the fallen tendency to focus on esoteric passages at the expense of the Scripture's plain teaching on a vast array of issues, including creation and the nature of God. Here, indeed, were two key areas where Gnostic teachers had wandered far from the truth, precisely because of the skewed belief that the mysterious should be the grid by which to interpret the clear and unambiguous, rather than vice versa.

Irenaeus unreservedly affirms "that the Scriptures are indeed perfect" but that biblical writers have not attempted to answer every question that a curious mind might pose. In his words, "If we cannot discover explanation of all those things in Scripture which are made the subject of investigation . . . let us not on that account seek after any other God besides Him who really exists."[23] *This is a key point for Irenaeus*, for the Gnostics' unbridled curiosity and unwillingness to live theologically and hermeneutically within the boundaries laid down by Scripture itself had led them into idolatry. They had actually created God in their image through their unwillingness to submit to God's silence on key questions they wanted answered.

Rather than follow this arrogant, undisciplined path, Irenaeus counsels us to "leave things of that nature to God who created us, being most properly assured that the Scriptures are indeed perfect, since they were spoken by the Word of God and His Spirit."[24] The problem is that while the Scripture is perfect, we are not. For "we, inasmuch as we are inferior to, and later in existence than, the Word of God and His Spirit, are on that very account destitute of the knowledge of His mysteries." This should not be a surprise to us, since we have a hard enough time making sense of "those things which lie at our very feet (I mean such as belong to this world, which we handle, and see, and are in close contact with)."[25]

If created reality is hard enough to understand, analyze and interpret, how much more so the wonder and mystery of God and God's actions on our behalf? In Irenaeus's words, "If, therefore, even with respect to creation, there are some things [the knowledge of] which belong only to God, and others which come within the range of our own knowledge," how can we complain? *Our ability to make sense out of creation or the Scripture is a gift of grace.* In short, "we are able by the grace of God to explain some of them, while we must leave others in the hands of God, and that not only in the present world, but also in that which is to come, so that God should for ever teach, and humanity should for ever learn the things taught it by God."[26]

The apostle Paul himself intimated that one of the joys of heaven will be the wonder of ever-increasing knowledge of God. When all else has passed away, Paul writes, "faith, hope, and love [will] abide" (1 Cor 13:13). Faith, Irenaeus writes, "endures unchangeably," while hope leads us to expect to "be receiving more and more from God, and to learn from Him, because He is good, and possesses boundless riches, a kingdom without end, and instruction that can never be exhausted."[27] Hence, we can leave some questions "in the hands of God."

Allow what is clear in the Scripture to shed light on what is foggy, Irenaeus coaches. If one does so, soon the melodies and harmonies of Scripture will reach the reader's ears. Despite the diversity of Scripture, "there shall be heard one harmonious melody in us, praising in hymns that God who created all things." Though we might be tempted to ask the Gnostic question, "What was

God doing before he made the world?" the boundaries of Scripture will bring us back to our senses. In Irenaeus's words, "that this world was formed perfect by God, receiving a beginning in time, the Scriptures teach us; but no Scripture reveals to us what God was employed about before this event." Thus, we should not search after answers to questions God has chosen not to answer. If we speak where God has remained silent, the result will be "foolish, rash, and blasphemous suppositions . . . so, as by one's imagining that he has discovered the origin of matter, he should in reality set aside God Himself who made all things."[28] This wise reticence equally applies to curiosity about the hour of Christ's return, as well as to inquiries into the nature of the Son's generation by the Father.[29]

Irenaeus wonders why anyone would listen to teachers such as Marcion when their teaching has deserted *the foundation of authority*: the Law, the Prophets, Christ and his chosen apostles.[30] The Gnostic cosmology, with its denigration of creation, ends up with little exegetical weight behind it. Why? Marcion has declared certain texts to lack authority, rather than dealing seriously with the theology they presented. One can only denigrate the created order, for instance, by willfully ignoring key biblical texts that link creation with the specific act of God.

The Pattern of Authority

Irenaeus's fundamental question is this: What is to be trusted more, the supposedly secret revelation received by Gnostic teachers or the authoritative Scriptures? His answer is obvious: "For these men are not more to be depended on than the Scriptures; nor ought we to give up the declarations of the Lord, Moses, and the rest of the prophets, who have proclaimed the truth."[31] Although the Gnostics may stridently insist that they have received divine revelation, Irenaeus teaches that all claims to divine communication must be run through the following grid of authority to determine their faithfulness to genuine Christian teaching: "the preaching of the apostles, the authoritative teaching of the Lord, the announcements of the prophets, the dictated utterances of the apostles, and the ministration of the law."[32]

Irenaeus develops this *pattern of authority* in book three of *Against Heresies*. Why is Irenaeus so convinced that Gnostic teaching cannot possibly be true? It does not fit the pattern of apostolic teaching handed down in the Scripture. The church, Irenaeus writes, "has received from the apostles" *a specific pattern of truth* founded upon the teaching of Jesus himself. He writes, "For the Lord of all gave to His apostles the power of the Gospel, through whom also we have known the truth, that is, the doctrine of the Son of God."[33]

It is important to note that Irenaeus couples the public teaching of the apostles with the later inclusion of that teaching in the body of Scripture itself. This is important because "we have learned from none others the plan of our salvation, than from those through whom the Gospel has come down to us, which they did at one time proclaim in public, and, at a later period, by the will of God, handed down to us in the Scriptures." Hence, apostolic teaching in the pages of the Scripture is "the ground and pillar of our faith."[34]

Gnostic teachers attempted to skirt the implications of Irenaeus's argument by asserting that the apostles occasionally spoke prematurely, before they had received full knowledge. Not so, Irenaeus responds. In fact, Irenaeus declares it "unlawful to assert that they preached before they possessed 'perfect knowledge,' as some do even venture to say, boasting themselves as improvers of the apostles."[35]

The only path left to the Gnostics, it seems, was to attempt to undercut the authority of the Scripture itself. According to Irenaeus's testimony, this is exactly what they attempted. When "confuted from the Scriptures, they turn round and accuse these same Scriptures, as if they were not correct, nor of authority, and [assert that] they are ambiguous. . . . For [they allege] that the truth was not delivered by means of written documents, but *viva voce*."[36]

Not only do the Gnostics reject the authority of the Scripture, but as we will discuss in some detail in our next chapter, they reject tradition as a valid means of ascertaining the meaning of the Bible. The Gnostics claim only "they have discovered the unadulterated truth. For [they maintain] that the apostles intermingled the things of the law with the words of the Savior." Therefore, only the Gnostics "themselves, indubitably, unsulliedly, and purely, have knowledge of the hidden mystery. . . . It comes to this, therefore, that these men do now consent neither to Scripture nor to tradition."[37]

Irenaeus leads his reader through the Gospels one by one, demonstrating from Matthew, Mark, Luke and John that Gnostic teaching simply cannot bear the weight of the gospel in its full presentation. He does so because of the tendency of heretical teachers to individualistically pick and choose which texts they will treat as authoritative. The Ebionites, for instance, placed great emphasis upon Matthew's Gospel. Marcion, as we have seen, relied heavily upon the Gospel of Luke, but only after "mutilating" it with his editorial scissors. Other heretics attempted to "separate Jesus from Christ, alleging that Christ remained impassible, but that it was Jesus who suffered, preferring the Gospel by Mark." Valentinus and his followers made "copious use of that according to John."[38] Other groups, such as the Montanists, disputed aspects of John's Gospel, largely because Johannine teaching appeared to contradict aspects of their teaching concerning the Spirit.[39]

Gnostic teachers not only employed a canon within the canon, asserting the authority of one text against that of another, but they argued that Jesus and the apostles purposely accommodated and incorporated the false ideas of their audience into their own teaching as a pedagogical bridge-building technique. That is, Jesus and the apostles would have taught the Gnostic cosmology if their audience had been able to receive this truth. Irenaeus writes, "some of these men impudently assert that the apostles, when preaching among the Jews, could not declare to them another god besides Him in whom they (their hearers) believed."[40] And so the apostles, accommodating themselves to the skewed worldview of the Jews, continued to preach the existence of only one God. Further revelation would have to occur in the future to correct this unfortunate accommodation—or so the Gnostics believed.

Irenaeus firmly believes that the Gnostics actually have inverted the concept of authority. In the Gnostic view, Christ and the apostles possessed a unique authority, but only when that teaching authority affirmed the positions already advocated by Gnostic teachers. Yet, Irenaeus teaches, the very purpose of apostolic teaching was to challenge peoples' ideas when and where they strayed from the truth. If the apostles knowingly embraced falsehood as a teaching methodology, "no one learned the truth from them, nor, at a much earlier date, from the Lord; for they say that He did Himself speak after the same fashion." Christ had come, Irenaeus emphasizes, not to confirm false ideas about God but to challenge them. To think otherwise would render the coming of Christ "superfluous and useless."[41]

The Church in the Pattern of Authority

It is important to observe at this juncture that Irenaeus refuses to separate the authority of the Scripture and the task of biblical interpretation from the community of the church itself, an idea we will explore in our discussion of the church fathers' understanding of the church. According to Irenaeus, the Gnostics err, not only because they fail to read the Bible well, but because they refuse to join "themselves to the Church." Instead, their highly individualistic interpretations of the Bible lead to doctrinal confusion and ethical disaster. They "defraud themselves of life through their perverse opinions and infamous behavior."[42]

The Gnostics remain confused in both their doctrine of God and in their understanding of theology, because they ignore "the beginning, the middle, and the end," that is, *the testimony of the Old Testament Scriptures, the witness of Christ and his apostles and the continuing guidance of Christ's church* in Irenaeus's own day. Irenaeus is convinced that in his response to Gnosticism he is simply preserving the gospel he and all Christians have received from previous generations of Christians. Through the preserving ministry of the Holy Spirit, the "entire dispensation of God" has been passed on faithfully over the years. As Irenaeus explains, "this gift of God has been entrusted to the Church, as breath was to the first created man, for this purpose, that all the members receiving it may be vivified; and the [means of] communion with Christ has been distributed throughout it, that is, the Holy Spirit . . . the means of confirming our faith, and the ladder of ascent to God."[43]

Because the Gnostics deserted the church in their quest for "knowledge," Irenaeus states that they are bereft of the Spirit and the life of Christ.

> For where the Church is, there is the Spirit of God; and where the Spirit of God is, there is the Church, and every kind of grace; but the Spirit is truth. Those, therefore, who do not partake of Him, are neither nourished into life from the mother's breasts, nor do they enjoy that most limpid fountain which issues from the body of Christ; but they dig for themselves broken cisterns out of earthly trenches, and drink putrid water out of the mire, fleeing from the faith of the Church, lest they be convicted; and rejecting the Spirit, that they may not be instructed.[44]

Foundation, Continuity and Fulfillment

Irenaeus observes that it is not only teachers such as Marcion who struggle to

understand the relationship between the Old and New Testaments. The Jewish
people themselves remain cloudy in their interpretation of Old Testament texts
because they lack the hermeneutical key to make sense of them. When the Old
Testament is read to a Jewish audience, Irenaeus argues, "it is like a fable; for they
do not possess the explanation of all things pertaining to the advent of the Son of
God, which took place in human nature."[45]

By way of contrast, the Christian community treats the Old Testament as a
treasure precisely because it contains Christ. According to Irenaeus, "it is a treasure, hid indeed in a field, but brought to light by the cross of Christ, and
explained, both enriching human understanding, and showing forth the wisdom
of God, and declaring His dispensations with regard to humanity."[46] Jesus himself, after his resurrection from the dead, turned the eyes of his disciples to the
Old Testament Scriptures, reminding them that the Scriptures had foretold
"that the Messiah is to suffer and to rise from the dead on the third day, and that
repentance and forgiveness of sins is to be proclaimed in his name to all nations"
(Lk 24:46-47).

Moses had spoken clearly of Christ. In fact, Irenaeus writes, "the writings of
Moses are the words of Christ." Jesus himself had rebuked his Jewish opponents
for not reading Moses well: "If you believed Moses, you would believe me, for he
wrote about me" (Jn 5:46). Not only had Moses written about Jesus, but also
"beyond a doubt, the words of the other prophets are His [words], as I have
pointed out."[47] Although some Jews rejected Jesus, this was not the fault of the
Law itself, "for the law never hindered them from believing in the Son of God;
nay, but it even exhorted them so to do, saying that people can be saved in no
other way from the old wound of the serpent than by believing in Him, who, in
the likeness of sinful flesh, is lifted up from the earth upon the tree of martyrdom
and draws all things to Himself."[48]

It should not surprise readers to discover Christ in the Old Testament, not
only because the story of the new covenant is imbedded in the narrative of the old
covenant, but also because *the same God inspired the Scriptures explaining both cove-
nantal stories.* The texts are unified because the same divine mind and purpose lies
behind both. The same God who said, " 'Let there be light'; and there was light"
(Gen 1:3), spoke in John's Gospel, "All things came into being through him, and
without him not one thing came into being" (Jn 1:3). The God who creates in

Genesis recreates humanity in Christ. Here we do not have a multitude of deities battling against one another, one erring by creating and another redeeming the effects of that cosmic mistake. On the contrary, as Paul clearly states, "[There is] one Lord, one faith, one baptism, one God and Father of all, who is above all and through all and in all" (Eph 4:5-6).

While the Gnostics insist that the god revealed in the Old Testament narrative is different from the God revealed in Christ, Irenaeus contends that the treasure present in both the old and new covenants is inseparable, since "one and the same householder produced both covenants, the Word of God, our Lord Jesus Christ, who spake with both Abraham and Moses, and who has restored us anew to liberty, and has multiplied that grace which is from Himself." The new covenant was "known and preached" by the prophets of the old, as God led them progressively to discern his redemptive purposes for all humanity.[49] Over time, "by means of the [successive] covenants," God's plan unfolded. As Irenaeus puts it, "there is one salvation and one God; but the precepts which form the man are numerous, and the steps which lead humanity to God are not a few."[50]

If we fail to discern Christ in the Old Testament, the treasure hidden in the field, we have failed to read Scripture through the eyes of Jesus and the apostles. For, Irenaeus writes, "if any one . . . reads the Scriptures with attention, he will find in them an account of Christ, and a foreshadowing of the new calling."[51] Stated differently, "Christ is the treasure which was hid in the field, that is, in this world. . . . The treasure hid in the Scriptures is Christ, since he was pointed out by means of types and parables." Now that the incarnation has occurred, "the prophecies have a clear and certain exposition." If we continue to read the Old Testament Scriptures apart from the light the incarnation of the Son sheds upon them, they will continue to seem like a fable. However, "when it is read by the Christians, it is a treasure, hid indeed in a field, but brought to light by the cross of Christ." Christ's birth, ministry, death, burial and ascension to heaven are all described in the Law and Prophets, but one must have ears to hear and eyes to see.

Hence, to read the Scriptures with the apostles and their successors in the church is necessarily to adopt an apostolic perspective toward inspiration and interpretation. Here, Irenaeus is convinced, is the path that leads to biblical, theological and hermeneutical consistency. For "then shall every word also seem consistent to him, if he for his part diligently read the Scriptures in company with those who are presbyters in the Church, among whom is the apostolic doctrine, as I have pointed out."[52]

Irenaeus reiterates his point: "For all the apostles taught that there were indeed two testaments among the two peoples." The first Testament "exhibited a type of heavenly things, inasmuch as humanity was not yet able to see the things of God through means of immediate vision." It "foreshadowed the images of those things which now actually exist in the church, in order that our faith might be firmly established; and contained a prophecy of things to come, in order that humankind might learn that God has foreknowledge of all things."[53]

To sum up, for Irenaeus *true* knowledge finds its heart and core in the narrative of the Scripture itself, a narrative passed on and authoritatively interpreted by the prophets, Jesus and the apostles. Although the canon of the Scripture is still somewhat fluid in Irenaeus's day, he remains convinced that the bishops of the church have faithfully preserved prophetic and apostolic texts, "without any forging of Scriptures." On the basis of this apostolic testimony the church is founded and itself teaches "a very complete system of doctrine . . . neither receiving addition nor [suffering] curtailment [in the truths which she believes]; and [it consists in] reading [the word of God] without falsification, and a lawful and diligent exposition in harmony with the Scriptures."[54]

Heretics such as the Gnostics, then, err seriously on a variety of issues. First, they have forgotten that they, like all Christians, are called to be students of the apostles, rather than their teachers. All the key Gnostic teachers "are of much later date than the bishops to whom the apostles committed the Churches." Second, because the Gnostics are faulty listeners, refusing to submit to apostolic doctrine as taught in the Scriptures and preserved by the church, Gnostic doctrine itself is confused and "scattered here and there without agreement or connection."[55]

By way of contrast, those who listen well to the Scripture and the apostolic doctrine it contains remain firmly planted on the pathway of truth. The "sure tradition from the apostles" makes plain for all to see that "the faith is one and the same, since all receive one and the same God the Father, and believe in the same dispensation regarding the incarnation of the Son of God, and are cognizant of the same gift of the Spirit, and are conversant with the same commandments."

Here within the teaching of the church, apostolically based as it is, the "one and same way of salvation is shown throughout the whole world. . . . For the Church preaches the truth everywhere, and she is the seven-branched candlestick which bears the light of Christ."[56]

The mark of heretical teachers is that they believe only they have discovered the truth. Only they "have hit upon something more beyond the truth." The problem, Irenaeus writes, is that when people each discover their own truth for themselves, truth itself ends up scattered and inharmonious. The blind end up leading the blind, and they "deservedly fall into the ditch of ignorance lying in their path, ever seeking and never finding out the truth." What is the remedy for this willful blindness? Run "to the Church . . . be brought up in her bosom, and be nourished with the Lord's Scriptures." Assume a humble stance before apostolic doctrine. Admit the limitations of human understanding. Do not be like the Gnostics, who have "formed opinions on what is beyond the limits of understanding," who have "set their own impious minds above the God who made them."[57]

If we are to run to the church, as Irenaeus suggests, surely a closer look at the church fathers' understanding of the church is warranted.

"It is said, 'In the church, God has set apostles, prophets, teachers,'
and all the other means through which the Spirit works.
Those who do not join themselves to the church are not partakers of these things.
Rather, they defraud themselves of life through their perverse opinions and infamous behavior.
For where the church is, there is the Spirit of God.
And where the Spirit of God is, there is the church, and every kind of grace."

IRENAEUS
Against Heresies

"Can he have God as his Father, before he has had the church for his mother?"

CYPRIAN
The Epistles of Cyprian

"If you do not wish to be deceived and if you want to continue loving one another,
be aware that each way of life in the church has hypocrites in her ranks. . . .
There are bad Christians, but there are also good ones.
At first glance you see a great number of bad Christians,
who as a thick layer of chaff prevent you from reaching the good grains of corn."

AUGUSTINE
Enarrations on the Psalms

TEN

ONE HOLY, APOSTOLIC CHURCH

What Is the Church?

Exactly what is the church? What is its relationship to Christ? What are the qualifications for membership? What characterizes it? How is the church related to the broader world around it? How does one enter the church? Can one leave it? How is the church to be led? How are the sacraments of the church to be administered? What is a sacrament? How is the church related to the earliest Christian community, that of the first century? What is the relationship between the church and the Scripture? What is the relationship between the Israel of the old covenant and the church of the new covenant? Is it possible or wise to attempt to discern who is a genuine member of the church and who is not? How is the church to respond to false teaching? Are there characteristics of a true church that set it off from a false one? How are genuine, trustworthy teachers of the church to be recognized? What distinguishes them from false teachers?

These and still many other questions faced the early Christian community from the first century forward. Even today, in the early twenty-first century, the answers we give to these questions are apt to distinguish and divide the Christian community. What still divides the Orthodox church from the Roman Catholic church? In what way is the Anglican church different from Rome, or from Protestant communions such as the Lutheran or Presbyterian churches? Ecclesiological questions, issues and answers still divide and unite Christians. Even if we cannot answer and resolve all these questions and issues or offer a final solution, surely a good look at the church fathers' understanding of the church is a *sine qua non* for making sense of our church life and community—or lack of it—today.

In this chapter we will view the church through the minds and hearts of three different fathers: Irenaeus, writing in the middle and later years of the second century A.D.; Cyprian, writing in a time of persecution and martyrdom in the middle of the third century; and Augustine, writing in the later fourth and early fifth centuries.

Irenaeus

What is the church? How is it to be identified? Who is to lead it? On what is the church founded? On what basis is the church to identify truth and discern error? These and other significant questions and issues faced Irenaeus, bishop of Lyon (ca. 130-200). In particular, Irenaeus found himself responding to Gnosticism, one of the most serious heresies facing the early Christian community. Exactly what was the message of Gnosticism, and why was it considered such a threat to the gospel and the community founded by Christ and the apostles?

As we have seen in the previous chapter, Gnostic teachers such as Marcion, Basilides, Carpocrates, Cerinthus and Valentinus taught that creation was the act, not of God the Father, but rather of the Demiurge, "either a wicked angel or a lesser deity."[1] Creation and its constituents were by definition evil, the creation of a lesser god. One attained salvation through the knowledge Gnostic teachers possessed of the Gnostic cosmology, rather than through faith in Christ's teaching, death and resurrection. Indeed, the resurrection of Christ's physical body from the dead made little sense to Gnostic teachers. Why in the world would God raise something from the dead that was inherently evil, the creation of a misguided lesser god? David Bercot's summary of Gnostic teaching is quite helpful:

> Because of the imperfections of the Demiurge, all material things (including man's flesh) are inherently flawed and incapable of salvation. The Gnostics taught that the God of the Old Testament was harsh and cruel and that he was this Demiurge. Some Gnostics labeled him as the "just God," in contrast to Jesus' Father, who is the "good God." Feeling pity on mankind, the ultimate God, the Father of

Jesus, sent his Son to show humans the way to salvation. Since the flesh is inherently corrupt, the Son never actually became man. . . . Most Gnostic teachers rejected the physical sacraments of baptism and communion as being inefficacious. They also rejected the teaching of the resurrection of the body. . . . Gnostic teachers often claimed that the apostles had secretly revealed their teachings to a few close followers. Without this revealed knowledge (*gnosis*), humans cannot be saved.[2]

The more important question that Irenaeus addresses concerns the authority of the Gnostic teachers. Where had they obtained this knowledge? On what basis was it authoritative? Some Gnostic teachers claimed to have received direct revelation from God, while others contended that the apostles themselves had revealed this fuller revelation to them in secret. Irenaeus meets these teachings and claims head on and in so doing provides us with significant teaching on apostolicity, tradition, authority and the nature of the church itself.

Apostolicity and the church. Irenaeus teaches that even though the church is "dispersed throughout the whole world, even to the ends of the earth," it "has received from the apostles and their disciples" a faith that is clearly defined and recognizable. The church, for instance, "believes in one God, the Father Almighty, Maker of heaven and earth," a teaching that clearly contradicts the Gnostic insistence that creation was the work of a lesser deity or evil angel. Even more important, however, Irenaeus teaches that the church has "received this preaching and this faith." Though the church is scattered geographically, "yet, as if occupying but one house, [it] carefully preserves it."[3] Whether a church is in Germany, Spain, Egypt or Libya, the faith remains "one and the same." Those who speak at great length upon the faith add nothing to it, "nor does one, who can say but little diminish it." Thus, one of the distinguishing marks of the church is its *preservation of apostolic teaching*, teaching that is markedly edited or absent in Gnostic circles.

Why should we pay such close attention to the apostles? Why and in what way is their teaching qualitatively different from that of Gnostic teachers such as Valentinus or Cerinthus? For Irenaeus, the progression of authority within the church looks something like this: Jesus himself, the apostles he has chosen as foundation stones of the church, the scriptures containing apostolic teaching, and finally those chosen to preserve the teaching of the apostles within the church and in the church's proclamation to the broader world.

Irenaeus writes, for instance, that the Christian community in his day has heard the gospel "from none others than . . . those through whom the Gospel has come down to us," a proclamation that, Irenaeus stresses, took place "in public."[4] Later, after the public proclamation by the apostles, their teaching "by the will of God [was] handed down to us in the Scriptures to be the ground and pillar of our faith."

Apparently some people, probably Gnostic teachers, were claiming that the apostles had preached before they possessed "perfect knowledge," which created a need to supplement the imperfect knowledge of the apostles by those who boasted "themselves improvers of the apostles." Irenaeus contends that it is impossible to improve upon the teaching of the apostles, however, precisely because they were chosen by the Lord and empowered on the day of Pentecost to teach the church authoritatively. He writes, "For after our Lord rose from the dead, [the apostles] were invested with power from on high when the Holy Spirit came down [upon them], were filled from all [His gifts], and had perfect knowledge."[5] If the apostles have "declared to us that there is one God, Creator of heaven and earth," how can Gnostic teachers insist that creation is the wicked result of the evil desire of a lesser deity? The Law, the Prophets and Christ himself have already taught that creation was the act of "one God, Creator of heaven and earth." To despise the created order, then, is to despise the teaching of the Father, Christ and "the companions of the Lord."

It is within the church that the teaching of the apostles has been faithfully passed on and preserved. How so? Apostolic teaching has been "preserved by means of the successions of presbyters in the Churches."[6] Irenaeus believes that anyone of good faith can observe the public record: "It is within the power of all, therefore, in every Church, who may wish to see the truth, to contemplate clearly the tradition of the apostles manifested throughout the whole world; and we are in a position to reckon up those who were by the apostles instituted bishops in the Churches, and [to demonstrate] the succession of these men to our own times."[7] If the apostles passed on secrets to a chosen few, as Gnostic teachers claim, would they not have communicated these secrets to those chosen by the church to succeed the apostles as leaders of Christ's body? Furthermore, would not the apostles have passed on this secret information to those they had publicly recognized as

leaders within the church, leaders who bore the responsibility for faithfully preserving the teaching of the apostles? Irenaeus adds, "For [the apostles] desired
that these men should be very perfect and blameless in all things, [men] they
were leaving behind as their successors, delivering up their own place of government to these men."[8]

Again, Irenaeus is deeply concerned to demonstrate the unbroken connection
between the apostles and the bishops or presbyters of the church, precisely
because Gnostic teachers were denying this connection. Apostolic truth finds its
source in the apostles and has been handed down publicly by them in the Scriptures to specific Christian leaders whose responsibility it was to pass on and preserve that same truth faithfully. This was not something done in a corner or
secretly. Thus, if leaders arise claiming to be teaching in the name of Christ and
Christ's church, their teaching must be tested by the standard of apostolic truth
preserved in the church. Why? Because the apostles passed on the truth to the
church and expect the church to preserve it and preach it. New teachings that do
not fit the apostolic pattern cannot be welcomed. To use an analogy, "the apostles, like a rich man [depositing his money] in a bank, lodged in [the church's]
hands most copiously all things pertaining to the truth: so that every person . . .
can draw from her the water of life."[9]

In addition, when questions arise, the "most ancient" churches should be lis-
tened to carefully. For instance, Irenaeus clearly gives the church of Rome a place of
eminence and authority within the wider church. First, it was "founded and orga-
nized at Rome by the two most glorious apostles, Peter and Paul." Second, the
apostolic teaching of these foundation stones has "come down to our time by means
of the successions of the bishop." That is, the bishops succeeding Paul and Peter
have preserved their teaching faithfully and publicly. Thus, "it is a matter of necessity that every Church should agree with this church, on account of its preeminent
authority." And what is this authority? The apostolic tradition that "has been preserved continuously by those [faithful] men who exist everywhere."

Who are these men? Irenaeus does not hesitate to name them publicly. The
record is present for all who wish to examine it. By the time of Irenaeus, there
had been twelve bishops of Rome, and he lists the name of each one. When he
can, Irenaeus stresses the connection between individual bishops and the apostles
themselves. Clement of Rome, for instance, "had seen the blessed apostles, and

had been conversant with them, and could be said to have the preaching of the apostles still echoing [in his ears], and their traditions before his eyes."[10]

Irenaeus does not limit his discussion to the church at Rome, however. Polycarp, the bishop of the church at Smyrna, was "instructed by apostles, and conversed with many who had seen Christ." Not only so, but Irenaeus himself had seen Polycarp in his early youth.[11] It was Polycarp who on arriving in Rome had preached the gospel faithfully, causing "many to turn away from the aforesaid heretics to the Church of God, proclaiming that he had received the one and sole truth from the apostles—that, namely, which is handed down by the Church."[12] Apostolic succession, then, focuses primarily on the role of the bishop as one who faithfully preserves and passes on the teaching of the apostles, who in turn are authoritative interpreters of Christ himself.

The church, in Irenaeus's thinking, is an inherently conservative institution. For Irenaeus, it is not the job of the church to innovate or to create new doctrines out of whole cloth. Whatever the church chooses to say must find its root in apostolic sources. If the source of a bishop's teaching, for example, cannot be traced to apostolic teaching, that bishop's instruction must remain suspect. When disputes over teaching and doctrine arise, Irenaeus argues that they must be adjudicated by turning to the "most ancient Churches with which the apostles held constant intercourse, and learn from them what is certain and clear in response to the present question."[13] Thus, teachers within the church must never place themselves above apostolic teaching. They are not free to undercut the apostolic tradition through appeals to further revelation, however secret, mysterious or elevated such revelation might appear to be.

Biblical interpretation and doctrinal formation, then, are communal, ecclesial functions. The task of biblical interpretation belongs to the leaders of the church, those who "possess the succession from the apostles; those who, together with the succession of the episcopate, have received the certain gift of the truth, according to the good pleasure of the Father."[14] Irenaeus is deeply suspicious of any teacher or group that willfully splits off from the church to advocate their own particular teaching. He links the willingness to split the church to perverse minds, pride, hypocrisy and the desire to profit financially. Irenaeus warns, indeed, that those who split the church, "who cleave asunder, and separate the unity of the church, shall receive the same punishment as Jeroboam did" (cf. 1 Kings 14:10).[15]

Irenaeus also warns of the possibility of a presbyter of the church falling into error. There are those who "are believed to be presbyters by many" but whose behavior or teaching undercuts their claim to the position. The apex of ecclesiastical disaster is the presbyter who fails in both in his teaching and behavior. "Keep aloof from all such persons," Irenaeus exhorts, and "adhere to those who, as I have already observed . . . hold the doctrine of the apostles, and who, together with the order of the priesthood, display sound speech and blameless conduct for the confirmation and correction of others."[16] Thus, the doctrine of the apostles remains the fundamental rule of life for faith and doctrine for all members of the church, from its highest leadership on down.

Marcion—a case study. It seems clear that Irenaeus would feel terribly uncomfortable with the idea of the "private judgment" of the individual as a fundamental hermeneutical principle. Why? Irenaeus's own experience had taught him firsthand the harm a renegade teacher could wreak on the church. Think, for instance, of Marcion.

Marcion, a teacher living in the second century A.D. whom we have already encountered in the pages of this book, founded his own church, based on his own unique and highly idiosyncratic interpretations of the Bible. Gnostic elements appear in his teaching, including the idea that the God revealed in the pages of the Old Testament, a God who creates the world and actively expresses his wrath and judgment, cannot possibly be the Father of Jesus Christ. Of course, if Marcion is going to advocate this position, he must sharply pare down the canon of Scripture, which is exactly what he does. Irenaeus observes that Marcion "mutilates the Gospel which is according to Luke, removing all that is written respecting the generation of the Lord, and setting aside a great deal of the teaching of the Lord." The epistles of Paul also come under Marcion's hermeneutical blade, for "he dismembered the Epistles of Paul, removing all that is said by the apostle respecting that God who made the world."[17]

The downward ecclesial and hermeneutical spiral in Marcion's life unfolded as follows: Marcion was a member of the catholic church and affirmed its doctrine. However, a "restless curiosity" afflicted Marcion and his followers, with the result that they were "expelled more than once" during the episcopate of Eleutherius. Finally, the Marcionite faction was excommunicated from the church, with the unhappy result of only furthering the expansion of Marcion's teaching. Tertullian mentions that Marcion "professed repentance" at the end of his life, but too late to restore his misled followers to the fold of the church.[18]

It is in light of disasters such as Marcion that Irenaeus points to the church as the only sure bearer, preserver and protector of genuine apostolic teaching. It is within the catholic or universal church that "the gifts of the Lord have been placed and there it behooves us to learn the truth, [namely,] from those who possess that succession of the Church which is from the apostles, and among whom exists that which is sound and blameless in conduct, as well as that which is unadulterated and incorrupt in speech."[19] It is the community of faith itself, founded upon Christ and the apostles, that is called to "expound the Scriptures to us without danger, neither blaspheming God, nor dishonoring the patriarchs, nor despising the prophets."[20]

True knowledge, in distinction to that of heretical teachers such as Marcion, "is [that which consists in] the doctrine of the apostles and the ancient constitution of the Church throughout all the world." Apostolic truth has been preserved and protected, as we have seen already in Irenaeus's thinking, by "the successions of the bishops, by which they have handed down that Church which exists in every place, and has come even unto us, being guarded and preserved, without any forging of Scriptures." Coupled to the church's interpretation of the Bible, Irenaeus insists, is "the pre-eminent gift of love, which is more precious than knowledge, more glorious than prophecy, and which excels all the other gifts [of God]."[21]

By now readers who have cut their exegetical teeth on Protestant luminaries such as Luther and Calvin are biting their lips. Did not Luther advocate the principle of "private judgment" in his interpretation of the Bible? How might Irenaeus respond to Luther's elevation of the individual conscience over the interpretation of the church's recognized teachers? While one is hesitant to respond on Irenaeus's part, we can at least hazard a guess.

First, we need to remember that Irenaeus's position was forged in the second century, not the sixteenth. Irenaeus was writing against individuals who were willfully following their own exegetical path and merrily disregarding apostolic teaching. Such was not the case with Luther. In fact, Luther argued that in his attempt to reform the church he was attempting to draw the church back to the apostolic tradition itself. Luther believed the Roman Church in the sixteenth century had wandered from its roots. Luther, at least at the beginning of his call for reformation, was issuing that call from within the boundaries of the Roman Catholic community. He came to argue increasingly that the bishop of Rome had deserted the apostolic tradition, an eventuality that Irenaeus does not appear to have imagined could take place.

Yet while those from a Protestant background can willingly affirm Luther's lasting contribution to the overall life of the church, Irenaeus might well point to other less healthy fruit that the principle of private judgment appears to have fostered. What of the hundreds, if not thousands, of Protestant churches and denominations, all claiming to possess the true interpretation of apostolic teaching? What of the broken body of Christ? What of the unity of the church? How might other fathers address these questions? We find ourselves drawn to the thought of Cyprian, for whom the unity of the church became a life-and-death issue.

Cyprian—On the Unity of the Church

What exactly was the situation facing Cyprian? Perhaps a word or two about Cyprian himself might prove helpful. Cyprian was bishop of the North African city of Carthage from roughly A.D. 248 to 258. The ten years of his episcopate were a rough, troubled, trying time for the church, a period of intense suffering during both the Decian and Valerian persecutions.

Imagine the following scenario. During the time of the Decian persecution, the emperor Decius issued an order that all Christians were required to obtain a *libellus*, a certificate showing that a person had sacrificed to the gods. While there was a religious background to Decius's order, in all likelihood the emperor was using his edict as a political means of pressuring the church to demonstrate political loyalty to Rome. Whether religious or political concerns motivated Decius, the result of his order was that many Christians faced a difficult decision: face the confiscation of one's property, incarceration or even possible execution, or deny one's faith by sacrificing to the Roman deities. Some Christians escaped this dilemma by purchasing a *libellus* without actually sacrificing to the emperor. Others, however, either suffered deeply for their faith or denied their faith by sacrificing.

To sacrifice or not? The following dialogue from the account of the martyrdom of Phileas, bishop of Thmouis, illustrates the cost faithfulness to Christ might entail. In the conversation between Phileas and the Roman governor Culcianus, the governor attempts to convince Phileas to sacrifice.[22]

Culcianus:	Sacrifice to the gods.
Phileas:	I don't sacrifice.
Culcianus:	Why?
Phileas:	Because the sacred and divine scriptures say, "Whoever sacrifices to the gods, and not to God alone, will be uprooted."
Culcianus:	Come on, sacrifice.
Phileas:	I do not sacrifice. I haven't learned how.

The lawyers stopped Phileas, who was speaking at length, and said to him: Why do you resist the governor?

Phileas:	I am answering his question.
Culcianus:	Sacrifice now.
Phileas:	I do not sacrifice. I spare my soul. Because not only Christians spare their souls, but also pagans. Take the example of Socrates. When he was being led to death, with his wife and sons standing by, he did not turn back, but took the hemlock eagerly.
Culcianus:	Remember the honor I showed you. I could have maltreated you in your city, but wishing to honor you, I did not.
Phileas:	I thank you. Do me the following favor.
Culcianus:	What do you want?
Phileas:	Use your full force. Carry out your orders.
Culcianus:	Do you want to die this way without a reason?
Phileas:	I ask as a final kindness that you apply your rigor and do as you've been commanded.
Culcianus:	If you were one of the yokels who give themselves up out of desperation, I wouldn't spare you. But since you have so much wealth that you could feed and take care not only

	of yourself but of the whole city, spare yourself for that reason, and sacrifice.
Phileas:	I do not sacrifice.

And, since he will not alter or budge, the lawyers and all the court, together with the fiscal officer, wanted the governor to give him [time for] reflection.

Culcianus:	Do you want me to give you a chance to think it over?
Phileas:	I have thought it over, often, and that's what I choose.

At that, the lawyers and the court, along with the fiscal officer, wanted to persuade the blessed Phileas to obey the commands. As he would not budge, however, they went at him, exhorting him to think it over. Peace to all the saints![23]

Forgiveness for the lapsed? The result of Phileas's decision was his execution by the Roman government. However, not all Christians were willing to pay this price. Some simply apostatized. Others attempted to live in two worlds by purchasing a *libellus* without actually sacrificing to the emperor. The terribly difficult question facing the leadership of the church after the persecution ended was precisely this: Could Christians who apostatized during persecution be forgiven and readmitted to the church? Cyprian argued that they could.

Cyprian was willing to offer forgiveness to the lapsed (those who had obtained *libelli* during the persecution), but only under certain conditions. While many of those who had lapsed were "insistent in pressing quickly to be received into communion," Cyprian advised the church to move slowly. The lapsed were to be helped in the process of repentance and restoration by those who had remained faithful during the persecution. If one who had lapsed fell into "some sickness or risk" and confessed his or her sin, such a one could receive "the laying of hands" as a sign the church recognized the penitence. What Cyprian did not tolerate, however, was disorder and insensitivity. It was "irreligious" and "mischievous," for instance, for those who had lapsed in persecution to rush back into the church, while genuine confessors of the faith remained in exile and "stripped of all their property."[24] Forgiveness was possible, but only through the church's order and discipline.

While Cyprian's response to the lapsed may seem quite astringent to modern sensibilities, some contemporaries felt he was far too lenient in his response to those who had sinned so greatly. Chief among these was Novatian, a Roman presbyter. Novatian argued that only God could forgive the lapsed. The church itself, Novatian argued, was called to be pure and holy, separate from the evil in the surrounding world and peopled by holy persons alone. Novatian, motivated at least in part by a desire to preserve a holy church, broke off from the catholic church and formed his own schismatic body. How was the catholic church to respond to the Novatianists' claim to represent Christ's body on earth? Where is the church to be found? What characterizes the church? In what and whom is the church's unity found? Cyprian responds to these questions in his treatise *On the Unity of the Church.*

On the church's unity. Cyprian pulls no punches. From the beginning of his treatise on the church's unity he insists that schism finds its root in the demonic. It is the devil's work, "a new fraud" that employs "the Christian name to deceive the incautious." It is the devil himself who "has invented heresies and schisms, whereby he might subvert the faith, might corrupt the truth, might divide the unity."[25] Schism is particularly deceptive because those who break away from the church believe they do so in the name of Christ. Indeed, "they still call themselves Christians, and, walking in darkness, they think that they have the light, while the adversary is flattering and deceiving."[26]

Cyprian turns quickly to a key text in his argument against Novatian's schism. Did not the Lord say to Peter, "You are Peter, and on this rock I will build my church, and the gates of Hades will not prevail against it. I will give you the keys of the kingdom of heaven, and whatever you bind on earth will be bound in heaven, and whatever you loose on earth will be loosed in heaven" (Mt 16:18-19)? In a similar vein, after the resurrection Jesus commanded Peter, "Feed my lambs" (Jn 21:15). While it is true, Cyprian admits, that after his resurrection Jesus gave all his apostles "equal power," it is equally evident that a principle of unity undergirds apostolic authority. Jesus, "that he might set forth unity . . . arranged by his authority the origin of that unity as beginning from one. Assuredly the rest of the apostles were also the same as was Peter, endowed with a like partnership both of honor and power; but the beginning proceeds from unity."[27] How, then, can Novatian believe he represents the true church when he has violated the fundamental principle of unity? "Does he who does not hold this unity of the church," Cyprian asks, "think that he holds the faith? Does he who strives against and resists the church trust that he is in the church, when moreover the blessed Apostle Paul teaches the same thing and sets forth the sacrament of unity?"[28]

It is especially the bishops of the church, Cyprian insists, who must uphold fervently the unity of the church. Thus he writes, "The episcopate is one, each part of which is held by each one for the whole." In turn, the "church itself is one." Granted, the church has spread throughout the world and is increasing in fruitfulness daily. Still, "as there are many rays of the sun, [there is] but one light; and many branches of a tree, but one strength based in its tenacious root. . . . Yet the unity is still preserved in the source."[29] Can one separate the light ray from the sun? The branch from the tree? If one does so, "it will not be able to bud; cut off the stream from its fountain, and that which is cut off dries up." It is the same way with the church. Although her light and fruit are dispersed over the whole world, . . . yet her head is one, her source one; and she is one mother, plentiful in the results of fruitfulness. From her womb we are born, by her milk we are nourished, by her spirit we are animated."[30]

Cyprian does agree with Novatian that the "spouse of Christ cannot be adulterous; she is uncorrupted and pure." Yet the church's very purity demands that "she knows one home; she guards with chaste modesty the sanctity of one couch."[31] If so, the schismatic "is separated from the church and is joined to an adulteress, is separated from the promises of the church; nor can he who forsakes the church of Christ attain to the rewards of Christ." The one who breaks away from the church is "a stranger," "profane" and "an enemy." These are strong words—but Cyprian is just getting started.

In words that continue to rumble through the ages, Cyprian insists that "he can no longer have God for his Father, who has not the church for his mother. If any one could escape who was outside the ark of Noah, then he also may escape who shall be outside of the church."[32] Jesus himself had warned that "whoever is not with me is against me, and whoever does not gather with me scatters" (Mt 12:30). Can we simply set his words aside? Can the very unity of the Father, Son and Holy Spirit be so easily broken in Christ's body? Cyprian asks, "Does any one believe that this unity which thus comes from the divine strength and coheres in celestial sacraments, can be divided in the church, and can be separated by the parting asunder of opposing wills?" Hardly, Cyprian contends, for to split the church is to disobey "God's law," to violate "the faith of the Father and the Son" and to forfeit "life and salvation."[33]

Cyprian draws his reader's memory back to the events surrounding Christ's death on the cross. As the Roman soldiers divided Christ's clothing among themselves, they left one of his garments in one piece. Cyprian comments that this "coat bore with it a unity that came down from the top, that is, that came from heaven and the Father, which was not to be at all rent by the receiver and the possessor, but without separation we obtain a whole and substantial entireness." Cyprian then deduces that just as Christ's coat was left undivided at the cross, so one "cannot possess the garment of Christ who parts and divides the church of Christ."[34] Although the twelve tribes of Israel experienced division as a sign of God's judgment upon them, "Christ's people cannot be torn, His robe, woven and united throughout, is not divided by those who possess it; undivided, united, connected, to show the coherent concord of our people who put on Christ." Christ's own clothing, then, is a "sacrament and sign [by which] He has declared the unity of the Church."[35]

Other Old Testament figures and events either prefigure or sacramentally model the unity of the church. Rahab, for instance, prefigured the church. How? All those who took shelter in her home were spared from the destruction that fell upon Jericho. The "sacrament of the Passover," with its insistence that the slaughtered lamb be eaten in "one house" (Ex 12:46), demonstrates that the "flesh of Christ, and the holy of the Lord, cannot be sent abroad, nor is there any other home to believers but the one church."[36] Only by remaining firmly rooted in the foundation of the church can the believer find stability and shelter in the storms of life. Cyprian explains, "The wind does not carry away the wheat, nor does the hurricane uproot the tree that is based on a solid root. The light straws are tossed about by the tempest, the feeble trees are overthrown by the onset of the whirlwind."[37]

Although the eruption of heresy is always a painful experience for the church, Cyprian believes it performs a needed sifting process by which the chaff is separated from the wheat. It is the "perverted mind that has no peace." Heresy forces the Christian to enter deeply into a process of discernment and discrimination, a testing of the mind and heart. In turn, through this testing true believers—identified by the ability to discern between truth and error—prove that they are genuine wheat rather than insubstantial chaff. "Thus, even here," Cyprian writes, "before the day of judgment, the souls of the righteous and of the unrighteous are already divided, and the chaff is separated from the wheat."[38] The church on earth is not a mixed fellowship of wheat and chaff, as Augustine will later argue in response to his Donatist opponents. Rather, Cyprian contends, even before the last judgment those believers who possess clear minds can engage in a discerning process with the goal of separating true believer from false. Of course, Cyprian insists that a clear mark of false believers is their willingness to enter into schism, motivated by a twisted desire for a purity that the church already possesses.

Cyprian briefly discusses various marks of the church, insisting that these marks cannot be present within schismatic groups. For example, Cyprian discusses baptism and argues that "there can be no other baptism but one." Although schismatic leaders such as Novatian may believe that the baptism they administer in schism is valid, in actuality they have deserted "the fountain of life." "People are not washed among them," Cyprian insists, "but rather are made foul; nor are sins purged away, but are even accumulated. Such a nativity does not generate human beings to God, but to the devil." How is it possible for schismatics to obtain peace with God, when they have already "broken the Lord's peace with the madness of discord"?[39]

But what of Jesus' promise that when two or three are gathered in his name, he will be in the midst of them (Mt 18:19-20)? Is not the church present where two or three are gathered in Christ's name? Yes, Cyprian agrees, provided that people are genuinely gathering "in Christ's name." To gather in Christ's name, however, by definition means to gather in peace and unity, for Jesus said in the same breath that "if two of you agree on earth about anything you ask, it will be done for you by my Father in heaven" (Mt 18:19). Thus, there is a clear order and progression in Christ's promise: "He placed agreement first; He has made the concord of peace a prerequisite."[40] To attempt to gather in Christ's name while splitting from his church is, at least for Cyprian, an exercise in demonic futility. He asks, "How can two or three be assembled together in Christ's name, who, it is evident, are separated from Christ and from His gospel? For we have not withdrawn from them, but they from us."[41] Jesus' promise applies to those "two or three who pray with one mind," what Cyprian labels "the law of prayer."

Schism is so serious precisely because it violates the two greatest commandments: "you shall love the Lord your God with all your heart, and with all your soul, and with all your mind, and with all your strength. . . . You shall love your neighbor as yourself" (Mk 12:30-31). Jesus inextricably links love and unity. How, then, can Novatian's schismatic church claim to represent the gospel when it violates the heart of the gospel? "But what unity does he keep," Cyprian asks, "what love does he maintain or consider, who, savage with the madness of discord, divides the church, destroys the faith, disturbs the peace, dissipates charity, profanes the sacrament?"[42]

In addition, the willingness to split Christ's church shows a shocking disregard for the order Christ has ordained for his body. "Does he think that he has Christ, who acts in opposition to Christ's priests, who separates himself from the company of His clergy and people? He bears arms against the Church, he contends against God's appointment." Korah, Dathan and Abiram made the same mistake in rebellion against the leadership of Moses and Aaron. Does the schismatic wish to join company with such and receive the same judgment?

> An enemy of the altar, a rebel against Christ's sacrifice, for the faith faithless, for religion profane, a disobedient servant, an impious son, a hostile brother, despising the bishops, and forsaking God's priests, he dares to set up another altar, to make another prayer with unauthorized words, to profane the truth of the Lord's offering by false sacrifices, and not to know that he who strives against the appointment of God, is punished on account of the daring of his temerity by divine visitation.[43]

At this point one must ask: Were not many members of Novatian's church faithful confessors of the church during the time of persecution? How could they be faithful confessors and even martyrs and yet so terribly wrong in their act of schism? Sadly, Cyprian responds, we have already seen this tragedy enacted in the life of Judas. Even though Judas had been chosen by Christ to be an apostle, he failed in his calling. Judas's failure, however, did not cause the "faith and firmness of the apostles" to fail. In the same way, "the holiness and dignity of confessors is not forthwith diminished, because the faith of some of them is broken." Rather, the greater number of confessors have remained within the church, refusing to follow Novatian in his schism.[44]

To sum up the Cyprianic understanding of the church: The church in this world is called to be a pure and holy church. Those with a discerning mind will readily discern between the wheat and the chaff. The call of the church is to be the wheat field of the Lord in the present time. Up to this juncture Cyprian is largely in agreement with Novatian. Novatian's great error, though, is to split from his mother, the church. To do so is to break the bond of unity and peace. As Cyprian notes, "God is one, Christ is one, and His Church is one, the faith is one." To sever this unity, Cyprian contends, is to sever oneself from Christ. In his words, "Unity cannot be severed, nor can one body be separated by a division of its structure, nor torn into pieces, with its entrails wrenched asunder by laceration. Whatever has proceeded from the womb cannot live and breathe in its detached condition, but loses the substance of health."[45]

Church history will soon repeat itself in the time of Augustine. Again a group of Christians will claim to represent Christ's pure church on earth, but only by splitting off from the larger body of Christ. How will Augustine respond? Surprisingly, he will offer a different model of the church than that of Cyprian. Why? A closer investigation is surely warranted.

Augustine—the Church as a *Permixta Ecclesia*

Augustine develops at least part of his understanding of the church against the backdrop of the Donatist controversy. The Donatists, a group of Christians located largely in North Africa and named after one of their early leaders (Donatus), were of a rigorist mentality similar to that of Novatian and his followers. The question at the heart of the Donatist controversy was this: Were the rites and sacraments of the church such as baptism and ordination validly exercised and practiced by those who had lapsed during a time of persecution? In a nutshell, the Donatists argued that the church was a pure society and must be led by pure and holy leaders. Hence, the Donatists contended that a leader who had lapsed in persecution could not rightly celebrate the sacraments of the church nor ordain other Christians to positions of leadership.

Augustine's response to the Donatist position is inextricably linked to his understanding of the church. What exactly is the church? Two possible views present themselves. The first model is that of the Donatists, who picture the church as a pure, holy society inhabited only by genuine believers. The second model, that advocated by Augustine, is that of the church as a *permixta ecclesia*, a mixed society of both genuine and false believers. Yet Augustine admits that the desire for a pure church in the present age can tempt the genuine believer to leave the church in a misguided quest for holiness and purity.

> If you do not wish to be deceived and if you want to continue loving one another, be aware that each way of life in the church has hypocrites in her ranks. . . . There are bad Christians, but there are also good ones. At first glance you see a great number of bad Christians, who as a thick layer of chaff prevent you from reaching the good grains of corn.[46]

As van Bavel points out, for Augustine the church in the present age is inevitably a mixed society, "for she is made up of human beings. Thus the church reflects the human condition. The parables of the fishing net, the weeds in the field, and the threshing floor (Matt. 3:12; 13:24-30; 13:47-49) are the main arguments in support of this view."[47]

Only God clearly knows who the genuine believers are in his *permixta ecclesia*. Because sin blurs the vision of all human beings, we are unable to distinguish the wheat from the chaff. To attempt to do so, as the Donatists did, is to court spiritual pride and to ignore the blurring effect of wickedness on all human judgments, both within and without the church. "First of all," Augustine writes, "we ought to know that we are all wicked in some respect. I tell you, even good people are in some way or other wicked, just as wicked people are under some aspects good."[48] Thus, the genuine church cannot be readily discerned because of the mixture of good and evil people in its body for the present.

> These two kinds of people are mixed. . . . Therefore, do not despair with regard to the citizens of the reign of heaven, when you see them busy taking care . . . of temporal affairs in an earthly society. On the other hand, do not immediately congratulate people occupied with heavenly things, for sometimes sons of perdition sit in the chair of Moses. . . . Those who care for earthly things should lift up their hearts toward heaven, and those occupied with the words of heaven, must keep their hearts upon this earth.[49]

Augustine says much the same thing in *The City of God*. Against the background of God's sovereign predestination, Augustine comments that the church's present enemies might well end up within its membership, while apparently genuine members could prove to be false Christians. The church "must bear in mind that among these very enemies are hidden her future citizens." The same principle allows for the possibility that the church "has in her midst some who are united with her in participation in the sacraments, but who will not join with her in the eternal destiny of the saints. Some of these are hidden; some are well known." For the present time, the city of God and the city of this world "are interwoven and intermixed . . . and await separation at the last judgment."[50]

This present evil age is a time of "humiliation" for the church in which she "is preparing for future exaltation." Presently, the church "is being trained by the stings of fear, the tortures of sorrow, the distresses of hardship, and the dangers of temptation; and she rejoices only in expectation, when her joy is wholesome."[51] During her pilgrimage home "many reprobates are mingled in the Church with the good, and both sorts are collected as it were in the dragnet of the gospel; and in this world, as in a sea, both kinds swim without separation, enclosed in nets until the shore is reached." It is when the sojourning, pilgrim church reaches her final destination "that the evil are to be divided from the good, and among the good, as it were in his temple, 'God will be all in all.' "[52]

Augustine discerns the model of the church as a *permixta ecclesia* within the apostles themselves. On the one hand, God chose the apostles as the beginning of a people who were to be "multiplied beyond counting" (Ps 40:5). Beginning with the ministry of John the Baptist, the church has been expanding. Augustine writes, "Christ chose disciples, whom he also called 'apostles.' They were men of humble birth, without position, without education, so that if there was any greatness in them or in their doings that greatness would be Christ himself present in them and acting in them."

Yet this original apostolic band itself was a *permixta ecclesia*. For here we find Judas, who at first appearance appears to possess the same faith as foundation stones such as Peter, James and John. Just as Jesus allowed Judas to remain part of the apostolic community, so the church forbears with wicked people in its midst. Judas, "though evil, he used for good, both to fulfil his destiny of suffering and to present to his Church a pattern of forbearance with wicked men."[53]

Augustine is convinced that the eruption of heresies such as Donatism forms a significant part of God's providential plan for the church. Granted, the devil himself foments heresies, theological positions that bear "the Christian name—as if they could be retained indiscriminately in the City of God without reproof, just as the city of confusion retained indifferently the philosophers who held diverse and contradictory opinions." Yet these distorted and perverse opinions actually serve to advance the health of the church. "In fact, all the enemies of the Church, however blinded by error or depraved by wickedness, train the Church in patient endurance if they are given the power of inflicting bodily harm, while if they oppose her only by their perverse notions they train her in wisdom."[54] Further, through facing opposition the church cultivates the virtues of "benevolence, or even beneficence," with the result that "love may be shown even to enemies, whether this takes the form of persuasive teaching or of stern discipline."[55]

Therefore, though the devil may continually attempt to harm the journeying church, either through physical persecution or through the infiltration of harmful ideas, he can "do her no harm." God will guide the church's course through this present age, occasionally providing prosperity "so that she is not shattered by adversity," and at times granting adversity, "so that she is not corrupted by prosperity." There will always be those within the church itself "who by their unprincipled behavior torment the feelings of those who live devout lives. For such people cause the name of 'Christian' and 'Catholic' to be defamed."

Perhaps the church experiences even more acute pain when the name "Christian" is mistakenly and deceptively attached to heretical doctrines and practices. That is, "when the heretics themselves are thought to have the Christian name and the sacraments, the Scriptures, and the creed, they cause great grief in the hearts of the devout." The unfortunate result is confusion among those considering conversion to the Christian faith and an opportunity for slander to the opponents of the church.

Thankfully, God is fully capable of identifying his true church. None known by God "can perish." Even the grief experienced by genuine Christians can have a fruitful outcome, as Augustine explains:

> For the actual behavior of bad Christians or false Christians is of profit to those who grieve, since it issues from a love which makes them hate the thought that these persecutors should perish or should hinder the salvation of others. Above all, great consolations appear also when they are brought out of error; and those con-

solations overflow the souls of the devout with a joy as great as were the pains that tormented them at the thought of their perdition.[56]

Augustine reminds his readers that the trials and tribulations of a pilgrim church are nothing new. They began neither with Christ's incarnation nor the ministry of the apostles. Rather, they "started with Abel himself, the first righteous man slain by an ungodly brother; and the pilgrimage goes on from that time right up to the *end* of history, with the persecutions of the world on one side, and on the other the consolations of God."[57]

At present, then, in this present evil age, the church remains a mixed society, *a permixta ecclesia*. Surprisingly, the kingdom of heaven includes both the good and the wicked, "the man who breaks what he teaches, and the man who practices it, though one is the least and the other is great in the kingdom, while in another sense it is a kingdom into which there enters only the man who practices what he teaches."[58] The pilgrim, journeying church encompasses both the good and the evil person. The church that has reached its destination, the church which at the end of this present age arrives at its heavenly home, will encompass "only one kind . . . when no evil person will be included." Our view of the kingdom, then, and who inhabits that kingdom, depends on our viewpoint. If we view the church in its present state, it is a mixed society. If we view the church in its final, glorified state, it is a holy society composed of genuine Christians. Even in its present state, however, it is "the kingdom of Christ and the kingdom of heaven. And so even now his saints reign with him, though not in the same way as they will then reign."[59] Indeed, the pilgrim church is made up of wheat and tares, but the "tares do not reign with him, although they are growing in the Church side by side with the wheat." The tares will remain "until the collection and removal of all stumbling-blocks at the end of the world."[60]

Augustine and Cyprian do appear to disagree on the nature and composition of the church in its present life in this age. As we have seen earlier, the Cyprianic model of the church pictures the church in this present age as a pure, holy community composed of only genuine believers. The Augustinian model of the church, on the other hand, sees the church in the present age as a *permixta ecclesia*, a mixed society of both genuine and false believers. In the Augustinian model, it is only in the future that God will separate true Christians from their false counterparts. Any attempt to do so in the present time, whether it be the schism of the

Novatianists in the third century or that of the Donatists in the late fourth and early fifth centuries, will ultimately prove futile, largely because only God knows those who are genuinely his.

Both Cyprian and Augustine would agree, however, that schism is always an evil. Indeed, in Augustine's work *On Baptism, Against the Donatists*, he understands Cyprian's earlier position against the Novatianists as supporting his own perspective. In the view of both Cyprian and Augustine, the fundamental unity of the church in Christ is the underlying principle that must be preserved. For instance, although Cyprian believed that baptism was valid only within the boundaries of the catholic church—a position with which Augustine disagreed—Augustine praises him for his humility and his refusal to countenance schism. Cyprian is praiseworthy precisely because of the "way in which he preserved unity with those from whom he differed in opinion."[61]

Augustine scolds his Donatist opponents for the presumptuousness of their schism. Do they really think they can look into the heart of a *traditor* (a church leader who had lapsed and handed over church property or scriptures to the Roman authorities) and determine his status before God? Had not the apostle Paul already taught that the servant "stands or falls" to his or her own master? (Rom 14:4). Did the Donatists not see that the apostle was speaking "to men who were wishing to judge, not of open facts, but of the hearts of other men"?[62]

Even worse than the Donatists' premature judgment is their willingness to split the church in their search for a pure community. Augustine warns the Donatists not to be misled into thinking that Cyprian would have supported their position. Rather than pointing to Cyprian's support of the rebaptism of those baptized outside the church, the Donatists should recall "the example of Cyprian for the preservation of unity." Augustine acknowledges that in Cyprian's day the question of rebaptism was a disputed issue. Although Cyprian "did not himself admit as members of the Church those who had been baptized in heresy or schism," he did maintain "communion with those who did admit them."[63] Unity was clearly a more fundamental issue for Cyprian, Augustine contends, than the question of baptism. Hence, the Donatists violate the more important principle, whether it was advocated by Cyprian or Augustine. If the Donatists will not listen to Augustine, can they not at least attune their hearing to the voice of Cyprian?

Seek counsel from the blessed Cyprian himself. See how much he considered to depend upon the blessing of unity, from which he did not sever himself to avoid the communion of those who disagreed with him. Though he considered that those who were baptized outside the communion of the Church had no true baptism, he was yet willing to believe that, by simple admission into the Church, they might, merely in virtue of the bond of unity, be admitted to a share in pardon.[64]

What is the final principle to be upheld? The fulfilling of the demands of love must always take precedence. Hence, the attempt to split the church over any lesser principle must be rejected. Cyprian fulfilled this principle, Augustine repeatedly argues, in his unwillingness to violate the unity of the church by tolerating Novatian's schism. Christ himself "came not to destroy the law, but to fulfill. But the fulfilling of the law is love. And in this Cyprian abounded greatly, insomuch that though he held a different view concerning baptism, he yet did not forsake the unity of the Church, and was in the Lord's vine a branch firmly rooted."[65] Those who would forsake the unity of the church, "the enemies of brotherly love," are in reality "false Christians, and antichrists." How can they be identified? When the opportunity to split the church occurs, they grab it. In fact, even if they remain within the church because the opportunity for schism is lacking, "they are severed from that invisible bond of love." How so? When the opportunity to split the church does arise, they quickly exploit it. The apostle John himself had warned of those who "went out from us, but they did not belong to us; for if they had belonged to us, they would have remained with us" (1 Jn 2:19). Augustine comments that John "did not say that they ceased to be of us by going out, but that they went out because they were not of us." That is, the mark of the false Christian, the wolf in sheep's clothing, is the willingness to split Christ's body into warring factions.

"Even if anyone is laboring under a defect of body,
yet if he is an observer of the doctrines delivered by Christ,
He will raise him up at His second advent perfectly sound.
He will make him immortal, incorruptible, and free from grief."

JUSTIN MARTYR
Dialogue with Trypho

"That same power can reunite what is dissolved.
It can raise up what is prostrate, and restore the dead to life again.
It can put the corruptible into a state of incorruption.
And the same Being, and the same power and skill,
can separate that which has been broken up and distributed
among a multitude of animals. . . . He can separate this, I say,
and unite it again with the proper members and parts of members.
And this is whether it has passed into one animal,
or into many, or even if it has passed from one animal into others."

ATHENAGORAS
On the Resurrection of the Dead

"And if the martyrs have had any limbs cut off, any parts removed,
they will not lack those parts at the resurrection;
for they have been told that 'not a hair of your head will perish.'
But if it will be right that in that new age the marks of glorious wounds
should remain in those immortal bodies,
for all to see, then scars of the blows or the cuts will also be visible
in places where limbs were hacked off,
although the parts have not been lost, but restored."

AUGUSTINE
City of God

ELEVEN

THE RESURRECTION
OF THE BODY
AND THE LIFE
EVERLASTING

The Question of the Resurrection

A constellation of concerns, interests and questions surrounds the fathers' discussion of the resurrection. Was it believable that Jesus had been raised from the dead? Why the necessity of a resurrection? Was Jesus' physical body raised from the dead? Would the bodies of believers also be resurrected in the same manner? If so, when? And what of the mechanics of the whole process? How, for example, could a body be raised from the dead if it had been burned to ashes or eaten by a wild animal? Was not God, after all, more interested in the soul than the body? What, indeed, was the relationship between the two? Could you genuinely be a human person if soul or body were lacking?[1]

Resurrection in the Apostolic Fathers

From the apostolic fathers on, the resurrection—both of Christ and of his followers—remained a topic of reflection. For example, *1 Clement*, a letter written toward the end of the first century, mentions a series of benefits related to Christ's incarnation. Among these is the "taste of immortal knowledge," a knowledge grounded upon Christ's resurrection from the dead.

The apostles received the gospel for us from Jesus Christ, and Jesus the Christ was sent from God. So Christ is from God and the apostles are from Christ: thus both came in proper order by the will of God. And so the apostles, after they had received their orders and in full assurance *by reason of the resurrection of our Lord Jesus Christ*, being full of faith in the word of God, went out in the conviction of the Holy Spirit preaching the good news that God's kingdom was about to come.[2]

Clement consistently argues that his audience, the congregation at Corinth, should be living in harmony rather than bickering. Why bicker if Christ is soon to return? At Christ's coming the dead will be raised, a resurrection previewed in Jesus' own resurrection. As Paul writes in 1 Corinthians 15, Clement reminds his readers that Christ is the firstfruits of the resurrection. Interestingly, Clement proceeds to see in the created order itself analogies of the resurrection.

Let us consider, beloved, how the Master continually points out that future resurrection which is to be, of which he made our Lord Jesus Christ the first fruits when he raised him from the dead. Let us observe, beloved, the resurrection that occurs in the regularity of the seasons. Day and night manifest resurrection: night falls asleep, and day arises; day departs, night returns. Or take for example the crops: how and in what way is the sowing done? The sower goes out and sows each seed in the ground, and they fall in the earth dry and bare, and decay. Then from their decay the wondrous providence of the Master raises them, and from each one more grow and bear fruit.[3]

Second Clement, in all likelihood a sermon, links a future resurrection with the necessity of repentance, and the reality of future rewards and punishments. As we have sinned in our bodies, so we will experience judgment and punishment in them if we fail to repent. As Joanne E. McWilliam Dewart summarizes Clement's argument, "Christians receive salvation themselves in the flesh, and Christ, the means of salvation, was himself enfleshed. It is therefore appropriate that the future reward should also be 'in the flesh.'"[4]

Not only will the saved receive rewards in the flesh, but those "who have gone astray or denied Jesus" will be punished in the flesh. If so, how are we to understand the relationship between the flesh and the soul or spirit/Spirit? This will be a key issue of investigation in this chapter, as the relationship between the soul, body, and spirit/Spirit remained a topic of inquiry for almost all the fathers.

Many people in the ancient world, particularly those from a Greek or Roman background, had a terribly difficult time making sense of a resurrection of the body from the dead, largely because of a prevalent dualism rooted in much Greek and Roman philosophy. Augustine, for instance, refers to Cicero's comment in *On the Commonwealth* that, while Hercules and Romulus "were deified human beings," their deification did not include their earthly bodies. Why? Cicero responds, "Their bodies were not taken up into heaven, indeed Nature would not allow what comes of the earth to dwell anywhere but on the earth."[5] For Cicero, the world of nature and the world of spirit simply do not mix.

However, 2 *Clement* remains unconvinced that this sharp division between spirit and flesh is correct, arguing that "this flesh is able to receive so great a life and immortality because the Holy Spirit is closely joined to it, nor can anyone express or declare 'what things the Lord has prepared' for his elect."[6] Perhaps the link between the flesh and the realm of the Spirit/spirit is much closer than one would have expected. At this early stage, 2 *Clement* points to such an intimate connection, and other patristic writers will develop this relationship.

Other apostolic writers plant seeds that will blossom in the writings of the great doctors of the church. Ignatius, an early Christian bishop and martyr, links the conquering of death and resurrection to the arrival of the age to come. Christ's death and resurrection were the sign this new age had begun. In his letter to the Ephesians Ignatius celebrates the destruction of the "old kingdom" as, in the incarnation, "God was becoming manifest in human form for the newness of eternal life; what had been prepared by God had its beginning. Hence everything was shaken together, for the abolition of death was being planned."[7] As Christians look to the "ensign" raised by Christ "through the resurrection," they can know that their own resurrection is assured. Thus Ignatius writes, "He was truly raised from the dead, when his Father raised him up, as in similar fashion his Father will raise up in Christ Jesus us who believe him—without whom we have no true life."[8] This future resurrection, Ignatius insists against all who would spiritualize it, will be a physical one. After all, Christ's own resurrection was surely that of a physical body.

> For I know and am confident that even after the resurrection he was in the flesh. And when he came to those with Peter he said to them, "Take, handle me, and see that I am not an incorporeal demon." And they immediately touched him and believed, being mingled with his flesh and spirit. Therefore they despised death

and were found to be above death. And after the resurrection he ate and drank
with them as a being of flesh, though he was spiritually united with the Father.[9]

Indeed, it is Ignatius's confidence in a future resurrection that fuels his deter-
mination to die as Christ's witness: "May I rise again in [my bonds] . . . so that I
may be found in the lot apportioned to the Ephesian Christians."[10]

Polycarp's letter to the Philippians highlights two key problems the early
Christian community struggled to understand concerning the resurrection. The
first was the delay of Christ's Parousia. If Christ had been raised from the dead
and was indeed alive and well at the right hand of the Father, why was he delay-
ing his return? Behind the question of Christ's delay was evidently, at least for
some, the question of his resurrection. In short, if Jesus had been resurrected
from the dead and ascended to heaven, surely he would have returned by now. A
second reoccurring question related to the nature of Christ's resurrection. Had
Christ's physical body been raised from the dead or not? The idea of a *spiritual* resurrection, as we have seen, frequently remained attractive to Gentile Christians
raised in a Greco-Roman context. A physical resurrection, at least to the Greek
mind, appeared to raise insuperable philosophical and physical problems.

Polycarp is quick to respond to both issues. First, regarding the delay in
Christ's second coming, Polycarp does not attempt to deal with timing. Instead,
in what Dewart describes as a "catena of New Testament phrases," Polycarp
links together a series of fundamental theological affirmations, none of which can
easily and logically stand on its own apart from the reality of Christ's resurrection.

> Serve God in fear and truth; give up empty vain discussion and the error of the
> crowd; believe "him who raised our Lord Jesus Christ from the dead and gave him
> glory" and a throne at his right hand, to whom were subjected all things in heaven
> and earth, whom every breathing thing serves, who is coming as judge of the living
> and the dead, whose blood God will require of those who disobey him. And "he
> who raised him" from the dead "will also raise us" if we do his will and walk in his
> commandments.[11]

For the Christian, Polycarp insists, belief in the true God necessarily entails
belief in the resurrection, for God is the one who raised Jesus from the dead. To
worship God is to worship the God of the resurrection. Because Jesus has been
raised, he is now reigning in heaven, sitting enthroned at the Father's right hand.

Though Christ's coming has been delayed, it is assured, and when Christ comes, both living and dead will be judged. Finally, Polycarp emphasizes, if Jesus has been raised from the dead, so those who have believed in him will also experience resurrection.

In light of these wondrous realities, the Christian is called to faithful witness. For instance, Polycarp himself was one of the first great martyrs or confessors of the faith.[12] The *Acts of the Martyrs*, written in the middle of the second century, records the words of Polycarp shortly before his death, words addressed to the God he had faithfully served all his life:

> "I bless you" because "you have considered me worthy" of this day and hour to receive "a portion among the number" of the martyrs, in the "cup" of "your Christ" unto the resurrection of eternal life "both of soul and body" in the "incorruption" of the Holy Spirit.[13]

Note carefully Polycarp's insistence on the resurrection of "both soul and body." He has little patience with those who would advocate a spiritual resurrection. For Polycarp, Christ's first coming was "in the flesh," as was his resurrection.

> For "everyone who does not confess that Jesus Christ came in the flesh is antichrist"; and anyone who does not confess the testimony of the cross is "of the devil"; and anyone who perverts the sayings of the Lord to suit "his own lusts" and says that there is neither a resurrection nor a judgment—that man is the first-born of Satan![14]

The Contribution of the Apologists

What insights do the apologists, writing in the second half of the second century, add to the fathers' understanding of the resurrection? Justin Martyr's work is particularly interesting, partly because he attempts to defend the tenets of the Christian faith against the objections of both a Jewish and a Roman audience. In Justin's *Dialogue with Trypho* Justin purposefully highlights an aspect of Christian belief that relates to Jewish perspectives: the return of a reigning Messiah to Jerusalem, where he will reign for one thousand years. It is the distinction between the first coming of the Messiah, during which the anointed one suffers, and his second coming in glory that the Jewish people failed to understand. Yet,

Justin argues, if Israel had been reading the Old Testament well they would have recognized this fundamental distinction.

> It was foretold by the Patriarch Jacob . . . that there would be two advents of Christ, and that in the first he would be subject to suffering, and that after this advent you people would have neither prophet nor king, and that the Gentiles who believe in the suffering Christ would look forward to his second coming.[15]

Justin is convinced that how one responds to the first coming of the Messiah holds significant, indeed, grave implications for what will occur when the Messiah returns a second time.

> Christ has come in his power from the almighty Father . . . calling all men to friendship, benediction, repentance and community, which should take place in the same land of all the saints [Canaan], of which he has pledged that there shall be an allotted portion for all the faithful. . . . Wherefore, men from every land, whether slaves or free men, who believe in Christ and recognize the truth of his words and those of the Prophets, fully realize that they will one day be united with him in that land, to inherit imperishable blessings for all eternity.[16]

Such a second coming and corollary inheritance demands not only the previous resurrection of the Messiah but also the future resurrection of those who place their faith in him. If the Jews had been reading the Old Testament carefully, Justin believes, they would have heard the prophets speaking just along these lines. Indeed, past righteous saints such as Jacob, Enoch and Noah will share in the resurrection.

> Since they who did those things which are universally, naturally and eternally good are pleasing to God, they shall be saved in the resurrection, together with their righteous forefathers . . . [and] with those who believe in Christ, the Son of God, who existed before the morning star and the moon, yet deigned to become incarnate, and be born of this virgin of the family of David, in order that by this dispensation he might conquer the serpent, that first sinner, and the angels who followed his example, and that he might thwart death and bring it to an end, so that, at the second coming of Christ, it would no longer have any power over those who believe in him and live according to his principles. At this second advent of Christ, some will be condemned to suffer eternally in the fires of hell, while others will be eternally free from suffering, corruption, and sorrow.[17]

Justin's responses to a Roman audience focus, wisely I think, on questions and concerns that a Latin audience would naturally have with the concept of a physical resurrection from the dead. Is it logical, Justin asks the Roman emperor Antoninus Pius, for the Roman mind to reject the resurrection outright? After all, did not Roman religious practices themselves affirm the idea of life after death?

> Let the oracles of the dead and the sorcery you perform through innocent children, and the invoking of the souls of the dead, let those whom the magicians call dream-sending and familiar spirits, and let whatever else is performed by those skilled in such arts convince you that even after death souls remain in a state of sensibility. Be convinced, likewise . . . by the teaching of the writers Empedocles and Pythagoras, Plato and Socrates, and by the ditch of Homer, and by the descent of Ulysses to see the dead, and by those who told similar stories. Treat us, therefore, in a similar manner as you treat them, for we believe in God not less, but more than they do, since we expect that our own bodies, even though they should be dead and buried in the earth, will be revived; for we claim that nothing is impossible with God.[18]

Justin's last point is especially significant, largely because the Roman mind had deep reservations about the possibility of the physical resurrection of a dead body. What if a shark had devoured someone at sea? How could such a body, now digested in the entrails of a fish, possibly be resurrected? Justin contends that only the vast, incomprehensible power of God could produce such a wonder. But, Justin argued, were there not markers already planted in the natural order pointing toward the mysterious, immeasurable power of God? Consider, for instance, human conception and gestation itself.

> And what would seem more incredible to a thinking person than if we were not in a body and someone were to affirm that from a little drop of the human seed it were possible to shape bones, muscles and flesh into the human form we now see? Now let us make this supposition: if you yourselves had not the form you now have, and were not born of parents like yours, and someone were to show you the human seed and the painted picture of a man, and were to affirm that from such a seed such a being could be produced, would you believe him before you saw the actual production? No one would dare deny [that you would not]. In like manner, because you have never witnessed a dead person rise again to life, you refuse to believe. . . . so now realize that it is not impossible that human bodies, after they are

dead and disseminated in the earth like seeds [1 Cor 15:35-44], should at the appointed time, at God's command, arise and assume immortality. . . . We [Christians] have learned that it is better to believe what is impossible to our own nature and to men than, like other men, to be unbelievers, for we know that our Teacher, Jesus Christ, has said: "What is impossible with men, is possible with God."[19]

Theophilus of Antioch makes much the same point but adds the essential element of *trust* in God's power to raise the dead. Note also how Theophilus connects the wonder of conception to the possibility of a future resurrection.

> If, then, the farmer trusts the earth and the sailor the ship and the sick man the physician, do you not want to entrust yourself to God, when you have received so many pledges from him? The first pledge is that he created you, bringing you from nonexistence to existence. . . . He formed you out of a small, moist matter and a tiny drop, which itself previously did not exist. It was God who brought you into this life. Second, you believe that statues made by men are gods and work miracles. Then do you not believe that the God who made you can later make you over again?[20]

A Closer Look: Athenagoras on the Resurrection

Before we turn to Athenagoras's analysis regarding the resurrection of decomposed or destroyed human bodies, a short look at the building blocks of his general argument may prove helpful. Athenagoras begins by asserting the reality of God's existence as the "cause of all things" and then explores the implications of God's existence, power and knowledge for a future resurrection. Can those who oppose the resurrection of the dead "show that it is either impossible for God, or contrary to His will, to unite and gather together again bodies that are dead, or even entirely dissolved into their elements, so as to constitute the same persons"?[21]

The notion of impossibility itself, argues Athenagoras, is inextricably linked to a lack of both knowledge and power. As he explains it, "A thing is in strictness of language considered impossible to a person, when it is of such a kind that he either does not know what is to be done, or has not sufficient power for the proper doing of the thing known."[22] If one lacks the knowledge of how to do something, how can one do it? Likewise, one might possess the knowledge of how to do something but lack the power to "do the thing known." Neither possibility is true of God.

What of destroyed or decomposed bodies? Consider the problem posed by the destruction and decomposition of human bodies to the possibility of bodily resurrection. Let us return, for instance, to our example of a hungry shark. Not only would an eaten body ultimately disappear, actually mingling with the body of a shark if devoured by such, but one wonders how in the world could ever God find such a body. It surely would have disappeared in the depths of the sea.

Athenagoras's response to this puzzling situation is multileveled and based on his confidence in *both God's knowledge and power*. First, Athenagoras contends that the dissolution of a human body is no problem for God, principally because of the comprehensive nature of God's knowledge. God knows the location of every human body, intact or not; in addition, God understands the human body's nature and composition.

> It is impossible for God . . . to be ignorant of the nature of our bodies which are destined to arise; he knows every part and member in their entirety. Nor indeed can he be ignorant as to where everything goes that decomposes and what part of the appropriate element receives what is decomposed and dissolved into its own kind.[23]

God's knowledge, though, would not be sufficient if it was not inextricably linked to divine power. What God knows God can infallibly accomplish. The marriage of divine power and knowledge guarantees the resurrection of the dead. If God has managed to create us from nothing in the first place, the re-creation of a decomposed body presents little problem.

> As to power, the creation of our bodies shows that God's power suffices for their resurrection. For if when he first gave them form, he made the bodies of men and their principal constituents from nothing, he will just as easily raise them up again after their dissolution, however that may have taken place. For this is equally possible for him.[24]

Interestingly enough, Dewart comments that Athenagoras is "the first christian writer to introduce (in lengthy and graphic detail) the notion of 'chain consumption' (humans eating beasts which have eaten humans),"[25] or to expand upon our earlier illustration, sharks who have eaten bodies and in turn are eaten by sailors. Such a chain of events, Athenagoras argues, presents no great difficulty to God.

After [the parts of the bodies devoured by beasts and eaten again by humans] have been separated again from the elements by the wisdom and power of him who links every kind of animal with its appropriate properties, they reunite intimately, one part with the other, even though they may be consumed by fire, rotted away by water, devoured by wild beasts or any animal that comes along, or have one part which has been cut off from the whole body and has decomposed before the others. They are united again to one another and occupy the same place as before so as to restore the harmonious composition of the body and effect the resurrection and the life of the body that has died and has totally decomposed.[26]

God, then, can surely surmount whatever practical problems the idea of a physical resurrection seems to pose. His power and wisdom guarantee such. Furthermore, though, Athenagoras accentuates God's willingness to raise the dead. God wills to raise the dead, because to do so fulfills the purpose behind humanity's creation, a purpose that surpasses that of other forms of animal life. It is humanity alone that is created in God's image, and thus is destined for immortality.

God made man for his own sake and out of the goodness and wisdom which is reflected throughout creation. . . .[And he made him for immortal life because] the Maker has decreed an unending existence to those who bear his image in themselves, are gifted with intelligence, and share the faculty for rational discernment, so that they, knowing their Maker and his power and wisdom and complying with law and justice, might live without distress eternally with the powers by which they governed their former life, even though they were in corruptible and human bodies.[27]

Because God wills the resurrection of human life, we can rest assured that death will not have the final word. Thus Athenagoras concludes:

We have put our confidence in an infallible security, the will of our Creator, according to which he made man of an immortal soul and a body and endowed him with intelligence and an innate law to safeguard and protect the things which he gave that are suitable for intelligent beings with a rational life. We full well know that he would not have formed such an animal and adorned him with all that contributes to permanence if he did not want this creature to be permanent. The Creator of our universe made man that he might participate in rational life and, after contemplating God's majesty and universal wisdom, perdure and make them the object of his eternal contemplation, in accordance with the divine will and the nature alloted to him. The reason then for man's creation guarantees his eternal survival, and his survival guarantees his resurrection, without which he could not survive as *man*.[28]

Why is this so? A human being is a composite being, a union of body and soul. That is, "human nature universally considered is constituted by an immortal soul and a body which has been united with it at its creation." Neither the soul nor the body is designed by God to exist alone, apart from its partner. Thus, "it is necessary, since all there is exists as one living being composed of two parts, undergoing all the experiences of soul and body . . . [that we] be fully integrated into one harmonious and concordant whole." Indeed, "without [the resurrection] the same parts would not be united with one another in a way that conforms with their nature, nor would the same men be reconstituted as they were."[29] God can be trusted to preserve human nature fully in its resurrected state.

Not only is God trustworthy, but, according to Theophilus of Antioch, the created order itself manifests a trustworthiness pointing to the power of God, a power more than equal to the challenge of resurrecting bodies from the dead.

God has given you many indications for believing him. If you will, consider the termination of the seasons and days and nights and how they die and rise again. And what of the resurrection of seeds and fruits, occurring for the benefit of mankind? One might mention that a grain of wheat or other seeds when cast into the earth first dies and is destroyed, then is raised and becomes an ear. . . . "All these things the *Sophia* of God works" . . . in order to demonstrate, even through these, that God is powerful enough to bring about the general resurrection of all men.[30]

The ethical necessity of a future resurrection. Not only is God all-powerful, but God is just. In this vein Justin warned his Roman persecutors that in light of God's power and justice their actions would some day warrant God's judgment; good deeds would be rewarded and evil deeds punished. Of course, such a recompense could only be possible if those who had committed good or evil acts still existed, even after death. Thus, there is an ethical necessity for a future resurrection. Human free will and human moral awareness demand a future righteous divine judgment. Justin explains:

Since God, from the very beginning, created the race of angels and men with free will, they will justly pay the penalty in everlasting fire for the sins they have committed. . . . The truth of this is shown everywhere by those legislators and philosophers who, acting according to right reason, have ordered some things to be done and others to be avoided. . . . Lest any one repeat the mistake of those so-called philosophers who claim that our statements that sinners are punished in everlasting fire are just boastful words calculated to instill terror, and that we want men to live a virtuous life through fear, and not because such a life is pleasant, I will make this brief reply, that if it is not as we say, then there is no God; or, if there is a God, he is not concerned with men, and virtue and vice are nothing, and legislators unjustly punish the transgressors of their excellent precepts.[31]

Athenagoras makes much the same point. Deeds done by both soul and body will surely be judged, and such a judgment can occur only if there is a resurrection.

It is necessary that such a man [made up of body and soul] should be held accountable for all his deeds and receive reward and punishment because of them. Just judgement requires the composite creature for his deeds. The soul alone should not receive the wages for deeds done in conjunction with the body . . . nor should the body alone be requited. . . . It is man, the combination of both, who receives judgement for each of his deeds. Our inquiry finds that this does not happen in our life-time. . . . Nor does it happen after our death; for the composite creature no longer exists when the soul is separated from the body and when the body itself is again dispersed among the elements from which it came and no longer preserves anything of its previous form or shape, still less any memory of its actions. What follows is clear to everyone: that this corruptible and dispersible body must, according to the apostle, put on incorruptibility, so that, when the dead are revivified through the resurrection and what has been separated or entirely dissolved is reunited, each may receive his just recompense for what he did in the body, whether good or evil.[32]

In the final analysis, Athenagoras contends, the "final cause" of humanity demands a resurrection. If the end of humanity is to love God and contemplate God forever, death must finally be overcome.

Huankind's end must surely be distinguished from that common to other creatures, since it has to do with a distinctive nature. Certainly it is not right to argue for the same end both for creatures who have no share in rational discrimination and for those who act in accordance with an innate rational law and can exercise prudence

and justice. . . . If the end has to do with the composite, and if this cannot be discovered either while men are still alive here below . . . nor yet when the soul is in a
state of separation . . . then the end of men must certainly be seen in some other
state of the same composite creature. . . . Since this is the necessary consequence,
there must surely be a resurrection of bodies that have died or even undergone
complete dissolution, and the same men must rise again. . . . The same body cannot
receive the same soul in any other way than by resurrection. When this takes
place, the end that suits human nature is the result.[33]

The arguments on the resurrection presented by early Christian apologists
such as Athenagoras maintained a long shelf life. It is interesting to note how
Augustine, the great Western church father, incorporated and developed these
key defenses of the resurrection. A closer look at Augustine's thoughts on the
resurrection in *City of God* might well prove worthwhile.

Augustine on the Resurrection

In *The City of God*, Augustine provides an extremely helpful roadmap through the
myriad questions surrounding the early Christian understanding of the resurrection. Whether it be the question of rewards and punishment after death (and
hence the necessity of some kind of resurrection), the nature of a resurrected
body, the rationale behind belief in the resurrection, miracles as attestations of
the resurrection, the problem of the future life for aborted children, the age of
people in the resurrected state, the question of gender after the resurrection, the
resurrection of a decomposed and dispersed body or the relationship between
Christ's resurrected body and that of the believer, Augustine has keen insights to
offer. As almost always, Augustine is worth spending an evening with, and book
twenty-two of the *City of God* will surely offer much food for thought.

Why should we believe in a future resurrection? Augustine believes that the
reality of either future blessing or punishment for all human beings demands a
resurrected state. He points his audience to the reality of Old Testament prophecies that have already been fulfilled and notes that prophecies predicting a future
resurrection have yet to reach fulfillment. That is, "by the lips of another prophet
we are told what God said to him: '. . . And many of those who sleep in the dust
. . . of the earth will rise up, some to go to eternal life, while the others go to
reproach and eternal shame.' "[34] If so, a resurrection of all people would seem to

be demanded. Is such an event either reasonable or possible?

Many in Augustine's world would say no. Cicero, as we have seen, in referring to the deified Hercules and Romulus, specifically states that "their bodies were not taken up into heaven, *indeed Nature would not allow what comes of the earth to dwell anywhere but on earth.*"[35] Augustine, to no one's surprise, finds Cicero's position less than convincing. Augustine asks us to "suppose that we were merely souls, that is, spirits without bodies." If we had once inhabited heaven simply as souls and "knew nothing of earthly creatures," we would have a terribly difficult time believing that "we were going to be linked with earthly bodies by some miraculous bond, to give life to those bodies." Surely our experience in heaven would have convinced us that "Nature does not allow an incorporeal substance to be bound by a corporeal tie."[36]

Yet the world we inhabit is filled with "souls animating these earthly frames, combined and bound up with them in a mysterious fashion." If so, why should we be surprised that if God wills "that an earthly body be raised up to a heavenly body," God should be able to accomplish this surprising feat? After all, God has already managed to couple the soul, belonging "to a more exalted order of being than any body," with an earthly body. If this much more difficult task has already been accomplished through God's will, knowledge and power, "will heaven distain to receive" the "earthly particle" now sustained and animated by the soul? Hardly. Rather, this resurrection has not yet occurred because "the time has not yet come when he has decided that it should happen." Only a cheap "familiarity" with the present state of affairs, in which souls indwell human bodies in our earthly existence, has blinded us to the "much more wonderful" state of affairs awaiting us in the future.[37]

The future resurrection remains inexplicable and mysterious to us because we "have never observed" anything like it. Yet if the greater miracle has already taken place, "the interweaving of material with immaterial substances, . . . the conjunction of the material with the immaterial," the terrestrial body with a heavenly one, should prove no problem.[38]

The nature of the soul and body, however, are not the linchpin of Augustine's response to the objections of philosophers such as Cicero regarding the possibility of resurrection. What of Christ's own resurrection? While in Cicero's day the idea of resurrection might have made little sense, one could no longer remain in doubt, since "the whole world has now come to believe that the earthly body of Christ has been taken up into heaven."[39] Granted, Christ's resurrection might remain incredible to the wider world, but "if it is incredible, then surely it is even more incredible that so incredible a thing should be so credited!" That is to say, if many believe in Christ's resurrection, in itself an incredible event, why should one be surprised if people also believe in the future resurrection of human bodies, "especially as both those incredibilities (one of which we see fulfilled, while we believe the other) are predicted in the same Scriptures by which the world has been brought to believe."[40]

Consider, Augustine encourages his readers, the remarkable fashion in which people came to faith in Jesus' resurrection. First one must consider the humble background and character traits of the earliest witnesses to the resurrection; they were hardly an impressive bunch. In Augustine's words, "There were just a few men, the merest handful, untrained in the liberal arts, completely uneducated, as far as pagan philosophy is concerned, with no knowledge of literature, no equipment in logic, no trappings of rhetoric."[41] Here, indeed, is a third great "incredibility."

Thus, Augustine asserts confidently, we have three incredibilities, all pointing to the reality of Christ's resurrection and of a wider resurrection in the future: (1) Christ himself has been raised from the dead and "with his flesh" has ascended into heaven; (2) the world has believed in Christ's resurrection; and (3) "it is incredible that men of no birth, no standing, no learning, and so few of them, should have been able to persuade, so effectively, the whole world, including the learned men."[42]

Why would people believe the testimony of the ragtag group of disciples? Belief was elicited not only by the apostles' words but by their miraculous deeds, signs pointing to the truth of the resurrection.

> For those who had not witnessed Christ's resurrection in the flesh, and his ascension into heaven in that same flesh, believed the report of those who told what they had seen, who not only spoke of it, but displayed miraculous signs. In fact, people who were known to have only one language, or two at most, were suddenly heard speaking miraculously in the languages of all nations; a man lame from birth stood up, sound and strong after forty years, cured at their word in the name of Christ; cloths taken from their persons had power to heal the sick; a countless number of

sufferers from various diseases were stationed along the road by which the disciples were to pass, so that as they passed their shadows might pass over the sufferers and, as a rule, the sick were restored to health; and many other amazing acts were performed by the disciples in Christ's name; indeed, even the dead were restored to life. All this was observed by those who had not witnessed Christ's resurrection.[43]

Augustine insists, then, that Christians from Jesus' day forward have held to three central beliefs: Christ himself has been raised from the dead and is alive in heaven; there will be a future resurrection of humanity; and the human body itself is immortal. Despite the fact that these central affirmations resulted in the suffering and deaths of many believers, they were "fearlessly proclaimed" and produced "a more plentiful harvest throughout the world when the blood of martyrs was the seeds sown."[44]

Augustine helpfully lists a number of common objections the "pagans" raise against the idea of a physical resurrection from the dead. For example, will aborted children rise from the dead? Moreover, what of the size of resurrected bodies? That is, "Will all bodies be the same height and size? Or will there be different shapes and sizes? And if they are all the same, what about abortive births?"[45] Even if aborted children do not rise, the same question applies to children: "How can they attain the size which they have not reached when they die at that early age?" In addition, Jesus' words that "not a hair of your head will perish" (Lk 21:18) raise a number of difficulties. When this text is compared with Paul's words that believers will attain "to maturity, to the measure of the full stature of Christ" (Eph 4:13) and his teaching that we are "predestined to be conformed to the image of his Son" (Rom 8:29), Augustine's pagan opponents raise a number of objections.

> If we are to take this to mean that all human beings who will be in his kingdom will have bodies of the same size and shape as Christ's body, then, say the pagans, "many people will need a reduction in size and height of body; and then what happens to that promise that 'not a hair will perish,' if such a great amount of the actual body is to be removed?" And indeed, in this matter of hair, one might ask whether all that the barber has cut off is to be restored! . . . And what of the fingernails? It seems to follow of necessity that all that has been removed in manicure must be replaced! And then what happens to the body's comeliness, which ought

surely to be greater, in that immortal condition, than it could be in the state of decay? And yet, if all this is not restored, it follows that it will perish; and then, they say, what about that assurance that "not a hair will perish"? They produce similar arguments about fatness and thinness.[46]

In addition, the process of decay and decomposition seems to pose insupera-ble difficulties for a physical resurrection of the dead, since "some in part are turned into dust, and in part evaporate into the air; some people are consumed by wild beasts, others by fire; others again perish by shipwreck or meet some watery end, and their flesh decays and dissolves."[47] The total loss of physical integrity in such cases seems *de facto* to preclude resurrection.

Will persons born with deformities, defects or other congenital difficulties retain this "unpleasantness" in the resurrection? If the Christian theologian says that they will not, Augustine observes, the wounds of Christ himself seemed to pose a problem. If "Christ rose from the dead with those marks on his body," why should one think that other marks or wounds would be eradicated in the resurrection?

Augustine believes "the most difficult question," however, concerns cannibal-ism: "When someone's body has been eaten by another man, who turns to canni-balism on the compulsion of hunger, into whose body will it return?"

> For it has been converted into the flesh of the man who has been nourished by such food, and it has supplied the losses which the emaciation of hunger had pro-duced. Is it then to be returned to the man whose body it had been originally? Or to the man whose flesh it became?[48]

Augustine proceeds to answer each question, laying out his understanding of the resurrection in the process. What, for example, of aborted babies? Augustine writes that "I cannot bring myself either to affirm or deny that they will share in the resurrection." "And yet," he continues, "if they are not excluded from the number of the dead, I cannot see how they can be excluded from the resurrection of the dead."

> For either it is not all the dead that will rise again, and there will be some souls eter-nally without bodies, although they had human bodies, even if only in the mother's womb, or else all human souls will receive again the bodies which they had, when those bodies rise again, wherever the bodies they left lived and died.[49]

Thus, the same question applies to both aborted children and young children who die outside the womb. What will be the nature of their resurrected body? Will they have the body of a child in heaven? Augustine does not think so. Rather, by what Augustine describes as a "marvelous and instantaneous act of God," those who have died young will "gain that maturity they would have attained by the slow lapse of time." All children possess the potential for growth and maturity, a potential that will reach its fulfillment in the resurrected state. If an early death prevented the "material realization" of the "potential stature" provided in conception itself, "what was lacking will be supplied."[50] Augustine explains:

> All parts of the body are already latent in the seed, although a number of them are still lacking even at birth, the teeth, for instance, and other such details. There is thus, it seems, a kind of pattern already imposed potentially on the material sub-stance of the individual, set out, one might say, like the pattern on a loom; and thus what does not yet exist, or rather what is there but hidden, will come into being, or rather will appear, in the course of time.[51]

Augustine clearly sees this future realization of the body's potential as promised in Christ's words, "not a hair of your head will perish." Even apart from Christ's promise, however, "it could not be beyond the resources of the Creator, who made everything from nothing, to make the additions that he, the Supreme Artist, knew to be required."[52]

What of the question of human stature in the resurrected state? For example, I am over six feet tall. Will I be such in the resurrection? Augustine would answer affirmatively. Just as the resurrected Jesus "appeared to the disciples in the form that was so familiar to them," so we too will experience the same continuity. Again, Augustine links his expectation here to Jesus' words that "not one hair will perish." If in my resurrected body I was under six feet tall, the promise would appear to be undercut. Augustine concludes, "It remains, therefore, that each person will be given the stature which he had in his prime, even though he was an old man when he died, or, if he died before maturity, the stature he would have attained."[53]

If we are raised in a fully realized or developed state, reaching the potential contained in our bodies from conception, the question of gender in the resurrection must be addressed. Will males be raised male, and females raised female? Will such distinctions be maintained in the age to come? Some were apparently arguing that women would be raised as men, because "God made man out of clay, and woman out of man." Augustine contends that a "more sensible opinion" would posit the continuation of sexual differentiation in the resurrection, with the sexual lust connected with the Fall eradicated in the resurrected state. After all, sexual distinctions were part of the created order before the sin of Adam and Eve.

God will remove all "defects" from human bodies in the resurrection, but Augustine insists that a body's "essential nature will be preserved" and that "a woman's sex is not a defect. It is natural.

> And in the resurrection it will be free of the necessity of intercourse and childbirth. However, the female organs will not subserve their former use; they will be part of a new beauty, which will not excite the lust of the beholder—there will be no lust in that life—but will arouse the praises of God for his wisdom and compassion, in that he not only created out of nothing but freed from corruption that which he had created.[54]

What of the question of human defect and deformity? Will deformities remain in the resurrection? Augustine argues that while nothing will be lost that was present in the earthly body—basing this conclusion on Jesus' promise that not a hair will perish—those constituents of the body that had caused deformity would no longer "be in places where they would disfigure the proportions of the parts." Such a healing redistribution does not necessitate a loss of anything essential to the body itself. Augustine illustrates his point through an analogy drawn from the potter's craft.

> If clay is used to make a pot, and then the material is brought back to the original lump to make a completely fresh start, it is not essential that the piece of clay which formed the handle should make the handle in the second attempt; and the same with the bottom of the pot, and so on. All that is required is that the whole pot should be re-made out of the whole lump, that is, that all the clay should go back into the whole pot, with nothing left over.[55]

Thus, no constituent of the body will be lost in the resurrection. Rather, each will occupy the place for which it was always designed. Augustine explains, "Such constituents will be returned to the same body, to take their place in its structure, undergoing a change of substance to make them suitable for the parts in which they are used." All that is part "of the essential nature" of the body will be restored. Any

aspect of the body that has experienced "the penal conditions of mortals in this life
. . . will be restored in such a way as to remove the deformity while preserving the
substance intact."[56] Cannot God the Almighty Artist, Augustine asks, "remove all
the deformities of the human body, not only the familiar ones but also the rare and
the monstrous, such as are in keeping with the miseries of this life, but are utterly
incongruous with the future felicity of the saints?"[57]

Indeed, God will fully perfect the potentials of the human body in the resurrection, removing the distorting effects of the Fall and its penalties, with beauty
the result. Those of us who are overweight and those who have always wished
they weighed more will find their wishes fulfilled in heaven. Why? Both "excess"
and "deficiency" will be erased, as the harmony expressed in physical beauty
becomes fully manifest. As a result, "there will be no ugliness, which is caused by
such disharmony, when distortions have been corrected and unpleasing deficiencies supplied from resources known to the Creator, and unprepossessing excesses
reduced without loss of essential substance."[58]

What of Christ's resurrected body? Did it not still manifest the marks of his
suffering? Yes, Augustine writes, but only for the sake of his disciples' weakness.
The "weak eyes of human beings" cannot bear to see the full glory of the risen
Christ, so Christ manifested his body in a manner that they could bear in testimony to his resurrection. He explains, "That was the purpose of his showing the
scars of his wounds for them to touch, and of his taking food and drink; it was
not that he needed nourishment but that he had the power to take it."[59]

The question remains of bodies that have been "consumed by wild beasts, or
by fire, or those parts that have disintegrated into dust and ashes," or even cannibalized. Augustine, rightly I think, considers it "unthinkable that the Creator
should lack the power to revive" all bodies "and restore them to life." It is equally
"inconceivable that any nook or cranny of the natural world, though it may hold
those bodies concealed from our detection, could elude the notice or evade the
power of the Creator of all things."[60]

> Even if because of some serious accident, or through the savagery of the enemy, it
> [the body] has been ground utterly into dust and scattered, as far as may be, to the
> winds or in the waters, so that it has ceased to be an entity in any particular place,
> even so it cannot possibly be withdrawn from the power of the Almighty Creator,
> and "not a hair of its head will perish."[61]

The most difficult question of all is that posed by cannibalism, where one body "has become part of the body of another living man."

Suppose that someone under compulsion of the last straits of starvation eats human corpses. This terrible thing has happened, as we know from the testimony of ancient history and even from the unhappy experiences of our own times. Now surely no one is going to maintain, with any show of truth or reason, that the whole of a body so eaten passes straight through the intestinal tract without any change or conversion into flesh of the eater? The former emaciation of the eater and its subsequent disappearance are sufficient indication that physical deficiencies are supplied by such nutriment.[62]

If such a blending of bodies has occurred, can it be undone? Well, Augustine replies, what was happening to the body of the man who was starving before he resorted to eating the body of another? His body was wasting away, "exhaled" into the air. In the resurrection God will restore all that has been lost. In the same way, God will restore those portions that have been cannibalized by the starving man to their original owners. In a manner of speaking, the starving man only "borrowed" them, "and like borrowed money" they must be returned to their original owner. Clearly, Augustine believes that God will reconstitute and resurrect every essential aspect of the human body. The only characteristics of bodily existence left in the grave are those connected to the effect of the Fall: "ugliness, . . . weakness, . . . sluggishness, . . . corruption [and] anything else that is inconsistent with that kingdom in which the sons of the resurrection and of the promise will be equal to the angels of God, in felicity if not in body or in age."[63]

Hence, "all that has perished from the living body . . . will be restored [and] changed." No longer will the body be an "old animal body." Instead, it will be transformed into a "new spiritual body, clothed in incorruptibility and immortality." This spiritual body will be "spiritual flesh . . . subject to the spirit, but it will be flesh, not spirit." Yet exactly what does Augustine understand this spiritual flesh to be?

Augustine is hesitant to attempt to describe a spiritual body, simply because it "is something of which we have had as yet no experience."[64] Whatever characterizes such a wondrous body in its details, we can know by extrapolating from the blessings God has already shown us in this life that his grace and power hold wonders in the future that will take our breath away.[65] Although the believer's resurrected, spiritual body may for a time remain ineffable, its reality is assured by the promise and power of God.

A final question remains. What will God's people "be doing in their immortal and spiritual bodies"? How will life in the age to come, when we will be living "according to the spirit" rather than "according to the flesh," be different? Augustine is clearly hesitant to respond to this question, explaining, "to tell the truth, I do not know what will be the nature of that activity, or rather of that rest and leisure. I have never seen it with my physical sight; and if I were to say that I had seen it with my mind—with my intellect—what is the human understanding, in capacity or in quality, to comprehend such unique perfection?"[66]

Augustine does assert that in the resurrected state there will be a peace that "surpasses all understanding," recalling Paul's words in Philippians 4:7. This surpassing understanding includes angelic knowledge itself. Only God knows the nature and characteristics of the peace awaiting us in the future. We and the angels can experience a taste of this peace, but only "according to our standard of perfection" and in our "measure." Augustine adds, "Human beings in their present state know it in a far lower degree, however highly developed may be their intellectual powers."[67]

A heavenly vision does await us, however, "as a reward of faith." As John expresses it, "when he is revealed, we will be like him, for we will see him as he is" (1 Jn 3:2). So at least we can be sure that one of the activities of the saints in heaven will be to see God, a vision that Augustine writes will take place "in the body." The mechanics of this vision remain mysterious both for him and for us: "but whether they [the saints] will see *through* the eyes of the body, in the same way as we now see the sun, moon, stars, sea and earth and all things on the earth—that is no easy question." For example, "it is hard to say that the saints will then have bodies of such a kind that they will not be able to shut and open their eyes at will." Yet, Augustine comments, "it is more difficult to say that anyone who shuts his eyes there will not see God."[68] Biblical examples such as Elisha's vision of Gehazi deceptively receiving gifts from Naaman the Syrian might reflect something of what heavenly vision is and how it operates. Gehazi assumed that because Elisha was not in the vicinity of his machinations, he was unobserved. Augustine comments, "How much more then in that spiritual body will the saints see everything, not only if they close their eyes, but even when they are not present in the body!"[69]

In heaven we will experience the perfection predicted by the apostle Paul. While at present our knowledge is partial, in the age to come this incompleteness will be overcome. For this present age, even the knowledge of apostles such as Paul remains incomplete. Thus, Augustine comments, "this life is as childhood to maturity, in comparison with the knowledge enjoyed in that life to come." Yet, on the basis of Elisha's vision of Gehazi's deception, Augustine argues that when the body "is freed from corruption . . . we will certainly need no bodily eyes to see what is there to be seen, since Elisha did not need them to see his servant when he himself was not present." Though Elisha's physical eyes did not see Naaman giving gifts to Gehazi, his "heart" observed what occurred, "with the miraculous assistance, as no one doubts, of the divine power." In the age to come, our vision will be even more clear, as God's gift to us will abound "much more richly."[70]

Although we will not need physical eyes to see in heaven, nonetheless, "those physical eyes also will have their own function and the spirit will make use of them through the spiritual body." How so? After the pattern of Elisha's relationship with Gehazi. Though Elisha did not use his eyes to observe Gehazi, "that did not mean that he did not use them to see things at hand, although he could have seen them by the spirit even if he had closed his eyes, in the same way as he saw things not present, when he was not in any physical relationship with them."

Yet the puzzle remains, for, as Augustine correctly notes, "if even those spiritual eyes will in this way have no more power in the spiritual body than the eyes which we now have, then without doubt it will not be possible to see God by their means." If so, "they will be possessed of a very different power, if that immaterial nature is to be seen by their means—that nature which is not confined to any space but is everywhere in its wholeness."[71] God obviously, then, is not a material substance seen in the same manner as objects in the created order. Rather, God "is wholly in heaven, wholly in earth, and that not at different times but simultaneously," a characteristic impossible for material substances. Hence, a resurrected body will possess eyes extraordinary in their potency, "in the sense of having the ability to see the immaterial."[72]

Although "no Christian doubts that it is with the eyes of the heart, or mind, that God will be seen, when he is seen," still Augustine ponders "whether God will be seen also with the physical eyes in that future life." Augustine has no doubt that we will see Christ by means of Christ's human body, but what of the immaterial God? The answer depends on "what new qualities the spiritual body will have, for we are speaking of something beyond our experience." The relationship between Elisha and Gehazi, however, has already shown us that "material things can be apprehended by the spirit, without the help of the bodily organs." If so, "why should there not likewise be such a mighty power in a spiritual body that the spirit may be perceived by such a body? For God is Spirit."[73] Augustine finally concludes:

> It is indeed most probable, that we shall then see the physical bodies of the new heaven and the new earth in such a fashion as to observe God in utter clarity and distinctness, seeing him present everywhere and governing the whole material scheme of things by means of the bodies we shall then inhabit and the bodies we shall see wherever we turn our eyes. It will not be as it is now, when the invisible realities of God are apprehended and observed through the material things of his creation, and are partially apprehended by means of a puzzling reflection in a mirror. Rather in that new age the faith, by which we believe, will have a greater reality for us than the appearance of material things which we see with our bodily eyes. . . . in the future life, wherever we turn the spiritual eyes of our bodies we shall discern, by means of our bodies, the incorporeal God directing the whole universe.[74]

This is an interesting idea, perhaps, but Augustine quickly acknowledges that "it is difficult, if not impossible, to support this suggestion by any evidence of passages in holy Scripture." Thus Augustine poses an "alternative suggestion." Perhaps our perception or vision of God will be mediated through the lives of believers and through creation itself, as we communicate the reality of God to each other through a kind of spiritual perception. We will perceive God "in one another, perceived by each in himself; he will be seen in the new heaven and the new earth, in the whole creation as it then will be; he will be seen in every body by means of bodies, wherever the eyes of the spiritual body are directed with their penetrating gaze."[75]

For the present, however, our vision will remain partial, obscure, as "in a glass darkly." In this present in-between time, lived by the Christian community between the ascension and parousia of our Lord, at best we receive glimpses of glory. Yet the glimpses we receive take our breath away. We have seen this glory manifested in the wonder of the incarnation, the holy Trinity, the Spirit, the cross and resurrection of Christ, God's providential governance of human history, the veracity of the Scripture and the beauty of the church. Could we ever say enough, write enough, in response to what God has done on our behalf? Hardly. We have simply made a beginning, attempting to listen carefully to teachers whose wisdom has met the test of time. How should we respond? With prayer, adoration, thanksgiving, worship. How can the theology we have studied be incarnated concretely and faithfully on a day to day basis? How did the fathers themselves link together theological inquiry and the life of prayer and worship? Here indeed are worthy questions that await further exploration and investigation. Volume three of this series, *Praying with the Church Fathers*, will devote itself to these very issues.

Abbreviations

ANF	Ante-Nicene Fathers
CCL	Corpus Christianorum. Series Latina
CSEL	Corpus Scriptorum Ecclesiasticorum Latinorum
NPNF[1]	Nicene and Post-Nicene Fathers, first series
NPNF[2]	Nicene and Post-Nicene Fathers, second series
PG	Patrologia Graeca
PL	Patrologia Latina
SC	Sources Chrétiennes

Notes

Preface

[1] Christopher A. Hall, *Reading Scripture with the Church Fathers* (Downers Grove, Ill.: InterVarsity Press, 1998).

[2] Anthony Ugolnik, *The Illuminating Icon* (Grand Rapids, Mich.: Eerdmans, 1989), p. 92, cited in Daniel Clendenin, *Eastern Orthodox Christianity: A Western Perspective* (Grand Rapids, Mich.: Eerdmans, 1994), pp. 52-53.

[3] Clendenin, *Eastern Orthodox Christianity,* p. 54.

[4] Ibid.

[5] Ibid.

[6] John Climacus, *The Ladder of Divine Ascent* (New York: Paulist, 1982), step 25, p. 218, cited in Clendenin, *Eastern Orthodox Christianity,* p. 55.

[7] All three volumes (*Reading Scripture with the Church Fathers, Learning Theology with the Church Fathers* and *Praying with the Church Fathers*) are published by InterVarsity Press.

Chapter 1: Preparing to Learn Theology with the Church Fathers

[1]For a fairly detailed discussion of the characteristics and qualifications for those designated "church fathers," see Christopher A. Hall, *Reading Scripture with the Church Fathers* (Downers Grove, Ill.: InterVarsity Press, 1998), pp. 49-55. The present discussion in *Learning Theology with the Church Fathers* is a synopsis of what can be found in *Reading Scripture with the Church Fathers*.

[2]Irenaeus *Adversus Haereses* 4.41.2, cited in *Encyclopedia of the Early Church*, ed. Angelo Di Berardino, trans. Adrian Walford (New York: Oxford University Press, 1992), 1:320.

[3]For the question of church mothers, see Hall, *Reading Scripture with the Church Fathers*, pp. 43-49.

[4]Vincent of Lerins *Commonitory* 41, cited in Johannes Quasten, *Patrology* (Westminster, Md.: Christian Classics, 1986), 1:9-10.

[5]Hall, *Reading Scripture with the Church Fathers*, pp. 51-52.

[6]See Boniface Ramsey, *Beginning to Read the Fathers* (New York: Paulist, 1985), pp. 4-7.

[7]Ibid., pp. 6-7.

[8]On the question of "church mothers," see Hall, *Reading Scripture with the Church Fathers*, pp. 43-49.

[9]Ibid., pp. 38-41, 54.

[10]Large portions of this reflection first appeared in my "What Hal Lindsey Taught Me About the Second Coming," *Christianity Today*, October 25, 1999, pp. 82-85.

[11]See Justin Martyr *1 Apology* 28; 45; 49; *2 Apology* 7; *Dialogue with Trypho* 32; 39; 85, all cited in Brian Daley, *The Hope of the Early Church: A Handbook of Patristic Eschatology* (New York: Cambridge University Press, 1991), p. 21.

[12]Justin Martyr *Dialogue with Trypho* 113, 139; cf. 80-81, cited in Daley, *Hope of the Early Church*, p. 21.

[13]Justin Martyr *Dialogue with Trypho* 113, cited in Daley, *Hope of the Early Church*, p. 21.

[14]Daley, *Hope of the Early Church*, p. 21.

[15]Irenaeus *Against Heresies* 5.32.1, cited in Daley, *Hope of the Early Church*, p. 31.

[16]Daley, *Hope of the Early Church*, p. 31; cf. Irenaeus, *Against Heresies* 5.35.1-2.

[17]Irenaeus *Against Heresies* 5.35.2; 5.36.1, cited in Daley, *Hope of the Early Church*, p. 31.

[18]Augustine *City of God* 20.7, in *Concerning the City of God Against the Pagans*, trans. Henry Bettenson (New York: Penguin, 1984), p. 907.

[19]Ibid., pp. 907-8.

[20]Daley, *Hope of the Early Church*, p. 134.

[21]John Chrysostom *Homilies on the First Epistle to the Thessalonians* 9.1, cited in Daley, *Hope of the Early Church*, p. 106.

[22]Vincent of Lerins *Commonitory* 22.27, cited in Thomas C. Oden, *Life in the Spirit* (San Francisco: HarperSanFrancisco, 1992), p. 486.

[23]Oden, *Life in the Spirit*, p. 487.

[24]Tertullian *Prescription Against Heretics* 20, cited in Henry Bettenson, ed. and trans., *The Early*

Christian Fathers: A Selection from the Writings of the Fathers from St. Clement of Rome to St. Athanasius (London: Oxford University Press, 1956), p. 190. I have slightly modified the translation.

[25]Ibid., cited in Bettenson, *Early Christian Fathers*, p. 190.

[26]Ibid., 21, cited in Bettenson, *Early Christian Fathers*, p. 191.

[27]Ibid., 32, cited in Bettenson, *Early Christian Fathers*, p. 191.

[28]Irenaeus *Against Heresies* 4.23.8, cited in Bettenson, *Early Christian Fathers*, p. 122.

[29]Ibid., 3.2-3, cited in Bettenson, *Early Christian Fathers*, p. 123.

[30]Ibid., 1.10.1-2, cited in Bettenson, *Early Christian Fathers*, p. 127.

[31]Athanasius *Four Discourses Against the Arians* 1.8, trans. J. H. Newman, rev. A. Robertson, NPNF[2] 4 (Peabody, Mass.: Hendrickson, 1994), p. 310.

[32]Ibid., 1.2, p. 307. I have slightly modified the translation.

[33]Ibid., 1.3, p. 307. I have slightly modified the translation.

[34]Hilary of Poitiers *On the Trinity* 2.1, NPNF[2] 9, p. 52, cited in Oden, *Life in the Spirit*, p. 470.

[35]Ibid., 2.2-3, NPNF[2] 9, pp. 52-53, cited in Oden, *Life in the Spirit*, pp. 470-71.

[36]See Constantine N. Tsirpanlis, *Introduction to Eastern Patristic Thought and Orthodox Theology* (Collegeville, Minn.: Liturgical, 1991); Jaroslav Pelikan, *The Emergence of the Catholic Tradition* (Chicago: University of Chicago Press, 1971); Frances Young, *From Nicaea to Chalcedon* (Philadelphia: Fortress, 1983).

[37]I am quoting from the text of the Nicene Creed found in *The Book of Common Prayer and Administration of the Sacraments and Other Rites and Ceremonies of the Church* (Kingsport, Tenn.: Kingsport Press, 1977), p. 358.

Chapter 2: Christ the Son, Begotten and Not Made

[1]Arius *The Letter of Arius to Eusebius of Nicomedia*, cited in Edward R. Hardy, *Christology of the Later Fathers* (Philadelphia: Westminster Press, 1954), pp. 329-30.

[2]Ibid., cited in Hardy, *Christology of the Later Fathers*, p. 330.

[3]Arius *The Confession of the Arians, Addressed to Alexander of Alexandria*, cited in Hardy, *Christology of the Later Fathers*, p. 333.

[4]Arius *Letter of Arius to Eusebius*, cited in Hardy, *Christology of the Later Fathers*, pp. 330-31.

[5]Arius *Confession of the Arians*, cited in Hardy, *Christology of the Later Fathers*, p. 333.

[6]For a brief biographical note on Athanasius, see Christopher A. Hall, *Reading Scripture with the Church Fathers* (Downers Grove, Ill.: InterVarsity Press, 1998), pp. 56-57.

[7]Athanasius *Four Discourses Against the Arians* 1.15, cited in Henry Bettenson, ed. and trans., *The Early Christian Fathers: A Selection from the Writings of the Fathers from St. Clement of Rome to St. Athanasius* (London: Oxford University Press, 1956), p. 381. Unless otherwise noted, subsequent references to *Orations Against the Arians* are from Bettenson, *Early Christian Fathers*.

[8]Ibid.

[9]Ibid., 3.1, pp. 393-94.

[10]Ibid., 1.14, p. 380.

[11]Ibid., 1.25, p. 382.

[12]Ibid., 2.33, p. 390.

[13]Both questions can be found in ibid., 2.34, p. 390.

[14]Ibid., 2.35, p. 391.

[15]Ibid., emphasis added.

[16]Ibid., emphasis added.

[17]Ibid., 2.31, p. 390.

[18]Ibid., 1.35, p. 383. Athanasius is convinced that the Arians are using language in a purposely deceitful manner: "Let us look at the replies which the Arians gave to Alexander (who is now in peace) at the beginning, when their heresy was being formed. They wrote, 'He is a creature, but not as one of the creatures; a work, but not as one of the works; an offspring, but not as one of the offsprings.' . . . What is the use of this disingenuous talk, saying that he is 'a creature and not a creature'?" (ibid., 2.19, p. 387).

[19]Ibid., 2.36, p. 392.

[20]Ibid.

[21]Ibid., 2.20, p. 388.

[22]Ibid., 2.50, p. 392.

[23]Ibid., 2.50-51, p. 393.

[24]Ibid., 3.3, p. 394.

[25]Ibid., 3.4, p. 395.

[26]Ibid.

[27]Ibid.

[28]Ibid.

[29]Ibid.

[30]Cornelius Plantinga Jr., *Not the Way It's Supposed to Be: A Breviary of Sin* (Grand Rapids, Mich.: Eerdmans, 1995), p. 91.

[31]Athanasius *Four Discourses Against the Arians* 1.34, trans. J. H. Newman, rev. A. Robertson, NPNF[2] 4 (Peabody, Mass.: Hendrickson, 1994), p. 326.

[32]For all quotes in the chart, see ibid.

[33]Ibid., 1.14, pp. 314-15.

[34]Ibid., 1.15, p. 315. Emphasis added.

Chapter 3: The Mystery and Wonder of the Trinity

[1]Cited in Alistair McGrath, *Understanding the Trinity* (Grand Rapids, Mich.: Zondervan, 1988), p. 110. Gregory of Nyssa is quoted in Alistair McGrath, *Understanding Jesus* (Grand Rapids, Mich.: Zondervan, 1987), p. 29.

[2]Roderick T. Leupp, *Knowing the Name of God: A Trinitarian Tapestry of Grace, Faith and Community* (Downers Grove, Ill.: InterVarsity Press, 1996), p. 16.

[3]This introduction to the fathers on the Trinity is lifted from my article, "Adding Up the Trin-

278 LEARNING THEOLOGY WITH THE CHURCH FATHERS

ity," *Christianity Today*, April 28, 1997, p. 26.

[4]R. P. C. Hanson, *The Search for the Christian Doctrine of God: The Arian Controversy 318-381* (Edinburgh: T & T Clark, 1988), pp. xx-xxi, emphasis added.

[5]Rather than providing an overall survey of patristic thought on the Trinity, I am purposefully choosing to explore the thought of two significant fathers in some depth. Other early Christian thinkers such as Tertullian and Origen had previously made significant contributions to trinitarian discussions, and in some ways both Gregory and Augustine are building on the foundation laid by their predecessors. For a general survey of patristic thought on the Trinity, see Roger Olson and Christopher A. Hall, *The Trinity* (Grand Rapids, Mich.: Eerdmans, 2002).

[6]Gregory of Nazianzus *The Second Theological Oration—On God*, in *Christology of the Later Fathers*, ed. Edward R. Hardy (Philadelphia: Westminster Press, 1954), p. 136. Unless otherwise noted, all references to Gregory's *Second Theological Oration* are taken from Hardy's *Christology of the Later Fathers*.

[7]Ibid.

[8]Ibid., p. 138.

[9]Ibid.

[10]Ibid.

[11]Ibid. I have modified the translation slightly.

[12]Ibid., p. 139.

[13]Ibid., pp. 139-40, emphasis added.

[14]Ibid., p. 140.

[15]Ibid., p. 141.

[16]Ibid., p. 142.

[17]Ibid.

[18]Ibid., p. 143.

[19]Ibid., p. 145.

[20]Ibid., p. 147.

[21]Ibid.

[22]Ibid., p. 150. Gregory adds that "the subject of God is more hard to come at, in proportion as it is more perfect than any other, and is open to more objections, and the solutions of them are more laborious."

[23]Gregory of Nazianzus *The Third Theological Oration—On the Son*, in *Christology of the Later Fathers*, ed. Edward R. Hardy, p. 161. Unless otherwise noted, all references to Gregory's *Third Theological Oration* are taken from Hardy's *Christology of the Later Fathers*.

[24]Ibid.

[25]Ibid., p. 162.

[26]Gregory admits the difficulty of understanding the Father's generation of the Son, but he does not find this surprising. If we have a difficult time understanding all the facets of human gener-

ation, should we be surprised that the divine generation is even more difficult to comprehend? It is best not "to speculate on the generation of God; for that would be unsafe. For even if you knew all about your own, yet you do not by any means know about God's. And if you do not understand your own, how can you know about God's? For in proportion as God is harder to trace out than man, so is the heavenly generation harder to comprehend than your own" (ibid., p. 165).

[27]Ibid.

[28]Ibid.

[29]Ibid., p. 167.

[30]Ibid.

[31]Ibid., p. 168.

[32]Ibid., p. 171.

[33]Ibid., p. 172. Note the catalog of biblical references provided by Gregory in paragraph 17 (ibid.). The church has produced a trinitarian model precisely because the Scripture has driven it to do so.

[34]Ibid., p. 173.

[35]Ibid.

[36]Ibid., pp. 174-75.

[37]Gregory of Nazianzus The Fourth Theological Oration—Which Is the Second on the Son, in Christology of the Later Fathers, ed. Edward R. Hardy, p. 177. Unless otherwise noted, all references to Gregory's Fourth Theological Oration are taken from Hardy's Christology of the Later Fathers.

[38]This is the translation Gregory cited. The NRSV reads, "The LORD created me at the beginning of his work, the first of his acts of long ago."

[39]Gregory of Nazianzus Fourth Theological Oration, p. 178.

[40]Ibid.

[41]Ibid., p. 188.

[42]Ibid., p. 189. He adds, the "best theologian is he who has, not indeed discovered the whole, for our present chain does not allow of our seeing the whole, but conceived of him to a greater extent than another, or gathered in himself more of the likeness or adumbration of the truth, or whatever we may call it" (ibid.).

[43]Ibid.

[44]Ibid., p. 190-91.

[45]Ibid., p. 191.

[46]Ibid.

[47]Ibid., pp. 191-92.

[48]Ibid., p. 192.

[49]Ibid.

[50]Ibid., pp. 192-93.

[51]Gregory of Nazianzus The Fifth Theological Oration—On the Spirit, in Christology of the Later

Fathers, ed. Edward R. Hardy, p. 194.

[52]Ibid., p. 195.

[53]Ibid.

[54]Ibid.

[55]Ibid., p. 196.

[56]Ibid.

[57]Ibid.

[58]Ibid.

[59]Ibid.

[60]Ibid., p. 198. Gregory comments that the limitations of the theologian must always be kept in mind. If we have a hard time explaining and describing matters close to us, how much more so with the attempt to describe God? "And who are we to do these things, we who cannot even see what lies at our feet, or number the sand of the sea, or the drops of rain, or the days of eternity, much less enter into the depths of God, and supply an account of that nature which is so unspeakable and transcending all words?" (ibid., pp. 198-99).

[61]Ibid., p. 199, emphasis added.

[62]Ibid.

[63]Ibid.

[64]Ibid., p. 202.

[65]Ibid.

[66]Ibid., p. 207.

[67]Ibid., pp. 207-8.

[68]Ibid., pp. 209-10.

[69]Ibid., p. 211.

[70]Ibid.

[71]Ibid., pp. 213-14.

[72]Ibid., p. 214.

[73]For a recent translation, see Augustine *The Trinity*, ed. John E. Rotelle, introduction, translation and notes by Edmund Hill (Brooklyn, N.Y.: New City Press, 1991).

[74]An abbreviated discussion of this sermon can be found in Olson and Hall, *The Trinity*, pp. 41-44.

[75]Augustine *Sermons on New Testament Lessons* 2, NPNF[1] 6 (Peabody, Mass.: Hendrickson, 1994), p. 259.

[76]Ibid.

[77]Ibid.

[78]Ibid.

[79]Ibid.

[80]Ibid., p. 260.

[81]Ibid.

[82]Ibid., p. 261. Augustine writes that "these three things which belong to the Son only [the virgin birth, the crucifixion and the resurrection], were wrought neither by the Father alone, nor by the Son alone, but by the Father and the Son" (ibid.).

[83]Ibid.

[84]Ibid., p. 262.

[85]Ibid.

[86]Ibid.

[87]Ibid. I have slightly modernized the translation.

[88]Ibid., pp. 262-63.

[89]Ibid., p. 263.

[90]Ibid.

[91]Ibid., pp. 264.

[92]Ibid. Augustine is careful to remind us that the divine and human "are indeed very far removed from each other, as the lowest from the Highest, as the changeable from the Unchangeable, the created from the Creator, the human nature from the Divine. . . . Remember that I have undertaken merely to show, that there are some three things which are separately exhibited, whose operation is yet inseparable" (ibid.).

[93]Ibid.

[94]Ibid.

[95]Ibid.

[96]Ibid.

[97]Ibid., p. 265.

[98]Ibid.

[99]Ibid.

[100]Ibid.

[101]Ibid., p. 266.

Chapter 4: Christ Divine and Human

[1]Frances Young, From Nicaea to Chalcedon (Philadelphia: Fortress, 1983), p. 241.

[2]Extract from Alexander Kerrigan, St. Cyril of Alexandria: Interpreter of the Old Testament, Analecta biblica 2 (Rome: Pontificio Istituto Biblico, 1952), p. 7, cited in Young, From Nicaea to Chalcedon, pp. 240-41.

[3]Cited in Young, From Nicaea to Chalcedon, p. 241.

[4]Nestorius Le Livre d'Heraclide de Damas, French. trans. F. Nau (Paris: Letouzey, 1910), p. 323; and Nestorius The Bazaar of Heraclides, ed. and trans. G. R. Driver and L. Hodgson (Oxford: n.p., 1925), p. 370, cited in Young, From Nicaea to Chalcedon, p. 229.

[5]Young, From Nicaea to Chalcedon, p. 229.

[6]Socrates Ecclesiastical History 7.29, cited in Young, From Nicaea to Chalcedon, p. 234.

[7]Ibid., 7.32, cited in Young, From Nicaea to Chalcedon, p. 234.

[8]Young, *From Nicaea to Chalcedon*, p. 234.

[9]Harold O. J. Brown, *Heresies: The Image of Christ in the Mirror of Heresy and Orthodoxy from the Apostles to the Present* (Garden City, N.Y.: Doubleday, 1984), p. 170.

[10]Ibid., p. 166.

[11]Ibid., p. 173.

[12]John McGuck, introduction to Cyril of Alexandria, *On the Unity of Christ*, trans. John McGuck in (Crestwood, N.Y.: St. Vladimir's Seminary Press, 1995), p. 18.

[13]Cyril of Alexandria *On the Unity of Christ*, p. 52.

[14]Ibid.

[15]Ibid., p. 51.

[16]Ibid.

[17]Ibid., p. 53.

[18]Ibid., p. 55.

[19]Ibid.

[20]Ibid., p. 58.

[21]Ibid., p. 59.

[22]Ibid.

[23]Ibid.

[24]Ibid.

[25]Ibid., p. 60.

[26]Ibid.

[27]Ibid., p. 61.

[28]Ibid.

[29]Ibid.

[30]Ibid.

[31]Ibid., p. 62.

[32]Ibid., p. 63.

[33]Ibid., p. 64.

[34]Ibid., p. 67.

[35]Ibid.

[36]Ibid., p. 68.

[37]Ibid.

[38]Ibid.

[39]Ibid.

[40]Ibid., p. 69.

[41]Ibid., p. 73.

[42]Ibid., p. 76.

[43]Ibid., p. 69.

[44]Ibid., p. 70.

[45]Ibid.

[46]Ibid., p. 77.

[47]Ibid., p. 73.

[48]Ibid., p. 77.

[49]Ibid., p. 78.

[50]Ibid.

[51]Ibid., p. 79.

[52]Ibid.

[53]Ibid., p. 83.

[54]Huston Smith, *The Religions of Man* (San Francisco: Harper & Row, 1986), p. 442.

[55]Cyril of Alexandria *On the Unity of Christ*, pp. 114-15.

[56]Ibid., p. 117.

[57]Ibid., p. 118.

[58]Ibid., p. 130.

[59]Ibid., p. 118.

[60]Ibid., p. 125.

[61]Ibid., p. 130.

[62]Ibid., pp. 130-31.

[63]Ibid., p. 131.

[64]Ibid., p. 101.

Chapter 5: On the Holy Spirit

[1]For the following summary and quotations, see David Anderson, introduction to Basil the Great *On the Holy Spirit*, trans. David Anderson (Crestwood, N.Y.: St. Vladimir's Seminary Press, 1980), p. 8.

[2]Clement of Rome *First Epistle to the Corinthians* 46.6, cited in Henry Bettenson, ed. and trans., *The Early Christian Fathers: A Selection from the Writings of the Fathers from St. Clement of Rome to St. Athanasius* (London: Oxford University Press, 1956), p. 41.

[3]Irenaeus *Against Heresies* 3.24.1, cited in Bettenson, *Early Christian Fathers*, p. 114.

[4]Ibid., 4.praef. 3, cited in Bettenson, *Early Christian Fathers*, p. 115.

[5]Origen *In Ioannem Fragmenta* 37, cited in Bettenson, *Early Christian Fathers*, p. 313.

[6]Anderson, introduction to Basil the Great *On the Holy Spirit*, p. 7.

[7]Ibid., p. 11.

[8]Basil the Great *On the Holy Spirit*, p. 16.

[9]Ibid., p. 28.

[10]Ibid.

[11]Ibid., pp. 28-29.

[12]Ibid., p. 29.

[13]Ibid.

[14]Ibid.

[15]Ibid., p. 30.

[16]Ibid.

[17]Ibid., p. 31.

[18]Ibid., p. 30. Basil will later scold his theological opponents for insulting "dogmas pertaining to the divine nature by confining them within human categories" (ibid., p. 80).

[19]Ibid., p. 33.

[20]Ibid.

[21]Ibid., p. 34.

[22]Ibid., p. 42.

[23]Ibid., pp. 42-43.

[24]Ibid., p. 43.

[25]Ibid., p. 44.

[26]Ibid.

[27]Ibid.

[28]Ibid.

[29]Ibid., p. 45.

[30]Ibid., p. 46.

[31]Ibid.

[32]Ibid., pp. 49-50.

[33]Ibid., p. 48.

[34]Ibid., p. 50.

[35]Ibid., p. 52.

[36]Ibid., p. 53.

[37]Ibid.

[38]Ibid.; cf. Jn 6:41.

[39]Ibid.; cf. Num 21:8.

[40]Ibid., p. 56.

[41]Ibid., p. 61.

[42]Ibid.

[43]Ibid.

[44]Ibid., p. 62.

[45]Ibid.

[46]Ibid.

[47]Ibid.

[48]Ibid., p. 63.

[49]Ibid. Basil adds, "It is impossible to maintain a life of holiness without the Spirit. It would be easier for an army to continue its maneuvers without a general, or for a choir to sing on key without its director" (ibid., p. 64).

[50]Ibid., p. 65.

[51]Ibid., p. 63.

[52]Ibid., p. 64.

[53]Ibid.

[54]Ibid., p. 65.

[55]Ibid.

[56]Ibid.

[57]Ibid.

[58]Ibid., pp. 65-66; cf. 1 Cor 12:28.

[59]Ibid., p. 66.

[60]Ibid., p. 66; cf. Jn 14:2.

[61]Ibid., pp. 68-69.

[62]Ibid., p. 70; cf. Mt 28:19.

[63]Ibid., pp. 70-71.

[64]Ibid., p. 75.

[65]Ibid., p. 72.

[66]Ibid.

[67]Ibid., p. 76.

[68]Ibid.

[69]Ibid., p. 77.

[70]Ibid.

[71]Ibid.

[72]Ibid.

[73]Ibid., pp. 78-79.

[74]Ibid., p. 84.

[75]Ibid.

[76]Ibid.

[77]Ibid., p. 85.

[78]Ibid., p. 87.

[79]Ibid., p. 88.

[80]Ibid., p. 96. Basil argues that *in* is used more appropriately to describe the Spirit's work in the believer, while *with* more adequately describes the Spirit's relationship to the Father and the Son. The two prepositions "are not antagonistic expressions; it is simply that each has a unique meaning, as far as true religion is concerned. The preposition *in* expresses the relationship between ourselves and the Spirit, while *with* proclaims the communion of the Spirit with God" (ibid., p. 102).

[81]Basil writes that "we are all powerless to sufficiently express in words the graces with which we have been filled. He passes all understanding, and exposes the natural inability of our speech to even remotely approach His dignity" (ibid., p. 106).

[82]Ibid., p. 97.

Chapter 6: Sin, Grace and the Human Condition

[1]Irenaeus *Against Heresies* 4.37.1, ANF 1 (Peabody, Mass.: Hendrickson, 1994), p. 518.

[2]Ibid.

[3]Ibid., 4.37.2, p. 519, emphasis added.

[4]Ibid., 4.37.3, p. 519. I have slightly modified the translation. Irenaeus adds: "If then it were not in our power to do or not to do these things, what reason had the apostle, and much more the Lord Himself, to give us counsel to do some things, and to abstain from others? But because man is possessed of free will from the beginning, and God is possessed of free will, in whose likeness man was created, advice is always given to him to keep fast the good, which thing is done by means of obedience to God" (ibid., 4.37.4, p. 519).

[5]Ibid., 4.37.5, p. 520.

[6]Ibid., 4.37.7, p. 520.

[7]Ibid.

[8]Ibid., 4.38.1, p. 521.

[9]Ibid.

[10]Ibid.

[11]Ibid., 4.38.2, p. 521.

[12]Ibid. I have slightly modified the ANF translation.

[13]Ibid., 5.1.1, p. 526.

[14]Ibid., p. 527.

[15]Ibid., 4.40.3, p. 524.

[16]Ibid.

[17]Ibid., 4.41.1, p. 524.

[18]Ibid., 4.41.2, pp. 524-25.

[19]Ibid., 4.41.3, p. 525.

[20]Ibid., 5.1.1, p. 527.

[21]Ibid.

[22]Ibid., 5.1.2, p. 527.

[23]Ibid., 5.1.3, p. 527.

[24]Ibid.

[25]Ibid., 5.2.1, p. 528.

[26]Ibid., 5.2.2, p. 528.

[27]Ibid., 5.2.3, p. 528.

[28]Ibid.

[29]Ibid.

[30]Gerald Bonner, *St. Augustine of Hippo: Life and Controversies* (Norwich: Canterbury Press, 1986), p. 316.

[31]Peter Brown, *Augustine of Hippo* (Berkeley: University of California Press, 1967), p. 346.

[32]Ibid., pp. 346-47.

[33]Bonner, *St. Augustine of Hippo*, p. 317.

[34]Augustine *Confessions* 10.29.40, cited in Bonner, *St. Augustine of Hippo*, p. 317. I have slightly modified the translation.

[35]Bonner, *St. Augustine of Hippo*, p. 318.

[36]Augustine *On the Good of Widowhood* 26, cited in Brown, *Augustine of Hippo*, p. 351.

[37]Brown, *Augustine of Hippo*, p. 351.

[38]Julian of Eclanum *Opus imperfectum* 3.67, cited in Brown, *Augustine of Hippo*, p. 388.

[39]I am indebted to the helpful summary of Pelagius's teaching in Bonner, *St. Augustine of Hippo*, pp. 355-56, 361-67.

[40]Pelagius, quoted by Augustine in *On the Grace of Christ and Original Sin* 1.4-5, cited in Peter C. Phan, *Grace and the Human Condition* (Wilmington, Del.: Michael Glazier, 1988), p. 242.

[41]See Bonner, *St. Augustine of Hippo*, p. 356.

[42]Cited in ibid.; cf. Augustine, *On the Grace of Christ and Original Sin* 1.5.4.

[43]Brown, *Augustine of Hippo*, p. 372.

[44]Bonner, *St. Augustine of Hippo*, p. 356.

[45]Pelagius, quoted by Augustine in *On the Grace of Christ and Original Sin* 2.15-16, cited in Phan, *Grace and the Human Condition*, pp. 242-43.

[46]Bonner, *St. Augustine of Hippo*, p. 357.

[47]Augustine *Confessions* 8.9.21, cited in Bonner, *St. Augustine of Hippo*, pp. 357-58. Emphasis added.

[48]Caelestius quoted in Augustine, *Perfection in Human Righteousness* 6.12, cited in Brown, *Augustine of Hippo*, p. 373.

[49]Brown, *Augustine of Hippo*, p. 373.

[50]Augustine *Enarrations on the Psalms* 118.4, cited in Brown, *Augustine of Hippo*, p. 373.

[51]Brown, *Augustine of Hippo*, p. 373; Augustine, *Sermons* 165.3, cited in Brown (p. 373).

[52]Brown, *Augustine of Hippo*, p. 374.

[53]Ibid.

[54]Augustine *Guilt and Remission of Sins* 2.18.28, cited in Brown, *Augustine of Hippo*, p. 374.

[55]Bonner, *St. Augustine of Hippo*, p. 359.

[56]See ibid., p. 360.

[57]Ibid.

[58]Augustine *Confessions* 1.5.6, cited in Bonner, *St. Augustine of Hippo*, p. 360.

[59]Pelagius *Letter to Demetrias* 16; PL 33.1110, cited in Bonner, *St. Augustine of Hippo*, p. 361.

[60]Brown, *Augustine of Hippo*, p. 342.

[61]Ibid.

[62]Pelagius *Letter to Demetrias*, cited in Phan, *Grace and the Human Condition*, p. 236. Emphasis added.

[63]Ibid.

[64]Ibid., p. 237.

[65]Ibid.

[66]Ibid., p. 238.

[67]Ep. "Honorificentiae tuae" 1, cited in Brown, *Augustine of Hippo*, p. 347.

[68]See Brown, *Augustine of Hippo*, pp. 342-45.

[69]Bonner, *St. Augustine of Hippo*, p. 362.

[70]Pelagius, quoted in Augustine *On Nature and Grace* 12.11, cited in Bonner, *St. Augustine of Hippo*, p. 362.

[71]Augustine *On Nature and Grace* 12.11, quoted in Phan, *Grace and the Human Condition*, p. 241.

[72]Bonner, *St. Augustine of Hippo*, p. 363.

[73]Ibid. I am indebted to Bonner's discussion of the Pelagian understanding of grace and Augustine's response (pp. 362-93).

[74]Bonner's word.

[75]Bonner, *St. Augustine of Hippo*, p. 363.

[76]Cf. ibid., p. 364.

[77]Pelagius, quoted by Augustine in *On the Grace of Christ and Original Sin* 1.8.7, cited in Bonner, *St. Augustine of Hippo*, p. 364, emphasis added.

[78]Bonner, *St. Augustine of Hippo*, p. 364.

[79]Ibid., pp. 364-65.

[80]Cited in Phan, *Grace and the Human Condition*, p. 243.

[81]Pelagius, quoted by Augustine in *On the Merits and Forgiveness of Sins* 3.2.2, CSEL 60.130, 141, 144, cited in Phan, *Grace and the Human Condition*, p. 243.

[82]Ibid., 3.5.3, cited in Phan, *Grace and the Human Condition*, p. 243.

[83]Ibid.

[84]Bonner, *St. Augustine of Hippo*, p. 365.

[85]Ibid.

[86]Pelagius, quoted by Augustine in *On Nature and Grace* 42.36, NPNF[1] 5 (Peabody, Mass.: Hendrickson, 1994), p. 135.

[87]Augustine *On Nature and Grace* 42.36, p. 135.

[88]Bonner, *St. Augustine of Hippo*, p. 366.

[89]Ibid.

[90]Augustine *On the Grace of Christ and Original Sin* 14.12, NPNF[1] 5, p. 222.

[91]Ibid.

[92]Bonner, *St. Augustine of Hippo*, p. 370.

[93]Augustine *On Nature and Grace* 3.3, CSEL 60.235, cited in Phan, *Grace and the Human Condition*, p. 250.

[94]Ibid., 4.4-5.5, cited in Phan, *Grace and the Human Condition*, p. 251.

[95]Bonner, *St. Augustine of Hippo*, p. 371.

[96]Ibid.

[97]Augustine *City of God* 13.14, cited in Bonner, *St. Augustine of Hippo*, p. 371.

[98]Bonner, *St. Augustine of Hippo*, p. 372.

[99]Ibid., p. 374. Bonner writes: "it is more likely that Augustine was so absorbed by his theory that he did not give it the critical examination which it required" (*St. Augustine of Hippo*, p. 372).

[100]Ibid., p. 374.

[101]Ibid., p. 375.

[102]Ibid., pp. 377-78. Bonner explains: "On a foundation of physiological fact, erroneously explained, and a sense of shame accurately observed and probably rightly associated with the physiological fact, Augustine rears the structure of his theory of the transmission of Original Sin. Because of the disobedience of our members and the fact of shame, an element has come into human sexuality since the Fall which is both a consequence and a cause of sin. The element is concupiscence or lust" (ibid., p. 375).

[103]Ibid., p. 378.

[104]Ibid., p. 378.

[105]Augustine *Sermons* 26.12.13, cited in Bonner, *St. Augustine of Hippo*, p. 380. Bonner comments that in "the case of unbaptized infants, Augustine holds that theirs will be the mildest penalty; but this is hardly an encouraging reassurance. Christ alone, who was born of the Virgin Mary by the overshadowing of the Holy Spirit, is free from the fatal legacy and could therefore be offered as a sacrifice for the sins of others" (ibid., p. 379). Augustine did hold to the hope that in the future God's inscrutable decisions would be revealed to the believer. "Then what is now hidden will not be hidden: when one of two infants is taken up by God's mercy and the other abandoned through God's judgment—and when the chosen one knows what would have been his just deserts in judgment—why the one chosen rather than the other, when the condition of the two was the same? Or again, why were miracles not wrought in the presence of certain people who would have repented in the face of miraculous works, while miracles were wrought in the presence of those who were not about to believe?" Augustine *Enchiridion on Faith, Hope and Love* 24.95, cited in Bonner, *St. Augustine of Hippo*, pp. 380-81.

[106]See Phan, *Grace and the Human Condition*, pp. 255-58.

[107]Ibid., p. 255.

[108]Ibid., p. 256.

[109]Ibid.

[110]Ibid.

[111]Ibid., pp. 256-57; cf. Jn 15:5.

[112]Ibid., p. 258.

[113]Bonner, *St. Augustine of Hippo*, p. 384.

[114]Ibid.

[115]Ibid., p. 385.

[116]Ibid.

[117]Pelagius, quoted by Augustine in *Against Julian: Opus Imperfectum* 6.9, cited in Bonner, *St. Augustine of Hippo*, p. 385.

Chapter 7: God's Transcendent Providence

[1]Much of the material found in chapters seven and eight is drawn from my introduction to my translation of Chrysostom's *On Providence*. I have also treated aspects of Chrysostom's understanding of providence in *Reading Scripture with the Church Fathers* (Downers Grove, Ill.: InterVarsity Press, 1998), pp. 96-101. Some repetition seemed both necessary and unavoidable.

[2]See Frances Young, "Patristics," in *A New Dictionary of Christian Theology*, ed. Alan Richardson and John Bowden (London: SCM Press, 1983), pp. 431-35.

[3]Richard Rubenstein eloquently addresses this difficulty when he writes: "How can Jews believe in an omnipotent, beneficent God after Auschwitz? Traditional Jewish theology maintains that God is the ultimate, omnipotent actor in the historical drama. It has interpreted every major catastrophe in Jewish history as God's punishment of a sinful Israel. I fail to see how this position can be maintained without regarding Hitler and the SS as instruments of God's will. . . . To see any purpose in the death camps, the traditional believer is forced to regard the most demonic, anti-human explosion in all history as a meaningful expression of God's purpose. The idea is simply too obscene for me to accept" (Richard L. Rubenstein, *After Auschwitz* [New York: Bobbs-Merrill, 1966], p. 153, cited in David McKenzie, "A Kantian Theodicy," *Faith and Philosophy* 1, no. 2 [April 1984]: 241).

[4]John Chrysostom *On Providence* 5.2, in Christopher A. Hall, *John Chrysostom's "On Providence": A Translation and Theological Interpretation* (Ann Arbor, Mich.: University Microfilms International, 1991), p. 193. Unless otherwise noted, references to Chrysostom's *On Providence* are from this edition; cf. *Sur La Providence de Dieu*, trans. Anne-Marie Malingrey, SC 79 (Paris: Cerf, 1961), pp. 160, 162.

[5]Ibid., 10.18; cf. Malingrey, *Sur La Providence de Dieu*, p. 162.

[6]See G. W. H. Lampe, *A Patristic Greek Lexicon* (Oxford: Clarendon, 1961), 2:1133-34.

[7]Chrysostom *Postquam presb. Gothus* 6 (my translation of PG 63:509 A), cited in Edward Nowak, *Le Chretien devant la Souffrance* (Paris: Beauchesne, 1972), p. 62.

[8]Chrysostom, *On Providence* 1.5; cf. Malingrey, *Sur La Providence de Dieu*, p. 58.

[9]Ibid., 1.3; cf. Malingrey, *Sur La Providence de Dieu*, p. 56. Emphasis added.

[10] Ibid., 2.16; Malingrey, *Sur La Providence de Dieu*, p. 70.

[11]Chrysostom *Homilies on Colossians* 8, NPNF[1] 13 (Peabody, Mass.: Hendrickson, 1994), p. 294. I have modified the translation provided in the NPNF.

[12]Chrysostom *Homilies on I Thessalonians* 7, NPNF[1] 13, p. 352.

[13]Chrysostom *Homilies on the Acts of the Apostles* 15, NPNF[1] 11 (Peabody, Mass.: Hendrickson, 1994), p. 99; cf. PG 60:126C-D.

[14]Chrysostom *On the Providence of God* 7.36.

[15]Ibid., 7.37.

[16]Ibid., 9.3.

[17]Ibid., 10.20.

[18]Ibid., 10.21. Emphasis added.

[19]Ibid., 10.24.

[20]Ibid., 10.30.

[21]Ibid., 10.31. Emphasis added.

[22]Ibid., 10.33.

[23]Ibid., 10.19.

[24]Ibid., 10.23.

[25]Ibid., 10.27-28.

[26]Ibid., 10.40.

[27]This specific classification is not found in *On Providence*, but it underlies Chrysostom's analysis of human response to providence and his use of key verbs such as *philosopheō*. I am indebted to Edward Nowak's discussion of this classification and its relationship to Chrysostom's thought.

[28]Chrysostom *Homilies on Philippians* 3, NPNF[1] 13, p. 196; cf. PG 62:202D. I have slightly modified the translation.

[29]Cf. Anne-Marie Malingrey, "*Philosophia*": *Etudes d'un groupe de mots dans la litterature grecque, des Presocratiques au IV siecle apres J.C.* (Paris: Klincksieck, 1961), pp. 263-69.

[30]Edward Nowak, *Le Chretien devant la Souffrance*, p. 71.

[31]Chrysostom *On Providence* 14.6, emphasis added.

[32]Ibid., 14.9.

[33]Ibid.

[34]Ibid.

[35]Ibid., 14.11.

[36]Ibid., 14.13.

[37]Ibid.

[38]Ibid., 15.1.

[39]Ibid., 22.11.

[40]Ibid., 7.1.

[41]Ibid., 16 (intro.).

[42]Ibid., 16.1-4.

[43]Ibid., 16.4.

[44]Chrysostom *Homilies on 2 Timothy* 9, NPNF[1] 13, p. 512, emphasis added.

[45]Cf. Christopher A. Hall, "Letters From a Lonely Exile," *Christian History* 13, no. 4, pp. 30-32; Hall, *Reading Scripture with the Church Fathers*, pp. 98-101.

[46]Chrysostom *Letters of St. Chrysostom to Olympias*, trans. W. R. W. Stephens, NPNF[1] 9 (Peabody, Mass.: Hendrickson, 1994), p. 297. I have slightly modified the translation.

[47]Ibid., p. 293. I have slightly modified the translation.

[48]Chrysostom *Homilies on the Gospel of St. John* 62, NPNF[1] 14 (Peabody, Mass.: Hendrickson, 1994), p. 231. I have slightly modified the translation.

[49]Chrysostom *Homilies on 1 Corinthians* 28, NPNF[1] 12 (Peabody, Mass.: Hendrickson, 1994), p. 166. I have slightly modified the translation.

[50]Ibid., Homily 41, p. 253. I have slightly modified the translation.

[51]Chrysostom *Homilies on Romans* 22, NPNF[1] 11, p. 507.

[52]Chrysostom *Homilies on the Acts of the Apostles* 43, NPNF[1] 11, p. 266. I have slightly modified the translation.

[53]Chrysostom *Homilies on the Gospel of St. John* 42, NPNF[1] 14, p. 231.

[54]Chrysostom *On Providence* 20.5-6; 22.10.

[55]Ibid., 22.3.

[56]Ibid., 22.8.

[57]Ibid., 22.10.

[58]Ibid., 2.1.

[59]Lampe provides the following definitions of *periergazō* in its neutral and negative sense: a. to exercise oneself about, be much concerned with. b. to investigate. c. to be inquisitive about, inquire into out of curiosity. d. to meddle with, be a busybody about. e. to pay attention to, be concerned about (Lampe, *Patristic Greek Lexicon*, 2:1064). Lampe defines the *polypragmoneō* word group as follows (in its neutral or negative sense): a. to be unduly concerned about, seek too eagerly. b. to take unnecessary trouble over, deal with unnecessarily. c. to be inquisitive about, inquire too inquisitively into, especially of matters beyond human understanding. The noun *polypragmonia* is defined as "inquisitiveness," while the adverb *polypragmonikōs* means "with over-eager curiosity" (ibid., 2:1118).

[60]Chrysostom *On Providence* 2 (intro.).

[61]Ibid., 2.1.

[62]Ibid., 2.16.

[63]Ibid., introduction.

[64]Ibid.

[65]Paul W. Harkins, introduction to John Chrysostom, *On the Incomprehensible Nature of God*, trans. Paul W. Harkins (Washington, D.C.: Catholic University of America Press), p. 18.

[66]Ibid., p. 24.

[67]Ibid., pp. 24-26.

[68]Chrysostom *On the Incomprehensible Nature of God* 2, p. 83.

[69]Chrysostom *On Providence* 2.1.

[70]Ibid., 2.3.

[71]Ibid., 2.6.

[72]Ibid., 2.11.

[73]Ibid., 2.18.

[74]Ibid., 3.11.

[75]Chrysostom *Three Homilies Concerning the Power of Demons* 1, NPNF[1] 9, p. 186; cf. PG 49:256D-257A.

[76]Chrysostom *On Providence* 8.14.

[77]Ibid., 9 (intro.).

[78]Ibid., 9.1.

[79]Ibid., 9.1-2.

[80]Ibid., 9.5, emphasis added.

[81]Ibid., 9.5-6.

[82]Chrysostom *Homily on the Paralytic Let Down Through the Roof*, NPNF[1] 9, p. 212; cf. PG 51:51A.

Chapter 8: God's Wise and Loving Providence

[1]John Chrysostom *On Providence* 6.1, in Christopher A. Hall, *John Chrysostom's "On Providence": A Translation and Theological Interpretation* (Ann Arbor, Mich.: University Microfilms International, 1991). Unless otherwise noted, references to Chrysostom's *On Providence* are from this translation.

[2]Ibid.

[3]G. L. Prestige, *God in Patristic Thought* (London: Hollen Street Press, 1952), p. 6.

[4]Ibid., p. 7.

[5]Chrysostom *An Exhortation to Theodore After His Fall* 1.4, NPNF[1] 9 (Peabody, Mass.: Hendrickson, 1994), p. 93, emphasis added.

[6]Chrysostom *On Providence* 6.3.

[7]Ibid., 6.8, emphasis added.

[8]Ibid., 6.5-6.

[9]Ibid., 6.10.

[10]Ibid., 6.12-13.

[11]Ibid., 6.16-19.

[12]Ibid., 6.20.

[13]Ibid., 6.22.

[14]Ibid., 6.14.

[15]C. S. Lewis, *The Problem of Pain* (New York: Macmillan, 1962), p. 40.

[16]In a homily on Philippians, Chrysostom strikingly illustrates the connection between the disease of sin and the incarnation: "But what does he do? As a most excellent physician, He prepares medicines of great price, and Himself tastes them first" (*Homilies on Philippians* 11, NPNF[1] 13 [Peabody, Mass.: Hendrickson, 1994], p. 238; cf. PG 62:269D).

[17]Chrysostom *On Providence* 8.5.

[18]Ibid., 8.6, emphasis added.

[19]Ibid., 8.8.

[20]Chrysostom *Homily Against the Marcionists and Manichaeans* 4, NPNF[1] 9, p. 205; cf. PG 51:38A.

[21]Chrysostom *Homilies on the Gospel of St. John* 67, NPNF[1] 14 (Peabody, Mass.: Hendrickson, 1994), p. 249; cf. PG 59:371D.

[22]Chrysostom *Homilies on Second Corinthians* 1.5, NPNF[1] 12 (Peabody, Mass.: Hendrickson, 1994), p. 274; cf. PG 61:387D-388A. I have slightly modified the translation.

[23]Augustine, "Commentary on Psalm 62:2," cited in *Divine Providence and Human Suffering*, James Walsh and P. G. Walsh, Message of the Fathers of the Church 17 (Wilmington, Del.: Michael Glazier, 1985), p. 175; cf. CCL 39:794.

[24]Chrysostom *On Providence* 8.8, emphasis added.

[25]Ibid., 8.7.

[26]Ibid., 14.6.

[27]Chrysostom *Homilies on the Statues* 16.6, NPNF[1] 9, pp. 447-48; cf. PG 49:165D.

[28]Chrysostom *Homily Concerning Lowliness of Mind* 8, NPNF[1] 9, p. 152; cf. PG 51:317B.

[29]Chrysostom *Homilies on First Corinthians* 4.5, NPNF[1] 12, p. 18; cf. PG 61:33D.

[30]Chrysostom *Homilies on Second Timothy* 2, NPNF[1] 13, p. 480; cf. PG 62:607B-C, emphasis added.

[31]Chrysostom *On Providence* 8.7.

[32]Ibid., 8.7-8; 15.1.

[33]It should come as no surprise that Chrysostom stresses the great reversal the cross introduces into history in his instructions to new Christians: "Do you not know what great result the cross has achieved? It has abolished death, has extinguished sin, has made Hades useless, has undone the power of the devil, and is it not worth trusting for the health of the body? *It has raised up the whole world, and do you not take courage in it?*" See Chrysostom *Instructions to Catechumens*, second instruction 5, NPNF[1] 9, p. 171; cf. PG 49:240B, emphasis added; I have slightly modified the translation.

[34]Chrysostom *On Providence* 14.8.

[35]Ibid., 4.13.

[36]Ibid., 15.4.

[37]Ibid., 15 (intro.); 17 (intro.).

[38]Ibid., 9.5.

[39]Ibid., 2.13.

[40]Ibid., 2.14.

[41]Ibid., 8.13, emphasis added.

[42]Ibid., 8.14.

[43]Ibid.

[44]Ibid., 9.1.

[45]Ibid., 10.3.

[46]Ibid., 10.7.

[47]Ibid., 10.12.

[48]Ibid., 10.16.

[49]Ibid., 13.4.

[50]Ibid., 10.19.

[51]Ibid., 10.40.

[52]Chrysostom *Homilies on the Statues* 2.9, NPNF[1] 9, p. 346; cf. PG 49:37C, emphasis added.

[53]Ibid., 2.17, p. 350; cf. PG 49:42A, emphasis added; I have slightly modified the translation.

[54]Chrysostom *On Providence* 8.9.

[55]Ibid., 9.6, emphasis added.

[56]1 Cor. 15:19.

[57]Chrysostom *Homilies on 1 Thessalonians* 2, NPNF[1] 12, p. 329; cf. PG 62:401C. I have paraphrased somewhat the awkward NPNF translation.

[58]Chrysostom *Homilies on Colossians* 8, NPNF[1] 13, p. 299; cf. PG 62:358D-359A.

[59]Chrysostom *On Providence* 24.1-2.

[60]Ibid., 24.3.

[61]Ibid., 22.6.

[62]Ibid., 22.7.

[63]Ibid., 22.8, emphasis added.

[64]Ibid., 22.10.

[65]Ibid., 24.4.

[66]Chrysostom *Homilies on Romans* 31, NPNF[1] 11, p. 558; cf. PG 60:674A.

[67]Chrysostom *On Providence* 11.3.

[68]Chrysostom *Homilies on Ephesians* 23, NPNF[1] 13, p. 166.

[69]Chrysostom *Homilies on the Gospel of St. John* 79.3, NPNF[1] 14, p. 293; cf. PG 59:429D-430A. I have slightly modernized the translation.

[70]Chrysostom *Homilies on the Statues* 17.12, NPNF[1] 9, p. 457; cf. PG 49:177D-178A.

[71]Chrysostom *Homilies on S. Ignatius and S. Babylas*, NPNF[1] 9, p. 138; cf. PG 50:592C-D.

[72]Chrysostom *On Providence* 11.5.

[73]Ibid., 21.1.

[74]Ibid., 21.3.

[75]Ibid., 21.4.

[76]Ibid., 19.11-12.

[77]Chrysostom *Homily on the Paralytic Let Down Through the Roof* 1, NPNF[1] 9, p. 212; cf. PG 51:50C. I have slightly modified the translation.

[78]Ibid., 2, p. 212; cf. PG 51:50D.

[79]Chrysostom *Homilies on the Statues* 20.21, NPNF[1] 9, p. 480; cf. PG 49:209D.

[80]Chrysostom *On Providence* 22.11.

[81]Ibid., 19,13-14, emphasis added.

[82]Ibid., 21.1. For a detailed analysis of Chrysostom's athletic metaphors, see J. A. Sawhill, "The Use of the Athletic Metaphors in the Biblical Homilies of St. John Chrysostom" (Ph.D. dis-

sertation, Princeton, 1928).

[83]Chrysostom *Instructions to Catechumens*, first instruction 5, NPNF[1] 9, p. 162; cf. PG 49:228B-C.

[84]Chrysostom *Three Homilies Concerning the Power of Demons* 2.1, NPNF[1] 9, p. 187. I have slightly modified the translation.

[85]Chrysostom *Homilies on Acts* 29, NPNF[1] 11, pp. 187-88; cf. PG 60:220B.

[86]Chrysostom *Homilies on St. Matthew* 33.6, NPNF[1] 10 (Peabody, Mass.: Hendrickson, 1994), p. 224; cf. PG 57:395B-C.

[87]Chrysostom *On Providence* 22.1.

[88]Ibid., 9.6, emphasis added.

[89]Ibid., 22.2.

[90]Ibid., 19.3.

[91]Ibid., 19.10.

[92]Ibid., 19.3.

[93]Athanasius *On the Incarnation of the Word* 27, NPNF[2] 4 (Peabody, Mass.: Hendrickson, 1994), p. 51; cf. PG 25:144B.

[94]Chrysostom *On Providence* 22.17, emphasis added.

[95]Chrysostom *Homilies on Acts* 15, NPNF[1] 11, p. 97; cf. PG 60:124A. I have slightly modified the translation.

[96]Chrysostom *On Providence* 23.3.

[97]Ibid., 21.1.

[98]Ibid.

[99]Chrysostom *Homilies on the Statues* 4.2, NPNF[1] 9, p. 364; cf. PG 49:59D-60A; see also ibid., 18.1, p. 459; cf. PG 49:180D, emphasis added.

[100]Chrysostom *On Providence* 8.8, emphasis added.

[101]See Chrysostom *Homily Concerning Lowliness of Mind* 7-8, NPNF[1] 9, p. 151; cf. PG 51:317A.

[102]Cf. Chrysostom *Homilies on the Gospel of Saint Matthew* 11.10, NPNF[1] 10, pp. 74-75; cf. PG 57:202C.

Chapter 9: The Sacred Scriptures

[1]For a detailed analysis of patristic hermeneutics, see Christopher A. Hall, *Reading Scripture with the Church Fathers* (Downers Grove, Ill.: InterVarsity Press, 1998).

[2]Irenaeus *Against Heresies* 1.3.1, ANF 1 (Peabody, Mass.: Hendrickson, 1994), p. 319. Irenaeus insists that a principal weakness of the Gnostic religious system is its nonbiblical foundation: "Such, then, is their system, which neither the prophets announced, nor the Lord taught, nor the apostles delivered, but of which they boast that beyond all others they have a perfect knowledge. They gather their views from other sources than the Scriptures; and, to use a common proverb, they strive to weave ropes of sand, while they endeavor to adapt with an air of probability to their own peculiar assertions the parables of the Lord, the sayings of the

prophets, and the words of the apostles, in order that their scheme may not seem altogether without support" (ibid., 1.8.1, p. 326).

[3]Irenaeus *Against Heresies* 3.1.1, cited in *The Church Fathers on the Bible*, ed. Frank Sadowski (New York: Alba House, 1987), p. 30.

[4]Ibid.

[5]Ibid., 3.1.1, cited in Sadowski, *Church Fathers on the Bible*, p. 31.

[6]Ibid., 3.1.2, cited in Sadowski, *Church Fathers on the Bible*, p. 31.

[7]Ibid., 3.11.8, cited in Sadowski, *Church Fathers on the Bible*, pp. 31-33.

[8]Ibid., cited in Sadowski, *Church Fathers on the Bible*, p. 33.

[9]Ibid., 3.14.1, cited in Sadowski, *Church Fathers on the Bible*, pp. 33-34.

[10]Ibid., cited in Sadowski, *Church Fathers on the Bible*, p. 34.

[11]Ibid., 3.14.3, cited in Sadowski, *Church Fathers on the Bible*, p. 35.

[12]Ibid., cited in Sadowski, *Church Fathers on the Bible*, p. 36-37.

[13]Ibid., 3.15.1, cited in Sadowski, *Church Fathers on the Bible*, p. 37.

[14]Ibid., cited in Sadowski, *Church Fathers on the Bible*, p. 37.

[15]Ibid., 1.27.2, ANF 1, p. 352.

[16]Ibid.

[17]Ibid.

[18]Ibid., 4.26.1, cited in Sadowski, *Church Fathers on the Bible*, p. 38.

[19]Ibid., 2.10.1, ANF 1, p. 370. I have slightly modified the translation.

[20]Ibid., 2.27.1, ANF 1, p. 398.

[21]Ibid.

[22]Ibid., 2.27.3, ANF 1, p. 399.

[23]Ibid., 2.28.2, ANF 1, p. 399.

[24]Ibid.

[25]Ibid.

[26]Ibid., 2.28.3, ANF 1, p. 399. I have slightly modified the translation.

[27]Ibid., ANF 1, p. 400.

[28]Ibid.

[29]Ibid., 2.28.6, ANF 1, p. 401.

[30]Irenaeus believes it is "easy to prove" there is only one Creator. How? By pointing to key sources of authority for the church and Christian: the "*very words of the Lord*, that He acknowledges one Father and Creator of the world, and Fashioner of man, who was proclaimed by *the law and the prophets*, while He knows no other, and that this One is really God over all" (ibid., 2.11.1, ANF 1, p. 370, emphasis added).

[31]Ibid., 2.30.6, ANF 1, p. 405.

[32]Ibid., 2.35.4, ANF 1, p. 413. Irenaeus repeatedly reminds his reader of this pattern of authority. "These [are the] voices of the Church from which every Church had its origin; these are the voices of the metropolis of the citizens of the new covenant; these are the voices of the

apostles; these are the voices of the disciples of the Lord, the truly perfect, who, after the
assumption of the Lord, were perfected by the Spirit, and called upon the God who made
heaven, and earth, and the sea—who was announced by the prophets,—and Jesus Christ His
Son, whom God anointed, and who knew no other [God]" (ibid., 3.12.5, ANF 1, p. 431).

[33]Ibid., 3 (preface), ANF 1, p. 414.

[34]Ibid., 3.1.1., ANF 1, p. 414.

[35]Ibid.

[36]Ibid., 3.2.1, ANF 1, p. 415.

[37]Ibid., 3.2.2, ANF 1, p. 415.

[38]Ibid., 3.11.7, ANF 1, p. 428.

[39]Ibid., 3.11.9, ANF 1, p. 429.

[40]Ibid., 3.12.6, ANF 1, p. 432.

[41]Ibid., 3.12.6, ANF 1, p. 432.

[42]Ibid., 3.24.1, ANF 1, p. 458.

[43]Ibid.

[44]Ibid.

[45]Ibid., 4.26.1, cited in Sadowski, Church Fathers on the Bible, p. 38.

[46]Ibid., cited in Sadowski, Church Fathers on the Bible, p. 37. I have slightly modified the translation.

[47]Ibid., 4.2.3, ANF 1, p. 464.

[48]Ibid., 4.2.7, ANF 1, p. 465. I have slightly modified the translation.

[49]Ibid., 4.9.1, 4.9.3, p. 472.

[50]Ibid., 4.9.3, pp. 472-73.

[51]Ibid., 4.26.1, p. 496.

[52]Ibid., 4.32.1, cited in Sadowski, Church Fathers on the Bible, p. 44. Irenaeus adds, "it is incumbent
to obey the presbyters who are in the Church—those who, as I have shown, possess the succession from the apostles; those who, together with the succession of the episcopate, have
received the certain gift of truth, according to the good pleasure of the Father"(ibid., 4.26.2,
ANF 1, p. 497). In a similar vein, he writes, "Where therefore, the gifts of the Lord have been
placed, there it behoves us to learn the truth, [namely,] from those who possess that succession of the Church which is from the apostles, and among whom exists that which is sound
and blameless in conduct, as well as that which is unadulterated and incorrupt in speech. For
these also preserve this faith of ours in one God who created all things; and they increase that
love [which we have] for the Son of God, who accomplished such marvelous dispensations
for our sake; and they expound the Scriptures to us without danger, neither blaspheming
God, nor dishonoring the patriarchs, nor despising the prophets" (ibid., 4.26.5, ANF 1, p.
498).

[53]Ibid., 4.32.2, cited in Sadowski, Church Fathers on the Bible, p. 44. I have slightly modified the
translation.

[54]Ibid., 4.33.8, ANF 1, p. 508.

[55]Ibid., 5.20.1, ANF 1, p. 548.

[56]Ibid.

[57]Ibid., 5.20.2, ANF 1, p. 548.

Chapter 10: One Holy, Apostolic Church

[1]Bercot, *Dictionary of Early Christian Beliefs* (Peabody, Mass.: Hendrickson, 1998), p. 305.

[2]Ibid.

[3]Irenaeus *Against Heresies* 1.10.1-2, ANF 1 (Peabody, Mass.: Hendrickson, 1994), pp. 330-31. Unless otherwise noted, all citations of *Against Heresies* are from the ANF volume.

[4]Ibid., 3.1.1, p. 414.

[5]Ibid, emphasis added.

[6]Ibid., 3.2.2, p. 415.

[7]Ibid., 3.3.1, p. 415.

[8]Ibid.

[9]Ibid., 3.4.1, p. 416.

[10]Ibid., 3.3.3, p. 416.

[11]Ibid., 3.3.4, p. 416.

[12]Ibid.

[13]Ibid., 3.4.1, p. 417.

[14]Ibid., 4.26.2, p. 497.

[15]Ibid.

[16]Ibid., 4.26.3-4, p. 497.

[17]Ibid., 1.27.2, p. 352.

[18]Tertullian *The Prescription Against Heretics* 30, ANF 3 (Peabody, Mass.: Hendrickson, 1994), p. 257.

[19]Irenaeus *Against Heresies* 4.26.5, p. 498.

[20]Ibid.

[21]Ibid., 4.33.8, p. 508.

[22]The dialogue is found in *Paganism and Christianity: 100-425 C.E.—A Sourcebook*, ed. Ramsay MacMullen and Eugene N. Lane (Minneapolis: Fortress, 1992), pp. 234-38. I have included only excerpts from the dialogue. During the Valerian persecution, Cyprian sent the following letter, hoping to replace rumor with fact: "Many various and uncertain rumors are going about, but the truth is as follows: Valerian had sent a rescript to the senate directing that bishops, presbyters and deacons should forthwith be punished; that senators and men of rank and Roman knights should lose their dignity and be deprived of their property, and if, when deprived of their possessions, they should still continue to be Christians, then they should lose their heads also; that matrons should be deprived of their property and banished; that whosoever of Caesar's household had either before confessed, or should now confess, should

forfeit his property and be sent in chains as conscripts to Caesar's estates" (quoted in ibid., p. 226; cf. Cyprian *Letters* 80.1, in *A New Eusebius: Documents Illustrating the History of the Church to A.D. 337*, ed. and trans. J. Stevenson [London: SPCK, 1957], p. 259).

[23]Excerpts from MacMullen and Lane, *Paganism and Christianity*, pp. 234-35, 237-38.

[24]Ibid., p. 227; cf. Cyprian *Letters* 13, 14, 18, 22, trans. Robert Ernest Wallis, ANF 5 (Peabody, Mass.: Hendrickson, 1994), pp. 293-97.

[25]Cyprian *On the Unity of the Church* 3, ANF 5, p. 422. Unless otherwise noted, all citations of Cyprian's *On the Unity of the Church* (cited by paragraph) are from the ANF translation.

[26]Ibid.

[27]Ibid., 4, p. 422; I have slightly modernized the ANF translation.

[28]Ibid.; cf. Eph 4:4.

[29]Ibid., 5, p. 423.

[30]Ibid.

[31]Ibid., 6, p. 423.

[32]Ibid.

[33]Ibid.

[34]Ibid., 7, p. 423.

[35]Ibid.

[36]Ibid., 8, p. 424.

[37]Ibid., 9, p. 424.

[38]Ibid., 10, p. 424.

[39]Ibid., 11, p. 425.

[40]Ibid., 12, p. 425.

[41]Ibid.

[42]Ibid., 15, p. 426.

[43]Ibid., 17, p. 427.

[44]Ibid., 22, p. 428.

[45]Ibid., 23, p. 429.

[46]Augustine *Enarrations on the Psalms* 99.13, cited in Tarcisius van Bavel, "Church," in *Augustine Through the Ages*, ed. Allen D. Fitzgerald (Grand Rapids, Mich.: Eerdmans, 1999), p. 172.

[47]Van Bavel, "Church," p. 172.

[48]Augustine *Enarrations on the Psalms* 63.9, cited in van Bavel, "Church," p. 173.

[49]Augustine *Enarrations on the Psalms* 51.6, cited in van Bavel, "Church," p. 173.

[50]Augustine *City of God* 1.35, cited in *Concerning the City of God Against the Pagans*, trans. Henry Bettenson (New York: Penguin, 1984), pp. 45-46. Unless otherwise noted, all quotations of *City of God* are from this translation.

[51]Ibid., 18.49, p. 831; cf. Mt 13:47-50.

[52]Ibid.; cf. 1 Cor 15:28.

[53]Ibid., p. 832.

[54]Ibid., 18.51, pp. 833-34.

[55]Ibid., p. 834.

[56]Ibid., p. 835.

[57]Ibid.

[58]Ibid., 20.9, p. 915.

[59]Ibid.

[60]Ibid.

[61]Augustine *On Baptism, Against the Donatists* 2.5-6, NPNF[1] 4 (Peabody, Mass.: Hendrickson, 1994), p. 428.

[62]Ibid., 2.7-10, p. 429.

[63]Ibid., 2.10-15, p. 432.

[64]Ibid., 2.13-18, p. 434.

[65]Ibid., 3.26, p. 445.

Chapter 11: The Resurrection of the Body and the Life Everlasting

[1]Joanne E. McWilliam Dewart comments that "from the fourth century B.C.E. on" the "jewish world" had been "presented" a "greek dualistic anthropology which taught the independent survival of the soul, happily released from the body" (*Death and Resurrection,* Message of the Fathers of the Church 22 [Wilmington, Del.: Michael Glazier, 1986], p. 23).

[2]*1 Clem.* 42.1-3, cited in Dewart, *Death and Resurrection,* p. 39. Emphasis added.

[3]*1 Clem.* 24.1-5, cited in Dewart, *Death and Resurrection,* p. 41.

[4]Dewart, *Death and Resurrection,* p. 43.

[5]Cicero *De republica* 3.28, quoted by Augustine *City of God* 22.4, cited in *Concerning the City of God Against the Pagans,* trans. Henry Bettenson (New York: Penguin, 1984), p. 1026. Unless otherwise noted, all citations of *City of God* are to this edition.

[6]*2 Clem.* 14.3, 5, cited in Dewart, *Death and Resurrection,* p. 45.

[7]Ignatius *To the Ephesians* 19.3, cited in Dewart, *Death and Resurrection,* p. 46. Dewart comments that the "emphasis in this passage is on the new age, but it is evident that Ignatius was more explicit than either of the two writers of the sub-apostolic age [1 and 2 *Clement*] . . . in describing the death and resurrection of Christ as its effective beginning" (*Death and Resurrection,* pp. 46-47).

[8]Ignatius *To the Trallians* 9.2, cited in Dewart, *Death and Resurrection,* p. 47.

[9]Ignatius *To the Smyrnaeans* 3.1-3, cited in Dewart, *Death and Resurrection,* p. 49.

[10]Ignatius *To the Ephesians* 11.2, cited in Dewart, *Death and Resurrection,* p. 48.

[11]Polycarp *To the Philippians* 2.1-2, cited in Dewart, *Death and Resurrection,* p. 50.

[12]Polycarp employs the resurrection as part of his encouragement to those facing martyrdom: "[Be persuaded] that all these [martyrs] 'did not run in vain' [but] in faith and righteousness" and that they are "in their due place beside the Lord with whom they also suffered." For they did not "love the present world [but] him who died for us and was raised by God because of

us" (Polycarp *To the Philippians* 9.2, cited in Dewart, *Death and Resurrection*, p. 51).

[13]*Acts of the Martyrs* 14.2, cited in Dewart, *Death and Resurrection*, p. 51.

[14]Polycarp *To the Philippians* 7.1, cited in Dewart, *Death and Resurrection*, p. 50. Polycarp clearly is suspicious that the attempt to spiritualize Christ's resurrection or to deny it outright is actually a smokescreen for licentious behavior. If one's body does not experience resurrection, it does not really matter what one does with it, a perspective similar to some in Paul's Corinthian and Thessalonian audiences (cf. 1 Cor 6:12-20; 1 Thess 4:1-8).

[15]Justin Martyr *Dialogue with Trypho* 52, cited in Dewart, *Death and Resurrection*, p. 62. Theophilus of Antioch also directs his readers to the Old Testament's prediction of future events: "Because I obtained proof from the events which took place after being predicted, I 'do not disbelieve but believe,' in obedience to God. If you will, you too must obey him and believe him" (Theophilus of Antioch *To Autolycus* 1.14, cited in Dewart, *Death and Resurrection*, p. 72).

[16]Justin Martyr *Dialogue with Trypho* 139, cited in Dewart, *Death and Resurrection*, p. 62.

[17]Ibid., 45, cited in Dewart, *Death and Resurrection*, p. 63.

[18]Justin Martyr *1 Apology* 18, cited in Dewart, *Death and Resurrection*, p. 66.

[19]Ibid., 19, cited in Dewart, *Death and Resurrection*, p. 67.

[20]Theophilus of Antioch *To Autolycus* 1.8, cited in Dewart, *Death and Resurrection*, pp. 70-71.

[21]Athenagoras *On the Resurrection of the Dead* 2, ANF 2, p. 150.

[22]Ibid.

[23]Ibid., 2.5, cited in Dewart, *Death and Resurrection*, p. 74. Tatian argues similarly: "If fire consumes my bit of flesh, the vaporized matter is still contained in the world. If I am annihilated in rivers and seas, or torn to pieces by wild beasts, I am still stored in a rich lord's treasury. . . . God the ruler, when he wishes, will restore to its original state the substance that is visible only to him" (Tatian *To the Greeks* 6, cited in Dewart, *Death and Resurrection*, p. 84).

[24]Athenagoras *On the Resurrection* 3.1, cited in Dewart, *Death and Resurrection*, p. 74.

[25]Dewart, *Death and Resurrection*, p. 74.

[26]Athenagoras *On the Resurrection* 8.4 cited in Dewart, *Death and Resurrection*, pp. 74-75.

[27]Ibid., 12.5-6, cited in Dewart, *Death and Resurrection*, p. 76.

[28]Ibid., 15.2-4, cited in Dewart, *Death and Resurrection*, p. 77.

[29]Ibid., cited in Dewart, *Death and Resurrection*, pp. 77-78.

[30]Theophilus of Antioch *To Autolycus* 1.13, cited in Dewart, *Death and Resurrection*, p. 71.

[31]Justin Martyr *2 Apology* 7 and 9, cited in Dewart, *Death and Resurrection*, p. 68.

[32]Athenagoras *On the Resurrection* 18.4-5, cited in Dewart, *Death and Resurrection*, p. 80.

[33]Ibid., 24.4; 25.2-3, cited in Dewart, *Death and Resurrection*, pp. 80-81.

[34]Augustine *City of God* 22.3, p. 1025.

[35]Cicero *De republica* 3.28, quoted in Augustine *City of God*, p. 1026, emphasis added.

[36]Augustine *City of God* 22.4, p. 1026.

[37]Ibid.

[38]Ibid., p. 1027. Augustine, arguing with Platonist opponents on their own turf, contends that

the soul is "the most rarified of substances." If so, "what is it doing in the gross mass" of the body? If the soul can indeed inhabit the present physical body, can we not deduce that through "its extraordinary quality of nature" it can raise "the body belonging to it . . . to heaven"? Augustine asks, "In our present state the natural substance of earthly bodies is able to keep the soul on the earthly level; will not the soul eventually have the power to raise the earthly body to a higher realm?" (ibid., 22.11, pp. 1050-51).

[39]Ibid., 22.5, p. 1027.

[40]Ibid.

[41]Ibid.

[42]Ibid., p. 1028.

[43]Ibid., pp. 1028-29.

[44]Ibid., 22.7, p. 1033.

[45]Ibid., 22.12, p. 1052.

[46]Ibid., p. 1053.

[47]Ibid.

[48]Ibid., p. 1054.

[49]Ibid., 22.13, p. 1054.

[50]Ibid., 22.14, p. 1055.

[51]Ibid.

[52]Ibid.

[53]Ibid., 22.15, p. 1056. What of Paul's statement concerning "the full stature of Christ"? Augustine offers two possible interpretations. Perhaps this stature "is reached when, with Christ as the head, all the members of his body come to maturity, represented by the peoples who accept the Christian faith." If Paul's "words refer to the bodily resurrection, we must take them to mean that the bodies of the dead will rise neither younger nor older than Christ. They will be of the same age, the same prime of life, which Christ, as we know, had reached. For the most learned authorities of this world define the age of human maturity as being about thirty years; they say that after that period of life a man begins to go downhill towards middle age and senility" (ibid.).

[54]Ibid., 22.17, p. 1057. Augustine sees Eve's creation from the rib of the sleeping Adam as a prophecy of Christ and his church. How so? "The sleep of that man clearly stood for the death of Christ; and Christ's side, as he hung lifeless on the cross, was pierced by a lance. And from the wound flowed blood and water, which we recognize as the sacraments by which the Church is built up. . . . The woman, then, is the creation of God, just as is the man; but her creation out of man emphasizes the idea of the unity between them; and in the manner of that creation there is, as I have said, a foreshadowing of Christ and his Church" (ibid.).

[55]Ibid., 22.19, p. 1060.

[56]Ibid.

[57]Ibid., p. 1061.

[58]Ibid.

[59]Ibid. Will all human scars and bodily losses be totally eradicated? Augustine speculates that in the case of the martyrs scars will remain "as the proofs of valor," visible trophies of their faith and courage. He adds, "if the martyrs have had any limbs cut off, any parts removed, they will not lack those parts at the resurrection; for they have been told that 'not a hair of your head will perish.' But if it will be right that in that new age the marks of glorious wounds should remain in those immortal bodies, for all to see, then scars of the blows or the cuts will also be visible in places where limbs were hacked off, although the parts have not been lost, but restored" (ibid., p. 1062).

[60]Ibid., 22.20, p. 1062.

[61]Ibid., 22.21, p. 1064.

[62]Ibid., 22.20, pp. 1062-63.

[63]Ibid., 22.20, pp. 1063-64.

[64]Ibid., 22.21, p. 1064.

[65]For example, Augustine describes in detail the wonders of the human body in its present state, aspects of the body that point to God's goodness and providence: "Are not the sense organs and the other parts of that body so arranged, and the form and shape and size of the whole body so designed as to show that it was created as the servant to the rational soul? For example: we observe how the irrational animals generally have their faces turned towards the ground; but man's posture is erect, facing towards the sky, to admonish him to fix his thoughts on heavenly things. Then the marvelous mobility with which his tongue and hands are endowed is so appropriate, so adapted for speaking and writing and for the accomplishment of a multitude of arts and crafts. And is not this sufficient indication that a body of this kind was designed as an adjunct to the soul?" (ibid., 22.24, p. 1073).

[66]Ibid., 22.29, p. 1081.

[67]Ibid., p. 1082.

[68]Ibid.

[69]Ibid., p. 1083.

[70]Ibid.

[71]Ibid., p. 1084.

[72]Ibid.

[73]Ibid.

[74]Ibid., p. 1086-87.

[75]Ibid., p. 1087.

Index

Scripture Index